ADVANCE PRAISE FOR *BOY WITH A VIOLIN*

"*Boy with a Violin* captivated me with the intimate, humanistic writing that was evident on every page, in every line. A true writer, his writing is direct and succinct, and skillfully conveys his deep understanding of that era of our history, and of the nature of humankind. As Yochanan describes the indescribable— the tale of his miraculous survival—the story progresses from a testimony that is both chilling and deeply moving, to a fine work of literature that will touch the heart of any reader."

—HAIM BE'ER, Israeli novelist
(translated from Hebrew to English)

"Such stories have been told before: a Jewish boy, a violin, the pounding of boots, death and grief. Yet this book overwhelmed me. I was swept away, so much so that as I read this book on the train, I was so immersed that I missed my destination."

—JOHN JANES VAN GALEN, literary critic
Het Parool (Amsterdam), 12/7/2006
(translated from Dutch to Hebrew to English)

"The heroes of Fein's story are individualists who fought for their lives under impossible circumstances and overcame, illuminating the darkness of those days. . . . The story is not told through the eyes of the young man in the story, but through the context of his accumulated life experience."

—PROF. MATITYAHU MINTZ,
Professor Emeritus of History at Tel Aviv University
(translated from Hebrew to English)

"As I began to read the manuscript of *Boy with a Violin*, I could not put it down. Against the hellscape surrounding him . . . the book has a breath of optimism, a belief in the future of mankind as a unique creature: capable of committing atrocities, but also of creating wonders. . . . This book must be published: to show the reasons why man can rise from the ashes, and continue to live."

—PROF. MENACHEM BRINKER,
literary scholar and philosopher, Israel Prize laureate, and peace
activist; Professor of Hebrew Literature and Philosophy at the
Hebrew University of Jerusalem; Henry Crown Professor of Modern
Hebrew Language and Literature at the University of Chicago
(translated from Hebrew to English)

BOY WITH A VIOLIN

YOCHANAN FEIN

TRANSLATED BY PENINA REICHENBERG

BOY
with a
VIOLIN

A Story of Survival

INDIANA UNIVERSITY PRESS

This book is a publication of

Indiana University Press
Office of Scholarly Publishing
Herman B Wells Library 350
1320 East 10th Street
Bloomington, Indiana
47405 USA

iupress.org

Manufactured in the United States of America

First printing 2022

Cataloging information is available from the Library of Congress.

ISBN 978-0-253-06056-3 (hardback)
ISBN 978-0-253-06059-4 (paperback)
ISBN 978-0-253-06057-0 (ebook)

Frontis: The boy, Yochanan Fein, photographed in the
garden of his home after his liberation, 1945.

English editing by Padraic Carlin

In memory of my father,
MENACHEM (MENDEL),
and my brother,
ZVI (HIRSCH'KE),
who were killed in the Holocaust, to
THE PAULAVIČIUS FAMILY,
my saviors,
and to my beloved wife,
NURIT (IRKA),
who passed away on September 26, 2020.

"The officer ordered the soldier to return the violin, and to test whether my father was telling the truth, he ordered me to play. I stood in the middle of the yard, and as the soldiers dragged, packed, and destroyed our property, I played with tears running down my cheeks."

CONTENTS

ACKNOWLEDGMENTS

MY HEARTFELT THANKS TO MY FRIEND, THE DUTCH WRITER, Philo Bergstein. Without Philo, and his relentless energy, my story would be among those untold.

To my friend Professor Matityahu Mintz, who was the first to read the manuscript, I want to thank you for your sage advice, as well as for the materials you made available to me, which allowed me to describe several events in my book more precisely.

My sincere thanks to my friend Aryvdas Sabonis, the man behind the publishing of this book in Lithuanian (2017). Arvydas initiated the Lithuanian translation and publishing and researched and verified the historical facts presented in this memoir. His meticulous literary editing and his attention to detail was of vital importance to both the Hebrew and the English editions of this book.

To Padraic Carlin, the editor of the English translation of this book, and to Jonnie Pekelny, who proofread the manuscript, thank you both for your meticulous and thoughtful editing, enabling my story to reach a broader audience and to continue to be told and passed on to the next generation. Both invested much of their time to diligently review the book. Your dedication is greatly appreciated.

Last but not least, I am deeply thankful to my beloved son, Hemi, and grandchildren, Sapir (Sapphire), Noam, and Osher: to Hemi, for initiating the English translation and for countless hours of proofreading across the Hebrew and English versions; to Sapir and Osher, for their continued proofreading and editing to maintain the book's integrity across translations; and to Noam, for the connections that propelled the completion of the English version of this book.

PART

I

PROLOGUE

IT WAS A BONE-CHILLING NIGHT IN THE WINTER OF 1942—A night when no one would leave their homes, not just because of the curfew imposed on them by the German occupiers, but because of the brutally cold wind and snow. On nights such as this one, no merciful farmer would even let a dog out. On such a night, a man crossed the Nemunas River from Šančiai, on the outskirts of Kaunas, to the other suburb, Panemunė, that was across the river. The Nemunas River waters were frozen, and the man walked across the ice to a house close to the shore, secluded and far from other homes. After much hesitation, he knocked on the door. It was an unusual time of night for a visit, so the man of the house hesitated for a minute. When he opened the door, standing there was a dirty, bearded figure dressed in rags with torn shoes. He was just skin and bones. The stranger entered and collapsed.

This was the home of the Paulavičius family, made up of four people: the father, Jonas Paulavičius; his wife, Antanina; the oldest daughter, Danutė; and the younger son, Kęstutis. The man who had just come to their home was a Russian prisoner who escaped from a POW camp on the shore of the Nemunas River. The river was meant to be a natural barrier to prevent escape. It was a tremendous risk to open the door to an escapee, but in spite of that, the man of the house welcomed him into his home. He fed him and provided him with clothes, and without any hesitation, Jonas invited the man to stay, hoping that he would survive until the Red Army's victory, which would bring defeat to the soldiers of the Third Reich.

The prisoner surprised him with his answer. He declined. And then he explained: he had come as a messenger for his friends in the Šančiai POW camp, and he left with the help of a merciful guard who had been willing to take a risk for him. He promised his friends and the guard that he would return with food. "If I save myself," he said, "they will die." The Paulavičiuses accepted his explanation and supplied him with food. Before his departure back to the POW camp, Jonas Paulavičius and the Russian prisoner (whose name I can no longer recall), made a pact. Jonas promised the man that if he would have a chance to escape again, he would have a safe place to stay with him. They departed with a handshake, the strong hand of the Lithuanian farmer meeting the weak hand of the Russian prisoner.

1

WHO WAS THIS MAN?

JONAS PAULAVIČIUS WAS BORN IN 1898 IN A POOR LITHU-anian farmhouse, and, I believe, he was the third of six children. A small plot of land, owned by the family, was primitively cultivated and barely provided for them. Considering this, it's no wonder that each child, from an early age, looked for a way out of a house that lacked warmth and sustenance. So, Jonas found himself, fourteen years old, having had no regular schooling, making his own way in life. He was taken in as an apprentice in a carpentry shop and slowly learned the secrets of the trade. The young boy grew to be a rough and sturdy man.

During World War I (1914–1918), Lithuania was conquered by the Germans and gained its independence at the end of the war. Jonas, having no home, volunteered in a unit of the young Lithuanian army that fought the war of independence for Lithuania. The independent Lithuanian government honored the group of volunteers (*savano-riai*) with medals of honor and granted them a special status with material benefits. Jonas received a plot of land, about three thousand square meters, in Panemunė, a partially agricultural suburb of Kaunas. One side of the land bordered the Nemunas River, and the other side bordered Vaidoto Street, the main thoroughfare of the suburb.

Jonas built his house with his own hands. It was a two-story wooden home with stairs on the inside. He never quite finished it, but his family had a roof over their heads. He worked as a carpenter in the railway's workshops in Šančiai, across the river. His life as a laborer was difficult, but in his heart, he remained a farmer who loved the land and knew its virtues. What he planted and harvested on his land helped to feed and provide for his family.

In the 1920s and 1930s, Jonas sided with the political left. He was open to the ideas of equality and a better future. Although he was not a member of the underground Communist Party, he was a supporter from the sidelines. Some say that before World War II, the heads of the party, who were being hunted by the Lithuanian Secret Police, found shelter in his home. Among them was the secretary of the party, Antanas Sniečkus, who at one point even operated an underground printing press from Jonas's house.

In 1940, Lithuania became a Soviet Republic, in accordance with the secret part of the Molotov–Ribbentrop Pact.[1] Jonas was then selected by his workplace as a representative to the professional union of railway workers.

2

---oo---

A JEWISH BOY AND HIS PARENTS

ON JUNE 26, 1941, ON THE FOURTH DAY OF THE GERMAN IN-vasion of the Soviet Union, the Germans reached Kaunas. The anti-Soviet, pro-Nazi "partisans" started going wild. Thousands of Jews were murdered in the first days of the invasion. Those same pro-Nazi partisans—known as Žaliukai ("the green ones")—impris-oned Jonas, among others. After a few months, the German conquer-ors took full control and squashed down any ideas about Lithuanian independence. This new German government excelled in rigidity. In an effort to expose Communist Party members, the Germans tested the prisoners in jail. Whoever "passed" the test was allowed to live, whereas anyone who was suspected of being a member of the party was murdered. Jonas found himself facing a German officer. Since he had a basic competency in German, he used it to prove that he was not a member of the Communist Party. He could not deny his activity in the labor union for workers in the workplace, but he explained that this was not a political role, and therefore the Nazi officer decided to release him.

Jonas returned home, knowing he had just been saved by a miracle and that the difference between life and death had depended on the snap decision of the Nazi officer. He asked himself what he ought to do with the freedom restored to him; how would he explain to his Communist friends upon their return (for he had no doubt they would triumph over the Germans) what he had done to resist the oc-cupation? First, he found the broadcast frequency of Radio Moscow, and he listened religiously to the Lithuanian-language broadcasts.

He recognized the voice of his favorite broadcaster, Balys Baranauskas, who would become a central figure in Soviet Lithuania: a colonel during the war in the Lithuanian Red Army, established on Soviet land. The man called on all Lithuanians to oppose the occupiers in any way possible: as partisans with weapons; through passive struggle; by sabotage in the workplace; or by saving fugitives.

Next, Jonas decided to save lives. As he was making his plans, something happened that hurried his efforts: A Jewish family named Schames was interned in the Kaunas Ghetto. Their son, Shima'leh, was born before the war. When the ghetto gates closed on August 15, 1941, Shima'leh was about a year or a year and a half old. In early 1944, the Schames family decided to do everything in their power to save the boy, who by then had already turned four. In a roundabout manner, the family made contact with their Lithuanian neighbor from before the war. The family lived in the suburb of Šančiai, the area around which my story unfolds as well. They begged the neighbor to save their child for a fee. But the neighbor refused, claiming he lived in a house with many neighbors and that he was well known in the area, as was his entire family. In spite of this, he promised to look for another refuge for the child. He said he knew a man with a compassionate heart who lived in an isolated house, and he hoped that the man would accede to the request and accept the child.

After a while, the plan came to fruition. The man turned to Jonas Paulavičius, and his answer was affirmative, though not final: "I must check with my wife," said Jonas. A day later, he came back with a final reply. Jonas and Antanina Paulavičius agreed to take a risk and provide shelter for the young Jewish boy.

The child's adjustment in the family's home was difficult since he grew up in the closed cage of the ghetto and never heard any language other than Yiddish. Suddenly, the boy was cut off from his family and his Jewish brothers and turned over to very grave people who spoke a strange foreign language. He cried nonstop because of all the limitations and restrictions forced upon him in a language he did not understand. He was forbidden to go downstairs or to leave his room. He was forbidden to make noise and was even forbidden to cry. But Shima'leh did not stop crying, and his spirit broke before his saviors' eyes.

The Paulavičius family lived in fear of their secret being revealed. One day, when the child was playing with pieces of paper and threw them into a burning oven, a flame burst in his room. The family had reached their limit and considered returning the child to his parents.

Jonas was in constant contact with the child's parents with the help of Aaron Neumark, a Jewish engineer in the ghetto. The engineer worked in forced labor outside the ghetto along with thousands of other Jews who would leave the ghetto in Jewish brigades. On occasion, when Jonas was to update the parents about their son and receive instructions, he would travel to Kaunas, to the brigade's place of work, and meet with Neumark. There were risks in doing this. The German guards were used to the sight of Lithuanians approaching the Jews and trying to trade with them. The Jews would sell objects and clothes for food in trade that was called *beitten zachen* in Yiddish ("barter of clothing"). This time, Jonas approached Neumark with a heavy heart; he had come to tell him that the child would have to return to the ghetto. The danger was just too great.

Several days later, Jonas returned to get the parents' answer from Neumark: the parents refused to take back their son. Was such a thing possible? No doubt the parents were convinced that the good-hearted Jonas would find a solution to the problem, would not expose their son to danger, and would continue to hide him as before. Under the circumstances, Jonas recommended that the parents quickly close things up in the ghetto and join their child. This was not a simple decision; there was a grandmother as well, the mother of Mrs. Schames, and she could not be left behind. And so, due to the circumstances, four members of one family arrived at the Paulavičius' house: the boy, Shima'leh; his parents, Lena and Itzhak Schames; and Mrs. Feinsilber, Lena's mother.

3

THE GOAL—SAVING THE INTELLECTUALS

JONAS DID NOT STOP COMING UP WITH NEW PLANS. HE lacked formal education, but his logic was ironclad. Since he did not want to leave his family and go armed into the forest, he chose to save Jews as his means of fighting against the Nazis. This was his only way of opposing the occupiers. He could take advantage of the geography of his secluded house, which bordered the Nemunas River and was surrounded by a three-thousand-square-meter garden with many hiding places. Another advantage was that only a few people visited his home because Jonas was a tough, unfriendly man, and the family maintained a position of seclusion toward their surroundings. He set his goal—saving Jews—as a communist and a humanist. Jonas assumed that rescue operations should begin at a relatively late stage, when the Soviet soldiers would be approaching and there would be a reasonable chance that the Nazi occupiers would soon be driven out. It was impossible to hide many Jews for long. The many dangers and difficulties in obtaining food were among the main factors preventing such a rescue operation.

Jonas contemplated which Jews he would save. He couldn't possibly save them all. Therefore, he came to a tough decision: to save Jewish intellectuals, on the assumption that after the mass destruction, the nation would need leaders and educated people. Those who would find refuge with him would be the educated, doctors, and engineers. He turned to the Schames family, who had already been in hiding in his house, and asked them for names of Jews who would meet the criteria. The Schameses told him about two doctors, husband and wife Chaim and Tanya Ipp, who lived in the ghetto and had saved the Schames' son from a bad bout with pneumonia. When the engineer, Aaron Neumark, came to Chaim Ipp as Jonas's messenger and told him that a Lithuanian wanted to save him and his family, the doctor refused to believe it. When Neumark explained that the offer was the result of a special ideology to save educated Jews, it seemed even stranger to Chaim. Dr. Chaim Ipp was convinced that Jonas was a provocateur, and therefore he became even more strongly opposed to getting involved with him. But when he told his wife, Tanya, she was angry at his rash reply to Jonas's offer. Due to the horrors of the ghetto and the hardships they encountered, she was willing to take the risk of examining the proposal. She did not believe that a man would actually seek out doctors and, instead of rescuing them, hand them over to the Gestapo. She demanded that her husband meet Jonas to get an impression of him.

Tanya and Chaim were young doctors who had graduated from school just before the outbreak of the war and went through a terrible ordeal. They had worked in the Jewish hospital in Kaunas. During the German invasion, a pogrom was carried out against the Jews in the Lietūkis garage, where dozens died of severe torture. The wounded and dead were brought to the hospital, and the young doctor Tanya, who saw the shattered heads and the shattered limbs, could not stand it. She and her husband decided to commit suicide, realizing that a similar fate awaited them too. It was only by coincidence that another doctor, who entered the bathroom as they were about to fatally inject themselves, gave them encouragement and hope that all was not lost and convinced them not to take their lives.

After that, Tanya had gained a deep sense that she was meant to survive. Now suddenly, a Lithuanian savior came along who wanted to rescue them. How could this be another coincidence? He could have chosen any other doctor, engineer, or educated person, but he chose them. Furthermore, there had been another event that further cemented Tanya's convictions: she had worked in the ghetto hospital and was supposed to be on call the night of October 4, 1941, but for some reason, she had asked another doctor to take her shift. That very night, the Germans set fire to the hospital. The building and all those inside it were consumed by flames. Tanya, who was sentenced to death, was saved twice by chance and now held to a deeply engrained belief that she was destined to live. It was therefore decided that Chaim would go to town to meet Jonas.

Chaim, who was a dedicated and known doctor in the ghetto, was able to arrange leaving for a day with one of the brigades without much difficulty. He joined Aaron Neumark's brigade, and, as was agreed upon ahead of time, Jonas came to their place of work. Chaim was puzzled. In front of him stood a simple man whose tone was confident and serious. His eyes brightened as he smiled and said, "I want to save you and your wife because you are doctors."

Chaim apologized, "But we have no money to pay you."

Jonas replied, "I am not asking for money."

"For free? Why?" the doctor wondered.

Jonas clarified his intentions, explaining that he wanted to save Jewish intellectuals.

Several days later, the married doctors Chaim and Tanya Ipp escaped from the ghetto, and the two of them made it to the Lithuanian family's house. And so began the path of the second group, who, due to the predetermined and deliberate decision of Jonas Paulavičius, found their savior.

4

—⦿—

THE VIOLIN OF MY LIFE

THE PROBLEM JONAS FACED WAS WHERE TO HIDE THE GROUP of Jews in his house. And so, once the decision was made, Jonas dug a safe room under his house near the basement. The digging took a few months, and so as not to spark the neighbors' attention, it was done mostly at night. Jonas and his son Kęstutis first scattered the dirt in the yard. Then, when the surface was getting too high, they filled sacks, and on the pretext that they were going out for night fishing, they would carry the sacks by boat to the middle of the Nemunas River and throw them into the water. Thus, a fairly large room was excavated, and Jonas lined the walls with wooden planks and supported the ceiling on pillars. In this way, a room was created with a primitive ventilation hole hidden in the vegetation. The entrance to the room was through the basement of the house, which was normally used as a carpentry shop. Chips, planks, and wood debris were scattered around, and Jonas deliberately did not clean the place to avoid suspicion if anyone were to happen upon it. Furthermore, he covered the entrance to the secret, underground room with waste. In this room, the four souls of the Schames family and the two doctors, Tanya and Chaim, were hidden.

After this operation, the engineer Aaron Neumark told Jonas, "And what about me? I meet your criteria. I'm an engineer!"

Jonas replied, "Absolutely, you're in. But first you have to contact the next person in line after you for rescue."

In order to feed all these people in his house, in addition to his family, Jonas had to make business deals. His vegetable garden did not suffice, so he and his wife, Antanina, made use of anything that came their way. Antanina bought a horse and carriage and would travel to her childhood town, Anykščiai, as well as surrounding villages; she would buy food and other supplies cheaply and sell them to starving city folk. With her accumulated profits and the extra food, she fed the mouths of those who found refuge in their home.

Jonas made contact with an older, anti-fascist German sergeant who hated the forced separation from his family and loathed the army, the war, and Hitler. Since he worked in a supply depot, he "appropriated" things from there and sold them through Jonas for money, meals, or other things. In the end, they divided the profits.

One day, the German sergeant brought Jonas a violin. He explained that it was his violin and that he decided to sell it to support his family on the home front, who were hungry for bread. And then he said, "Buy the violin for yourself and teach your son to play!"

Jonas foresaw the practical possibility of his son learning to play, giving him the opportunity to then be able to perform at all kinds of events and weddings to please the invited guests and make an honorable living.

The purchase included violin lessons for Kęstutis. The deal consequently opened the doors of the house to the German, who at any time would come, wash, rest, and eat to his heart's content. He would also take with him smoked pork and fat––all for his family. The lessons did not work out, because Kęstutis had no musical inclination and did everything in his power to escape this punishment. The violin deal was therefore a waste of money. But then Kęstutis told his father, "In the prewar school, we had a prodigy, a Jewish boy who played the violin. At every event and holiday, the same child appeared and excited the audience. Maybe we should look for him and save him."

Jonas considered this and reached the conclusion that a young prodigy, a violinist, also belonged to the Jewish intelligentsia—those who could preserve the Jewish spirit and restore the culture after the war. He, too, could meet the necessary criteria to be saved.

I was that boy. I was then fourteen years old. As a child, I played the violin very seriously, and my parents treated my playing even more seriously and even predicted a violinist's future. And so, without lifting a finger to save myself, fate summoned Jonas to me. I remember that one evening a man appeared in our small, dilapidated, dark apartment in the ghetto. It must have been the winter of February 1944. The man introduced himself as Aaron Neumark. After an exhaustive search, he had finally managed to locate us. By then only my sister and I remained in the ghetto from our immediate family. At the time, we were living with relatives, the Pruzhans, and the Kronzons, whose story comes later. It turned out that Neumark knew about me and also knew our family because he had studied engineering in Bordeaux, France, together with my brother-in-law Asher Waldstein.

Neumark had a secret, which he refused to discuss in front of everyone else. He asked my sister to accompany him outside and by doing so aroused everyone's curiosity. From the window, I saw the two of them walking back and forth. My sister Yehudit came back with a strange story. A Lithuanian from Panemunė, where my father's house was, wanted to save me without any monetary compensation, just because I played the violin and went to school with his son. On the surface, it seemed illogical and incomprehensible. "And yet," my sister said, "you cannot refuse such an amazing offer . . . God sent you a savior."

We were so incredibly excited, and although we didn't really understand it, we wanted so much to believe it. There were other children in our house. Berta Kronzon, whose husband was sent away to the Riga Ghetto during one of the Actions, remained in the Kaunas Ghetto with her elderly parents and her three children. So naturally there was a hidden jealousy, but no one spoke openly about it. "They'll save Yochanan," everyone thought, "but what about Berta's three children?" The Pruzhans, Berta's parents, said that this was a blatant provocation and that it would be prudent not to be dragged into it. I, myself, did not remember any boy named Kęstutis Paulavičius in my class. And playing the violin—I thought, "What a ridiculous reason!" Berta Kronzon suggested to my sister Yehudit that she meet with Neumark and see if he could save her three children. Yehudit made arrangements with Neumark to continue their

Jonas and Antanina, 1945.

communication. It was decided that she would meet Paulavičius, get an impression of him, and listen to his offer directly.

None of this would be easy. Neumark had to wait at his workplace for Jonas to come and report to him in what brigade Yehudit was working. Then, as was decided, Jonas would come from Panemunė, a few kilometers away, and look for her there.

Totally determined, the Lithuanian went to see my sister. She listened to his strange story. The explanation of the violin alone did not convince her. When he said that his son had studied with me in the same class and that because he was so impressed with my playing, he sought to rescue me, my sister replied that we had no money. When this explanation did not dissuade Jonas, she added that for her, being separated from me would be too difficult: we had come a long way together, and she took care of all my needs as best she could, so she could not send me on such a dangerous path alone. Jonas dismissed all of these obstacles and suggested that she herself join me in hiding.

Yehudit promised to consider it and to give Jonas an answer one way or another. When she returned to the ghetto, she spoke of the meeting. My relatives, who had occasionally hinted to my sister and me that we were a burden to them, suddenly realized that Yehudit was the only young worker in the house, who contributed the lion's share to the family's sustenance. When she went to forced labor, she carried extra clothes on her back and replaced them with pounds of food. Suddenly, it became clear to them that if Yehudit and I were to leave, Berta's parents, the older Pruzhans, would remain in the ghetto, and Berta and her three children would be left without any help. Berta, who was assertive and authoritative, pleaded, "Do not leave us! Please do not run away with Yochanan without trying to save my children as well! If you manage to arrange shelter for my three children, we will not stop you. You owe us a moral debt; if you fulfill it, I will have no objections. My life and the lives of my parents don't matter as long as I know there is safety for the children."

We debated what to do. The separation from Yehudit would be unbearably difficult for me. I was scared. There were days when we thought that this offer might be a death trap, with malicious intent. On other days we thought that perhaps it was a real lifeline. So we debated, and occasionally Jonas would visit Yehudit's place of work and beg her to respond to his offer. Finally, hesitantly, we accepted the offer and decided that I would go alone to the hiding place in the Lithuanian's house.

5

—◦◦◦—

THE STORY—BACK TO
THE BEGINNING

WHEN WAR BROKE OUT BETWEEN THE SOVIET UNION AND Germany on June 22, 1941, our family was made up of seven people: my parents, Mendel and Ronia; my grandmother, my mother's mother, Malca Broide (née Fishman); and four children: my eldest sister, Devorah-Vera; my oldest brother, Zvika-Hirsch'ke; my sister Yehudit; and me. Our family owned a flour mill and some land, so our family was considered wealthy, and my father was considered prominent in the Panemunė community.

Even before the war, when the Russians invaded in 1940 and Lithuania became a Soviet Republic, our financial situation had worsened significantly. Since my father was a landowner and business owner, and thus considered to be "bourgeois," the authorities began to impose restrictions on him. He had to report, register, and manage his business in accordance with new rules and procedures, and high taxes were imposed. Despite these burdens, my father was an incurable optimist.

The war in Europe had already escalated by then. France had surrendered and London was being bombed. Yet my father saw a silver lining:

"Even though the Soviet regime is placing an economic burden on us, they are guaranteeing us life."

From a Polish Jewish refugee named Barash, who lived in our home for a while, and from stories of other Polish refugees to Lithuania, we already knew something about the fate of Polish Jewry. My father was convinced that the might of the Red Army would protect us from the Nazis.

Early in the morning of June 22, when we heard the German bombs from their planes, we still believed that the Soviet Red Army would destroy Hitler's army. Soviet Foreign Minister Vyacheslav Molotov's words were being broadcasted at the time: "Victory will be ours; the enemy will be eliminated."

On the second night of the war, my father understood from his sharpened senses and wisdom that the situation was really bad. That night, we saw the Russian troops retreating, and in the morning, we were met with panic and disorder. My authoritative father came to a decision that my mother found difficult to accept; we were to hitch a pair of horses to the largest wagon, load it up with as much as it could carry, lock the house, and travel to our relatives in the center of the city of Kaunas. From experience, my father knew that pogroms were more dangerous in small towns and city outskirts, whereas in the big city there was some security. Mother shed tears . . . our secure, rich, comfortable, pampered lifestyle and warm home collapsed in one day as if it were a house of cards.

We climbed on the wagon and traveled to Kaunas's center. Unfortunately for us, the bridge was no longer passable. Soviet sappers had mined it. My father pleaded with the officer "We are a Jewish family, and you have to understand what's waiting for us." In the process, he placed a "gift" into the officer's hand. The officer let us pass, and so we reached the Pruzhan and Kronzon families, who lived in a luxury apartment house owned by the Pruzhans.

On the fourth day of the war, the Germans entered. Jews were chased and murdered by Lithuanians. Our liberties were stripped, and we were forced to wear a yellow star. We hoped that my sister Vera (Devorah) and her husband, Asher Waldstein, who lived in Vilnius, had succeeded in escaping to Russia and were saved. We assumed that my brother, who was studying at the university in Vilnius, also escaped.

We were so horribly disappointed when my brother came back to Kaunas rather than fleeing. He didn't want to abandon us. Instead

Zvika (Hirsch'ke) Fein, 1938.

of escaping east with my sister and her husband, he returned home. This was the biggest mistake of his life. Since he was friendly with communists, he was caught by the Lithuanians; as a Jew and a communist, he was imprisoned in the city jail. We saw him a few times being led along with a group of prisoners. Our contact with him ceased. We believed that Hirsch'ke was alive, but later we found out that just a few days after he was imprisoned, he was murdered. He was nineteen years old.

On August 15, 1941, approximately two months after the German invasion, the gates of the ghetto closed on the Jews of Kaunas and its surroundings. The ghetto was established in the Slobodka (Vilijampolė) suburb. The Lithuanians living there were forced to leave their homes and find homes vacated by the Jews: "apartment exchanges." It was a sham. Beautiful homes were exchanged for miserable cabins. Even still, while it was clear that you were making an unjust exchange, there was an illusion that what you did receive was actually yours.

I remember the day a man from Slobodka came to my father and said, "Look, Mr. Fein, you have a house and a flour mill, and I also have a house and a flour mill in Slobodka. Let's trade!" My father went to see the property offered to him: it was a miserable house with one large room, in the middle of which stood a stove for cooking and heating, with a chimney going up through the middle of the ceiling; life was lived around this central stove. The miserable flour mill was no longer needed by anyone, so it would serve as a storeroom for us.

The trades were baseless, but my father understood that if we dallied, we wouldn't even get this much. My mother could not fathom how my father was agreeing to this. But my father was the one making the decisions, and wisely so. At first, we believed the sham—that the property in the ghetto was ours. But, in October, following the Great Action—where a third of the Jews in the ghetto were murdered, leaving only twenty thousand of the thirty thousand in the ghetto—the area of the ghetto was reduced. We were forced to leave our minimal property and became refugees with nothing.

Every move we were forced to make, from apartment to apartment, first from Panemunė and then inside of Slobodka, depleted our property, and all of our clothes remained packed in very few suitcases and boxes. Back when we were living in the house we got from the Lithuanian, Father was intrigued by a small wooden-fenced field right next to our home, where the Lithuanian had grown potatoes. Father figured that the produce we would pick from the field would feed us for a whole year. For him, a year was no small matter: the winter would pass, and the German army would not survive in the Russian cold and would be defeated. The exchange of houses thus promised food for the family.

Soon enough, hunger struck the ghetto. The regular portions we received—one hundred grams of bread a day and other meager rations—were just not enough. Even before autumn arrived, we started digging every day and taking out a few potatoes that were not yet ripe in order to complete what was lacking in our daily food basket. When the bulbs began to mature fully, the neighbors raided our field and began to dig out bulbs for themselves. My mother argued with them, saying that it was our property. But my father understood that arguing would not help, so he ordered us to stop arguing with the trespassers, saying that they were our brothers in trouble and were as hungry as we were. The only thing we could do was dig, and the more bulbs we took out, the better. We enlisted to the task and recruited all the family members: my cousin Michael'eh Lifshitz and others. Within a few hours, there was almost nothing left in the field. We packed a number of bags, dragged them into the house, and took them down to the flour mill cellar. I remember that many days after the attack on the field we would go out to check if there were still some potatoes left by the neighbors, and from time to time, we would find additional bulbs.

Soon, word spread that the Feins were a rich family and that they had sacks of potatoes. Friends and acquaintances began to visit our home, some of whom we knew rather superficially. They would ask us how we were, remind us who they were, what connection we had with them in the past, the favors they had once done for us or not done to us, and at the end of the conversation they would say, "Give us some potatoes!" My father could not stand the pressure of the requests, and nobody left our house empty-handed. My mother begged him to stop, but to no avail. Within a short period of time, all the potatoes had run out, and we, too, became hungry like everyone else.

This is what my father, Mendel Fein, was like, and in spite of his age—around sixty-two—he went out to do forced labor so that he would get the status of "productive Jew." Anyone holding a work permit was assumed to have an advantage for the upcoming future. My father's motto was *"Men darf zein a mentsch"*—"You have to be a mensch"—and he was, in fact, in every meaning of the word: gentle, kind, good-hearted, educated, loving. For us, our father was everything.

6

THE GREAT ACTION
AND THE LOOTING OF THOSE
WHO REMAINED

I REMEMBER HOW IN THE GREAT ACTION, WHEN ALL THE Jews in the ghetto were ordered to come out to the Democrats Square, we went through a selection: "Left, right; left right!"

We all knew which was the good side, where you would survive. While those sent to the right were not guarded, those sent to the left were heavily guarded by armed Nazis.

I remember how, as darkness fell, we got to the group making the selections, Nazi officers dressed in black. My sister tried to take advantage of her young age, her beauty, and her blond Aryan looks. She stood in front of our family and said, "This is my family, and we work." Indeed, we had permits. That's how we survived the Great Action.

A day earlier, we were trying to figure out how to deal with Grandma, who was more than ninety years old and could not walk to the square with us. The morning before the Action, her condition worsened, and late in the afternoon, she passed away. Since the Germans made note that they were going to search the houses and anyone found would be killed, we decided to leave Grandma's body unburied. Father covered her and left a note in German stating that she had passed the day before.

The day after the Action, I awoke at dawn, earlier than usual, and I heard shots from a distance. When I got up, I did not find my father in his bed, and I went outside. He was standing in the yard, and when I approached him, I saw that he was crying. Until then I had believed that only children cried. He explained that the shots we were hearing were killing our brothers. I refused to believe it. He pointed at a long line of people winding outside the ghetto between the mountains. Those were the people taken yesterday during the Action and brought to the Ninth Fort.[1] There, group after group was murdered . . . a whole day of murders. In the endless line of those awaiting their deaths was my father's sister, as well.

After the Action, our lives became much darker. A third of the people in the ghetto were murdered in one day.

The Germans looted the ghetto. They went from house to house searching closely. They dug around the houses and under the foundations and plundered whatever they could. The ghetto was depleted and impoverished. Being separated from our property was in effect tantamount to removing our means of subsistence since the clothes were used to trade for food. I remember very well how Nazi officers accompanied by soldiers entered our house and began emptying it. Until it came to my violin's turn. One of the soldiers took the violin and left with it. My father, who had a strong relationship with the violin and my playing it, rushed to the officer and urged him: "This boy plays well. Please, leave him the violin. Take anything you want, but, please, leave the violin!"

The officer ordered the soldier to return the violin, and to test whether my father was telling the truth, he ordered me to play. I stood in the middle of the yard, and as the soldiers dragged, packed, and destroyed our property, I played with tears running down my cheeks. My violin was returned to me.

This was an organized plunder, but robberies that were private initiatives of the Lithuanians followed. They saw the ghetto as an endless opportunity to get rich. There were legends spread among them of the Jews being wealthy, millionaires hiding their gold. More importantly, since Jews had been outlawed, they could do whatever they wanted to them. During the evenings and at night, the Lithuanians guarding the gates would leave their posts, visit a house, and at gunpoint search for possessions to loot. There was no one to complain to.

I remember one night, there was wild knocking at our door. My father asked, "Who is it?"

From outside, they answered in Lithuanian, "Open up!" It was clear that it was a thief, and my father refused to open the door. The Lithuanian did not give up: "Open up—or I will kill you!" and he slammed the door with the butt of his rifle.

My father remained steadfast in his refusal. He relied on the order that robbery by individuals was forbidden. The Germans had declared that "anyone who plunders will be killed!" (*Wer plündert, wird erschossen!*) He hoped that the Lithuanian would finally leave, but the man broke down the door and pointed his rifle at my father. However, Father did not retreat; he grabbed the rifle. Mother joined in, and they both tilted the barrel aside. The Lithuanian was astonished for a moment and evidently was at a loss; as the guard of the fence, he was not allowed to leave his post, and had expected a swift robbery. Yet the two Jews, an elderly man and woman, held the rifle and would not let go. The Lithuanian held the rifle with one hand, and with the other, he hit my parents, but they, covered with blood, still did not let go of the rifle.

Suddenly, a shot was fired. A Nazi officer, who was probably inspecting the fence, turned in the direction from which the shot was heard and presented himself in our yard during the struggle with the Lithuanian guard. At threat of gunpoint, the quarrel stopped. My parents and the Lithuanian stood in front of the Nazi, who demanded explanations. The Lithuanian, who did not speak German, had no way of justifying his presence in the ghetto. My father, who spoke German well, explained that the man had come to rob them and that he defended himself because the Lithuanian threatened to kill his family. Since the Germans did not like private theft (only organized robbery on their behalf), the Nazi took the rifle from the guard and ordered my parents and me to go inside. He led the Lithuanian away. We sat holding each other tight and wept. Again, I realized that adults cry too.

7

——◈◈◈——

THE SEPARATION FROM
MY PARENTS

ON FEBRUARY 6, 1942, I WAS SEPARATED FROM MY PARENTS. It was a bitter day, and I was all of twelve years old. That same day, the Germans demanded that the Jewish Committee ("Der Yiddisher Komitet") hand over five hundred working-age people to be sent to the Riga Ghetto. (The committees were also known as *Judenrats*, but I don't like to use the term).[1] Rumor had it that the Jewish Committee refused. In the early days of the ghetto, five hundred men had been called upon for special work, and it had been emphasized that they had to be intelligent and educated. Some of them had even come dressed nicely for their special work. Every last one was murdered. It was a bitter experience that prompted the Jewish Committee's refusal to cooperate and carry out this new demand.

The armed Germans, who realized that there were too few people in the Democrats Square, raided the area, and anyone they came across was removed from their homes. Our dwelling was close to the square—it was the second place we lived in because when the ghetto area was reduced, the house with the flour mill was no longer within the ghetto fence, and we were forced to uproot ourselves from there. We lived in a building that had once been a school, in the janitor's room. Gestapo men raided the house and took my parents and my sister to the square. They left me in the house. It was a cold, snowy day, and I went out to the steps of the house and watched what was going on. I saw that the Germans were carrying out a selection.

Masses of armed Germans were threatening with their weapons, and a group of four or five officers, wearing dark uniforms and wrapped in fur coats, were carrying out the selection.

I noticed my parents approaching, and when they reached the decision makers headed by the commander of the ghetto, Jordan, they were ordered to go to the right. All those sent there were under heavy guard, while the others who did not meet their criteria were released and ordered to go in another direction. I realized that they were taking my parents and my sister away from me. No one believed the Germans when they said that they would be transferred to another ghetto; the fear was that they were being taken to their execution. The thought that I would be left alone, a lonely child in the ghetto, frightened me, and I burst into tears. I went down the steps of the house and ran toward the group that was being guarded, so that I could stay with my parents. With no coat, I was freezing cold, and my tears froze on my face. A compassionate Jewish policeman noticed a lone child running frantically and asked why I was running. I explained that my parents had just been taken, and he advised me to report to the commander of the ghetto, Jordan, and ask that he release my parents. I should explain to him that I was left alone; maybe it would help. "You must try!" Since I hesitated, he pushed me forward.

Sending a Jewish boy to confront Jordan was like sending him straight to the Angel of Death. Even still, the policeman took me by the hand and walked me over to him. When we were twenty or thirty meters away from the officers, the policeman retreated and left me by myself since, of course, he, too, was afraid. I took a look back; I had come a long way, and the distance between the officers and me was just a few meters. I trembled from the cold and fright; my knees buckled beneath me and did not let me continue forward. You could hear a pin drop in the field: a Jewish child approaching the monster, the ghetto's officer, Jordan. He ordered me to approach. I moved forward, but not within reach of the whip in his hand. "*Was willst du den?*" ("What do you want?")

A German nanny (whom I will speak more about later) had raised me. I therefore spoke enough German to be able to explain that my parents were "there," and I pointed with a shaking hand to the guarded group. "So, what do you want?" I said that I wanted to be with my parents, and he answered: "Good, run over to your parents!" I believed I had succeeded.

But when I happily ran toward them, my mother screamed out horribly that I should run away and not come near them. My sensible father too, in a very commanding but loving tone, told me to stay away: "Go back! Ask them to release us to you!"

I went back and once again stood before Jordan, continuing to keep my distance so that his whip could not reach me. I said, "I don't want to go to my parents; I want my parents to come to me."

The officers burst out laughing. "This Jewish boy is not stupid . . ." Jordan spurted in his sharp, disgusting voice and sneered. "You can go to your parents or you can get out of here fast! You have one second to decide!" His voice and face were threatening, and he waved his whip in the air as if he were training animals in the circus.

Being separated from my parents was impossible for me. Again I ran back to them, and once more my mother screamed and my father ordered "Go home!" with his finger pointing toward our house.

I had to obey my father's orders. I knew he meant them out of love and that he said them to save me. I backed away.

Trembling from the cold, fear, and emotion, I entered our home. How horrible those next few hours were. A Jewish boy all alone in the ghetto. I remember crawling under the pile of blankets, still fully dressed, and covering myself up to my head to get warm.

Once I regained my composure, I had to consider what to do next. First, I ate all of the family's food for that morning. I was so hungry. I finished four hundred grams of bread all by myself. Then I decided to go to some relatives. I chose the Kronzons. Aunt Chava, my mother's sister, was married to Motel Pruzhan, and their daughter Berta was married to Abrasha Kronzon. The elderly Pruzhan couple, along with their daughter, son-in-law, and their three children, lived together in a remote apartment, on Bajorų Street, near the ghetto fence. So, I ran there, stumbling my way.

When I arrived, I thought they would ask me, "What happened?" But I found them sitting and crying. I was sure they were crying over my parents and my sister Yehudit. It turned out that they didn't know what happened to us at all. They were crying over Dr. Abrasha Kronzon, Berta's husband, who had also been taken. Berta tried to rescue her husband. She reached Dr. Elkes, who was the head of the Jewish Committee and knew Dr. Kronzon from before the war. She pleaded, explaining that she was left alone with her elderly parents and three children. Dr. Elchanan Elkes, a compassionate man, but helpless, said he would present the Germans with a list of Jews out of the five hundred who were essential to the ghetto, especially the doctors. But to what extent his request would be answered, he did not know and could not promise anything.

I stayed in their home, a two-room apartment, and we all waited for what was to come. Some releases were promised from the train station, which would probably happen at night. The hours dragged on. Night fell, and none of us closed our eyes. The only thing we could hear was the crying of Chava Pruzhan and the children; Berta held her tears. We sat mourning and waited. In the middle of the night, we heard a knock at the door. Everyone came to life, and they hurried to the door hoping that Abrasha, the head of the family, had returned. And how devastated were they, when at the door stood not Dr. Kronzon, but my sister Yehudit. Despite the bitter disappointment, they were happy for her return as well. Still, no one was happier than I was; I leapt toward her and hugged her with all my might: I would not be left alone anymore. Even with this joy, there was a heaviness in the air. Yehudit knew it too; Abrasha had not been released.

She told us that they had brought everyone to the train station. They had waited many hours. When the train arrived, the Germans had squeezed everyone into the train cars. When darkness fell, they ordered everyone to keep quiet and listen to the announcement. A German announced on a loudspeaker, "I will call out fifteen people. Anyone whose name I call will get off the train."

Everyone understood that fifteen people were going to be saved and sent back to the ghetto. There was complete silence, and the German called out one name after another monotonously. Anyone whose name was called shouted out loudly that they were there and got off the train. All five hundred hoped that they would be the one . . . ten had already gotten off, and then another one and another one . . . and then it was time for the last one.

The German then called out the name of a woman, and there was no answer. Perhaps the German botched the pronunciation of the name, or perhaps there was a mistake, or perhaps the lady did not hear, or perhaps she just wasn't among the deportees. He again called her name out loud, and there was no response. And then, my father told my sister Yehudit to get out of the train and stand forward. She didn't dare. Father ordered her, and she did not listen to him. How could she be saved in place of someone else and leave her parents alone! Again, the German's voice was heard, "I'm calling for the last time!"

My father pushed my sister out, and she fell on the platform; she got up and said, "That's me!" The German cursed and asked why he had to call her three times. All fifteen were taken to the vehicle and returned to the ghetto.

I never saw my father again. I did not know then that our separation at the Democrats Square on February 6, 1942, would be permanent. My parents were taken to the Riga Ghetto with nothing but the clothes on their backs. It was a hard winter. Generous people donated clothes to them, and the internal ghetto organizations took care of their needs as best they could. They were made to do forced labor, and when the ghetto was eradicated, they were taken to camps in Germany. My father died at the Dachau concentration camp near the end of the war. My mother miraculously survived and returned after the war to our home in Panemunė.

Sometimes I return in my memories to those terrible days. I think a lot about my parents, how at their advanced age they dealt with the daily hardships in the ghettos and forced labor in the camps, how

Parents of the author, Menachem and Ronia (née Broide) Fein ob"m.
(Note: *Ob"m* stands for "of blessed memory" and is used to
indicate a person has passed away.)

my mother fed us dishes that she managed to make out of nothing.
I remember the arguments between them about the distribution of
potatoes. My mother was in the right. "Every potato given away,"
she said, "hastens the arrival of our own famine." Yes, she was in
the right, and so it did. But in my soul, even now in my later years,
never have I ceased to long for my father, that wonderful man who
was in the wrong.

8

AT MY RELATIVES' HOUSE

AND SO BEGAN AN UNBEARABLE LIFE FOR MY SISTER AND ME at the home of our relatives. My aunt, Chava Pruzhan, was known as a difficult, bitter soul. Her marriage to her husband, Motel, did not go well, and they were like strangers until the end of their lives. They had two children, their daughter, Berta, and their son the doctor, Chaim'ke Pruzhan, who uprooted his family to Kėdainiai, where he had opened a private clinic. There were persistent rumors that at the outbreak of the war, the Jews of Kėdainiai were murdered and no one survived. Chava refused to believe it. She created a world of imagination and fantasy. Day and night, in a sort of frenzy, she spoke to an imaginary Chaim'ke, telling him all her troubles. When Motel implored her to stop and let them sleep a little at night, she would shout at him and accuse him of not loving their son. It was as if every living and breathing person was alive at the expense of Chaim'ke. Sometimes, Yehudit and I were also the victims of her complaints.

Motel (whom we often called Motel'eh), a reserved and quiet man, had had colon cancer before the war. He had undergone surgery, and, surprisingly, survived, but he needed medical care, medicine, and sanitary conditions. Furthermore, he couldn't always control his bowel movements. His life in the ghetto became, therefore, a living hell. He suffered and was very bitter. I, more than the others, started to feel fond of him, because he used to talk to me and tell me stories. Together, we sawed wood for the winter and did various house chores. His daughter, Berta, who was responsible for three children herself, wasn't an easy person, but she was wise and chose her battles

33

carefully. Her life was dedicated to her children, and there was no price she wasn't willing to pay for them and their well-being.

It was into this already crowded house, struggling for survival, that we moved in: myself, twelve years old; and my sister, eighteen. But, there was no time for childhood in the ghetto. You had to grow up fast, and we did. At first, we seemed like two spoiled children to our relatives, unqualified to live in this harsh new reality and unfortunately two more hungry mouths to feed. Only with time did they understand that Yehudit was their salvation. They never admitted as much out loud, but they knew it in their hearts. All the people in the ghetto had to go out to forced labor. But Berta Kronzon wasn't young anymore, and she suffered chronic pain in her legs. The hard day's work was unbearable for her. In various ways, she occasionally managed to free herself from forced labor, but three times a week she had to go, and she returned exhausted, unable even to carry food on her back. This was done by Yehudit, my sister. Every day she would get up before dawn and go out with the brigades to the Aryan side, packing a knapsack with clothes and various objects to be traded and sold for food. And so, every day, it was she who sustained the household. All our surplus belongings were traded or sold, and with the deutsche marks she received, even in the ghetto, it was possible to obtain necessary items. Although business transactions were forbidden, the laws of survival were stronger than any prohibition since the people had to live. Therefore, everyone bought and everyone sold.

I was given jobs as well. I would help Yehudit smuggle things into the ghetto. In the evening, before the brigades returned, I would lie in wait near the fence. The street that ran nearby curved along the length of the fence. When the brigades would reach the gate, their entrance was handled slowly because of the careful searches by the Lithuanian and German guards, who would mainly confiscate food products. There were many smuggling schemes, including bribing the guards. One way or another, the inspection took a long time, and the members of the brigades lingered by the fence waiting for their turn.

I would be waiting for Yehudit on the Jewish side of the ghetto, while she was on the road on the Aryan side. When the guard would turn his back—sometimes because he was bribed—Yehudit would dash to the fence, remove her backpack, and leave it there. I would press my foot down against the bottom wire and through the gap drag the heavy pack into the ghetto. After the inspection, we would meet and go home, happy that we managed to trick the Germans.

This was very dangerous because the Germans would shoot even into a crowd of children, though they were often satisfied with just a horrible beating. Hempfler, a notorious Nazi, excelled at this. I don't think I ever saw him without his thick crop, with its leather straps woven into a thick braid. More than once I was at the receiving end of his heavy blows.

As soon as we got home, Aunt Chava would start with her criticism. We never heard a positive word from her, and my relatives never praised my sister for making good deals. When my aunt thought that an object was sold for less than its real price, she would yell at her. At the same time, I think our hosts appreciated the efforts made by Yehudit, the beautiful blonde girl with "classic" Aryan looks. In our house, she had had a reputation of being spoiled and frightened, but in the ghetto, she became known for rare courage. After the brigade left the ghetto with the huge crowd of workers, she would remove her yellow star and take off in different directions to the many hiding places referred to as *malinas*, where business was carried out. She was able to establish contact with some Lithuanians, especially with one woman involved in business, who subsisted from these transactions.

Yehudit's trips on the Aryan side without the yellow star were very dangerous; however, she continued with them for the family's survival. Once, Yehudit brought home meat that was sold to her as lamb, and Aunt Chava realized that it was dog meat. There was a huge, bitter argument. Yehudit was reprimanded, and Aunt Chava decided that I, her brother, would need to accept the punishment; I would have to sell the meat wrapped in newspaper. In the evening, I went out to the square near the Jewish Committee, where there was always business being transacted.

On my way there, I had already decided that I would not sell the meat. Instead, I would stay out for several hours, as though I had

Yehudit, Yochanan's sister, 1946.

made an effort to sell it, and I would return with a story that I could not find a buyer. That night was dark and rainy; I made my way home via the dark alleyways of the ghetto, with my feet sloshing in puddles and mud. When I got closer to the house, I sensed that someone was following me; I could feel that something bad was going to happen. I turned around instinctively, and a blurry figure stood in front of me; I recognized that he was a Nazi officer. His coat buttons and the symbols of his rank sparkled in the dark. His hands were covered by black leather gloves, and he held a stick in his hand. He stopped me and asked what I had in the basket. I answered, "Nothing."

"Open it!" he ordered. He shone his flashlight into it, rummaged around with his stick, and found the meat. Without any warning he punched me in the face. I fell, my vision blurred, and lost consciousness. When I awoke, I found myself lying in the mud. Once I was convinced that the officer had disappeared, I stood up and went home crying and shaken, my face swollen, covered with blood and mud.

That night, I was actually greeted with love and compassion; even stern-faced Aunt Chava gave me praise and encouragement. I was forgiven for all my sins, both real and imagined.

9

--- oʘo---

GENERAL WINTER

I MUST TELL AN EXTRAORDINARY STORY, BORDERING ON UN-
believable, about how we earned our keep in our relatives' home.

I first heard the term "General Winter" from my father, who was
an incurable optimist and was generally encouraged by his cheery
prophecies, in sharp contrast to my mother's character, who was
constantly in a state of melancholy. When my mother delivered a
eulogy for the financial well-being of our family before the Russians
came to Lithuania, my father replied humorously that this should be
considered a fair price for the Red Army protecting us from Hitler.

The news of the persecution of Jews in Nazi-occupied areas, rein-
forced by the tens of thousands of refugees who had arrived in Lithuania from Poland, strengthened my father's confidence in the "deal"
he had reluctantly made with the communist regime in his mind.
But unfortunately, his optimism was misplaced. The Red Army retreated in panic, and on the fourth day of the war, the Wehrmacht
arrived in town.

My good father did not get depressed. He assumed that the war
would reach resolution quickly because of the greatest of the Russian
generals: General Winter. But the war lasted longer than expected,
and General Winter struck the inhabitants of the ghetto before he hit
the Germans. In normal times, the Eastern European winter had its
charm: a warm, heated house; the inhabitants dressed in wool; a hat
wrapped around the head and ears; gloves tied with a string through
the sleeves so that they would not get lost. We, the children, would

make and hold snowballs with our bare hands and have snowball fights. On a happy day, when school was canceled because of the cold, we would slide down the street on sleds into the middle of the frozen Nemunas River. The snowmen we built showcased our sense of creativity. But happy days were a thing of the past. Now, in the ghetto, we only knew the hardships of winter, the grip of its icy arms.

In the first winter of 1941–1942, fences were dug up, trees were up-rooted, the bushes—anything that could be burned—was gathered, collected, and thrown into the oven. The ghetto now looked like a giant field with no partitions.

The arrival of the second winter of 1942–1943 brought with it terrible suffering. Cold prevailed in the homes, clothes were running out, and the children's games lost their charm. General Winter beat us with all his might. What were we to do?

If only we had the wood that we had left behind in our previous home, just over the fence. We began to consider how to retrieve it. Eventually, Berta came up with a daring idea for bringing the wood we left behind at Daukanto Street—or at least some of it—to the ghetto. The idea took on a life of its own, and we could not put it to rest. The plan that was finally drawn up was quite far-fetched. Worse, it involved a life-threatening situation.

Dr. Elkes and Dr. Kronzon were friends from earlier days. Now, when Dr. Elkes—a man of stature, kindness, and compassion—was the head of the Eltestenraht (literally "the Council of Elders," or in the words of the locals—Der Yiddisher Komitet, or the "Jewish Committee"), Berta Kronzon once again asked him for help. The exact details of their conversation were not told to the children, but from the adults' whispered conversations, I knew that the risky plan of bringing the wood into the ghetto was being put into action.

Berta painted an already gloomy situation even worse: an elderly couple, four children, one of them a baby, a very sick father, and everyone freezing from the cold. Her husband, as mentioned earlier, had been exiled to the Riga Ghetto, and the burden of responsibility for the family's fate rested entirely on her. She was able, she said, to bring a small amount of wood in from what they had left at their home. What was needed was some kind of arrangement that would enable the wood to be brought through the gate. The quantity was described as a "horse-drawn wagon of wood."

And this remarkable person, Dr. Elkes, over whom the fate of the ghetto hung like a millstone, for whom any mistake could seal his fate, promised to help even with the littlest things, such as bringing wood for Berta Kronzon, his friend's wife.

He turned to a senior officer in the Jewish ghetto police, an officer who commanded the unit responsible for the gates. That same officer, Ernstam, knew the arrangements and procedures relating to the order of guard duty and personally knew many of the Lithuanian and German guards. The most easygoing were the most corrupt, and he managed to contact them and arrange matters. In all the smuggling and bribery transactions there was grave danger, but at that dark time, when life itself was in great danger, the instinct to live dictated the risks one would take to survive.

After the officer confirmed that he could arrange the smuggling of the wood, Berta was asked to organize the delivery and bring the wood on the day and time that they would tell her. In addition, it was determined that the wood wouldn't arrive at the main gate, but at a different gate, where the guarding was sparser.

And how did Berta intend to arrange the delivery? The main role in this drama was given to my sister.

Yehudit, who was familiar with danger, removed her star and went to the *nyanya*'s ("nanny" in Russian) house. The nanny was faithful and good to the Kronzon family. She was stunned when she saw Yehudit, but she received her with emotion, hugged and kissed her, and whispered "*Dochenka, dochenka*" ("my little daughter" in Russian). She listened, pained, to what had happened to the family in the ghetto and expressed sincere sorrow for their suffering.

Yehudit asked her to do a good deed for the Krozon family, by serving as a messenger. The nanny would talk to the groundskeeper, who had been employed by the Pruzhans, Berta's parents, for many years. His loyalty would be tested; he would be asked to give the Pruzhans a small amount of wood from what was left with him before they were exiled to the ghetto. It was dangerous to consent to the request, and it would not have been hard to refuse. What would be simpler than saying that all Jewish property had been confiscated and that there was no more wood for the Pruzhans? Everything now belonged to the municipal authority—the Jewish homes and their wood.

Nevertheless, the nanny approached the groundskeeper, and he acceded to the request. Whether he took wood from the existing lot in the large house or purchased other wood with the money paid to him, that I will never know—and it is totally unimportant in any case. Finding a wagon driver who, for pay, would bring the wood to the ghetto—at every obstacle, someone was willing to help. Even in Sodom, a few righteous people could still be found. Thus, after meticulous planning and a properly arranged timetable, the improbable operation began. We could hardly believe that our far-fetched scheme was becoming a reality. That day, I spent a long time by the ghetto gate, hidden behind a nearby house, waiting for what was to come.

The cart left with Yehudit walking alongside it on the sidewalk so that the wagon driver would not be connected to her in the event that she was caught and identified. The wood arrived at the gate at the intended time. A police officer waited at the gate inside the ghetto, while two Lithuanian policemen stood outside.

After a cursory check of the contents of the wagon, the lock was removed, the gate was opened, and the valued delivery made it inside. As she approached the gate, Yehudit climbed onto the cart and sat down beside the wagon driver as if she were an innocent traveler who wanted to accompany him. Everything was done quickly and hurriedly—a testimony to the power of bribery. The wagon came at a gallop into the courtyard of our house, the wood was quickly unloaded (to the neighbors' astonishment), and the driver fled toward the gate as fast as possible to ensure getting out before the changing of the guards.

For days, my Uncle Motel'eh and I sawed the tree trunks to an appropriate length, and with an ax we chopped them to the desired thickness. Mostly, attention was given to protecting the wood from theft. We installed locks on the shed, and my Uncle Motel'eh, who did not sleep well, kept an eye on what was going on in the yard.

An oven made of dark tin was installed in our house with two openings for cooking—made by a resourceful metal worker in the ghetto. From the oven, a chimney spun through the room and out the window. So, while the cooking of the ghetto food went on, usually in the evening, the house heated as well by the heat emitted from the chimney.

The project of bringing the wood required endless resourcefulness, good-heartedness and mercy, good people, and courage. However, every act of courage requires a bit of luck, and once again, luck played its part in a big way for my sister Yehudit. Thousands of people froze from the cold in the ghetto: children, parents, and elders. But we had something they lacked, which in the ghetto was known as "vitamin P"—*protektzia* ("protection" based on who you knew and having the right connections).

10

❧

ACTIVITIES

AMONG MY OTHER DUTIES, I HAD TO REDEEM OUR RATION cards for the food we had coming to us. The queues for the food were very long, irregular, unjust, and violent. People pushed each other, and what was needed was chutzpah and elbows. I, a skinny kid, could not stand this battle. So I found a method: I would come early, wait hours until the store opened, and be the first, or at least one of the first. I'd get up before dawn with my sister. We would each go our own way—she to the forced labor and I to the breadline. In addition to bread, sometimes they also distributed another food item. Once they distributed butter. That morning I came especially early because I knew the pressure would be enormous, and I did in fact manage to get the family's portion.

On occasion they distributed spoiled food as well. Once they distributed little fish that we called *kilkes*. They were so rotten that they were dangerous for consumption. In spite of the hunger, the ghetto organizations decided to bury the fish and not distribute them. Once they distributed meat that turned out to be horse meat from those killed in battle. We actually debated eating it over throwing it out. In the winter, they distributed frozen, rotten potatoes that looked like congealed mud. You would have to come with a bucket into which the distribution was poured. Of course, they weighed it so that you should not, God forbid, get more than your share. They would pour the portion into the bucket with a shovel because you could not touch the muck with your hands, and when it was brought home and the mud and rot were rinsed off, there remained very few potatoes,

43

which were also blemished. Still, they were supposedly suitable for eating.

I took on an important job: managing the implementation of the ration cards. Reliably and consistently, I carried out my duty. When they sliced the bread ration for my family, sometimes it was necessary to add a slice or half a slice to the weight, since the seller was not always accurate when he distributed the bread. Despite being perpetually hungry, I never touched an extra crumb. My family knew I could be trusted to fulfill my responsibility, and I was proud of the trust they placed in me.

I had another job with a side benefit. I was even called "rich boy" from time to time. In the evenings, the ghetto was dark, without electricity. Other sources of light used were candles, oil lamps, and carbide. The most important and efficient commodity was, therefore, a flashlight.

Before the war, flashlights were sold in the shape of a cylinder, operated by round batteries. From my youth, I remembered that having a flashlight was a symbol of maturity. The children would save every penny to buy a flashlight. During the war, the production of round batteries ceased, causing a shortage, because the German Army needed square batteries. A few of us kids developed a method of transforming the round flashlight into a square. We would cut into the side of the flashlight, remove a piece of tin, straighten it, and place a three-millimeter-thick delicate box made of plywood with a closure on the flashlight, which would move on an axle made of a thin nail. When the closure was locked, the battery would press against the bulb and light it. These flashlights were in demand in the ghetto, and I could make four or five a day, which meant I always had money in my pocket. I could buy many things with those deutsche marks, even extra food to add to the family ration.

This was the first business I ran in my life, but there were other enjoyable pastimes that made us forget our hunger, problems, and sadness.

I learned to play chess in the ghetto. Leibke Solski was the boy who taught me. Through him, I made my acquaintance with a group of children who were addicted to chess. Even I lost myself in the game. The whole group adopted for themselves a well-known chess master from Berlin named Kopelman as their "rabbi." He had moved from place to place, escaping Hitler's wrath. In Lithuania, he first ended up in Klaipėda, a port city (known as Memel in German), and when it was taken over from Lithuania by the Germans (1939), he escaped to Kaunas, which they took over as well (1941).

Kopelman didn't know how to do anything except play chess. His wife was a violinist, and their charming son was a good dancer. The Kopelmans' house in the ghetto was run-down, and his family was poor and hungry all the time, but Kopelman ignored it. He would sit on a stool at the entrance to his home, next to a small table, with the chessboard arranged in front of him as though he were waiting for a partner. In the evening, when the boys would free themselves up from their duties—some of them were older and worked in forced labor—they would gather at the Kopelman's narrow, cramped house.

We would play chess by the light of a candle. Thanks to Kopelman, I learned to love the game and its secrets. Whenever I had free time, I would run over there. Kopelman, who loved me, honored me with a gift. They had a bookcase in their house with a broad selection of subjects. Some of the books, of course, were about chess. There were books in Russian, a language Kopelman did not speak, and a book about the international chess competition of 1935 in Moscow, in which two Jewish Grandmasters, Botvinnik and Flohr, tied for first place. All the games in the competition were in this book, with an analysis and notes on the moves. Kopelman gave me this book as a present, and I went home so happy.

As I stated, the book was written in Russian, but I only knew how to speak it and not read it. So, late at night, when everyone else was sleeping, I would sit in the corner, by the light of a candle, joining letter to letter, simultaneously learning the chess games of the greats and how to read Russian.

I learned the names of the masters, and I fell in love with chess. One evening, as I sat opposite the checkered board, I did not get up from there until early morning when I had to get in line for bread.

The truth: sleep in the ghetto was not so pleasant; I shared a bed with the two bigger Kronzon children, Sima and Shmuel (Samuel). Everyone tried to hog the blanket.

It seemed to me that I was in control of my dreams. At night I would dream of food, or sometimes I would order up a dream of a movie I had seen in the past. However, I wasn't sure whether I was dreaming or hallucinating.

Besides my enjoyable pastime of chess, I kept busy with other things, as well. Throughout this unforgettable period, I continued studying the violin. Today, I find it difficult to explain to myself how, in the hell of the ghetto, we had the will to continue with luxury pastimes, to study violin in the inferno of the ghetto. But this was one of those things that characterized the will to live. Efforts were made to teach children in the ghetto, in spite of the fact that it was forbidden, and there were parents who made sure of their children's violin lessons at any price.

It was understood that studying piano was no longer possible— there were no pianos in the ghetto, but my sister Yehudit insisted that I continue playing the violin and demanded of our relatives that they disburse funds from the income she provided as payment for her work. A teacher was found named Stuppel, who was a famous violinist in Kaunas before the war and the first violinist in the ghetto orchestra. Yet a problem emerged: my violin was a three-quarter size, but over time I grew, my hands got longer, and I needed a full-size violin. There was such a violin in the house. Dr. Abrasha Kronzon played violin as a hobby, having studied at the conservatory, and once he was taken to the Riga Ghetto, his violin went unused. However, Berta forbade anyone touching his violin, especially me, whose playing was almost forced upon those I was living with. My teacher's explanations, that playing an instrument does not harm it, but exactly the opposite, it is actually good for it, did not help. My teacher, Stuppel, was so kind as to give me his second violin, and the problem was solved.

It was hard to practice in the overcrowded apartment. The members of the household did not have the patience for this. But

I continued and actually progressed from student pieces to more complicated compositions. I started playing Bach, the Concerto in A Minor and the Concerto in E Major, in addition to other captivating compositions.

I met several gifted children at Stuppel's. One of them, Intriligator, was an outstanding musician. Another was especially talented. I don't remember his name, but I would sit for hours listening to him play. Afterward, I would accompany him to his home, where he would continue to play for many more hours. I came to know Beethoven's concerto from him, and I listened to his rendition of Bach's Chaconne and other wonderful compositions.

11

THE MALINA

AS TIME WENT ON, ESPECIALLY AFTER THE SURRENDER OF the Germans in Stalingrad, fears about the fate of the ghetto increased. How would one survive? Everyone was preoccupied with this question. To escape? Where to, how, to whom? Escape plans were feasible for individuals, not for families with children.

What would the German defeat look like? Would the Red Army come storming in, not leaving the Germans time for so-called minor details such as the liquidation of a small concentration of Jews in the Kaunas Ghetto, or would there be a cruel and total annihilation of all the inhabitants of the ghetto?

What crystallized in our heads was perhaps typical of all the residents in the ghetto. The general conclusion was, given our bitter experiences and knowing the Germans' murderous inclinations, that with a slow retreat, the ghetto would be liquidated in the most horrific way imaginable. At that time the illusions ceased. We already knew all too well what Nazis were capable of. But we hoped that if the withdrawal would be fast, and the Red Army would beat them and chase them by storm, as was the case in several battles we heard about, and if we could find a short-term hiding place until the fury subsided, there would be a chance of survival. That was how the idea of a *malina* (a hiding place) was born, a short-term hiding place until the storm passed—hours or days—hoping to make it to liberation. Building a malina was the only thing that our family, with the means at our disposal, could actually manage practically. After much thought, discussion, and more than a few arguments, our malina plan was formulated. And this is how things were planned.

Our house in the ghetto had three entrances: The first entrance, adjoining Bajorų Street, led to the apartment we lived in. In the third entrance lived the family of Dr. Matis, a well-known ear, nose, and throat doctor in Kaunas, married to a German woman. She had had the opportunity to leave her husband, live on the Aryan side, and survive, but she chose to follow him. She was confined with him and their children in the ghetto, and so she come to share the fate of the Jews of the Kaunas Ghetto. None of their family survived.

The second entrance, the middle one, led to the second floor of the house, where several families lived, and also to the basement of the house, most of which was under our apartment, but much smaller. The entrance to the basement was through a square door, one meter square in size, on the side of the stairs. To enter the basement, one had to lift the door that moved on its hinges toward the wall, where it was attached by a hook installed for that purpose, and climb down a ladder that stood on the floor of the basement.

Our plan was to pile boards on the basement door, parts of broken furniture, rusted tins and metals, and all kinds of scraps found in yards, and place them in a disorganized manner, as though they were items that no one needed. And that was exactly what we did. People would see it—and unless they decided to investigate further—they would see the corner of a filthy, disorderly warehouse. The original entrance to the cellar would as such be hidden from the human eye.

Now we had to dig an entrance from our apartment. After a lot of measuring and calculations, we figured out that we had to do it from the floor near the wall, under the three-door wardrobe. The wardrobe stood on four short legs, and to see the floor underneath it, one would have to kneel and bend down. The wardrobe stood in its place as though it were planned that way. At the bottom of the wardrobe, at each of its doors, there were shelves made of plywood cut perfectly to close off the bottom of the wardrobe without being attached to the sides. This way, the bottom board could easily be lifted.

Moving the bottom revealed the wooden floor of the room, into which I cut with a fine saw, creating a rectangular opening just big enough for a person to crawl inside. When we removed the rectangle in the floor, a concrete floor was revealed—which was the ceiling of the basement. With painstaking and exhausting work, my uncle Motel Pruzhan and I broke through, using a chisel, a hammer, and an iron bar. Once a hole was made in the concrete floor, widening it was relatively easier. With the banging of the hammer and the iron bar, the opening was widened to the required size.

The rectangle that was cut out of the floor was strengthened with fitted wooden beams and served as a little door to the opening. Two hinges were screwed to the door, upon which it hung open downward. A ladder was positioned by the door. Those who climbed down into the basement closed the door from inside and locked it in a manner that leveled it with the floor. The cut in the floor was painted the right color, and thus the work was complete.

We practiced going down into the basement-turned-malina. Everyone had to climb down as quickly as possible; the last one down had to replace the floor of the wardrobe while standing on the ladder, climb down one more rung, and close the floor door, lock it, and climb the rest of the way down. We brought blankets into the malina, as well as toasted bread and a barrel to collect water. All of this work required the neighbors' consent, which was given because no one needed the basement. However, there was an expectation, unspoken: in return for their consent, when the time came, the malina would serve everyone.

And so we became owners of a malina. From there, we drew a sliver of hope for the future.

12

THE GIRL, GHETTA'LEH

WE NOW ARRIVE AT THE STORY OF THE YOUNGEST GIRL IN the Kronzon family.

Berta Kronzon was in the last months of her pregnancy when the war broke out, and in the family's eyes, this pregnancy was thought to be an absolute disaster. When the Kronzons thought to bring a baby into this world, they thought of their beautiful, rich home on the affluent Daukanto Street, in the area between Laisvės Alėja ("Freedom Lane") and the military museum, Karo *muziejus*. They had a big yard with fruit trees and ornamental plants and a small pool that had a statue and fountain in the middle. There was a gated entrance for those who came on foot and a main gate that would open when the doctor would enter and leave in his black Ford—a symbol of his standing and quite rare at that time.

The Kronzons' house was rich and comforting, and the children were pampered by the nanny, the Russian nyanya. She was devoted and trustworthy and served in their home even after the Germans came, up until the family was confined to the ghetto.

On the eve that the ghetto closed, August 15, 1941, their daughter was born. She did not enjoy the same pampering as her siblings did. Her parents named her Ghettah, and we called her Ghetta'leh. Her name was derived from the fatal combination of the birth and closure of the ghetto. Ghetta'leh was a wonderful, marvelous, beautiful baby. She started walking and talking very early for her age. She was incredibly intelligent. She would entertain us and make us laugh, making our lives in the ghetto a little more bearable. Her parents swore they would do everything in their power to ensure Ghetta'leh would want for nothing. And so, despite the hunger and hardship, and despite the fact that we were in the depths of hell, the little girl lacked nothing. The Kronzons sold everything, and there was nothing too expensive for them to sell to obtain the necessary food, as though there were no war and as though there were no ghetto at all.

The child grew up in a ghetto surrounded by fences in an environment where there was shooting at night, where there was candlelight or carbide and kerosene lamps, and surrounded by starving people. Yet she knew no hunger. Every day she ate semolina porridge enriched with a spoonful of butter and an egg; she drank milk, and they even got meat for her. Her grandmother fed her, and like every child whose stomach was always full, she developed a resistance to food. Today, it is hard to explain how in a hungry ghetto a little girl was satiated, dressed well, and lacked nothing.

She was the flower of the ghetto. All the residents of the street and the area close by knew the beautiful Ghetta'leh. When I went walking with her, people would stop us and marvel at her appearance. The family's situation worsened tremendously when Dr. Kronzon was taken to the Riga Ghetto. But even then, the family continued to take care of all of dear Ghetta'leh's needs. However, as time went on, and Ghetta'leh celebrated her second birthday, concern for her fate grew. It seemed as though we, the older ones, if given the opportunity, could escape with some chance of survival, but what would a two-year-old toddler do? Therefore, the plans for Ghetta'leh's rescue depended on removing her from the ghetto. We still didn't know how that would happen, but we started getting ready.

Ghetta'leh was a chatterbox, and we had to get her used to being quiet. Slowly and steadily we practiced being silent with her. We got to the point that, when we declared in a scary voice, "*a Deutsch!*" ("a German" in Yiddish), Ghetta'leh would become silent. Afterward, we taught her to hide. The code word a Deutsch meant she was to go hide and sit quietly until we said, "*Er iz avek!*" ("He has left" in Yiddish). Whether as a game or seriously, Ghetta'leh learned to be quiet in her hiding place for hours.

In the next stage of her training, the phrase a Deutsch meant that she had to hide not in some corner or under the bed, but to curl up in a big backpack and lock the opening from inside. And Ghetta'leh would sit in the backpack in total silence. Once, when we took her out, she was all red and wet from sweat. Sometimes it seemed we were tormenting the child unnecessarily, but Berta, her mother, who had a tough personality, did not let up.

She pressured Yehudit to do her best to save Ghetta'leh. She came up with an idea of finding the nyanya, the Russian nanny who had served them for so many years, and asking her for help once more.

And indeed, Yehudit, who didn't shy away from taking a risk, did so. Even today, I still find it hard to grasp the extent of her bravery. Yehudit would go out early in the morning with the work unit, and there, at the airport or somewhere else where she worked with hundreds of forced laborers from the ghetto, she would remove the yellow star from her clothes, disappear from the sight of the guards, and go into town for her errands and her business. One day, she arrived at the Kronzon's nyanya. After a short reconnaissance of the area, when she realized that she was not being followed by any strangers, she gathered her courage and knocked on the door. The door opened, Yehudit crept in, and the door closed again.

Hugs and tears, stories, honest empathy for the family's troubles. "God, when will it all end?" The nyanya told Yehudit that life was difficult for her as well, and she had many worries. There were shortages, her two sons were drafted into the army, and for some time there had been no word from them. What was their fate? Everything was said briefly. Time was pressing, and fear filled the room; a long absence from the work brigade was dangerous.

Yehudit expanded on her story of Ghetta'leh: beautiful, bright—a flower! Tears welled up in the nyanya's eyes. Here, Yehudit revealed the purpose of her visit. She asked, pleaded: "Please accept Ghetta'leh into your home. We won't ask for anything else," she promised. "Please, save only her. The others are less important."

The woman cried bitterly as she considered the proposition. "Money and valuables are not part of the equation—perhaps something, for subsistence, if you have it, if possible, nothing more."

Finally, the good, wonderful nyanya agreed to the request. Weeping, she hugged Yehudit and blurted out in a strangled cry, "*Dochenka* ['my little daughter' in Russian], how can I refuse the Kronzons?"

The dangers were beyond belief. They would have to make up a story for the neighbors that the girl was a relative. And what would happen if she was caught speaking Yiddish ("Some kind of German," they would assume), the only language she knew? Today I think that the woman's consent in accepting the child was an act of tremendous bravery and was a testament to her big heart, humanism, and compassion.

Yehudit visited her several more times. A date was set for bringing the child, plus an alternative date because you could never plan exactly. The plan was to place Ghetta'leh in a backpack and pass her through the fence to the Aryan side. Luckily, the Kronzon's house in the ghetto was adjacent to the fence.

On the Aryan side, about ten meters away, stood the house of a Lithuanian family with whom we had regular contact. Every morning, we saw their window from our window, and when the guard walked away, we talked to them. From time to time we even did some business with them, such as bartering clothes or other necessities for food. In fact, one could say, a certain closeness developed between us, a kind of friendship. In any case, our impression was that the Lithuanian woman was understanding of our bitter fate.

Now we turned to her with a request, that she accept Ghetta'leh into her house for just a few hours after she is smuggled through the fence. Then Yehudit would come for her posing as an Aryan, without her yellow star, as though she were taking her for a walk. That would end the part of the Lithuanian neighbor in the operation.

The woman wanted to help, but she was scared to death. It was such a big risk. Yet Berta, and all of us, did not stop begging her. We offered her valuables in exchange. Finally, the Lithuanian neighbor agreed. Even though she was paid, we considered her act to be very humanitarian. She risked her life and the lives of her household for the sake of the little one.

The day came to say goodbye to Ghetta'leh. I cannot describe the feelings of the entire household: the parting from a flower who made our lives more pleasant in the ghetto, as well as the fear that the complex operation might end in disaster. But we knew we had to try and that there was no going back.

I remember that early morning, when we all trembled with fear and helplessness. I, the boy, was the man of the family. We yelled, "a Deutsch!" and Ghetta'leh hurried into her backpack. This was preceded by days of explanations and practice. She already knew that she would find herself on the other side of the fence.

Ghetta'leh cooperated as though she were older. After she climbed into the backpack, we tied it loosely so that she would have air to breathe. I left with the bag and hid in the bushes a meter or a meter and a half from the fence. We bribed the Lithuanian guard without revealing to him the type of "merchandise" we were transferring. The Kronzon's younger son was with me, a ten-year-old boy named Samuel (we called him Sammy). When the guard disappeared, Sammy stood with all his weight on the barbed wire, and with his two hands, he lifted the top parallel barbed wire. Through that hole I passed the bag, which I left behind the fence, and whispered a few words of encouragement. When we moved away, the Lithuanian neighbor came out quickly and brought the bag into her house.

I returned home. We opened the window and witnessed a crying Ghetta'leh, not believing that this step of the risky and complicated operation had passed successfully. But this was just the start. There were still difficulties and dangers ahead.

That same day, my sister Yehudit left for work early, at dawn, and as she often did, removed her yellow star, and disappeared from work. She walked the entire city of Kaunas to the Aryan side of Slobodka, to the Lithuanian woman's home across from our own. This took immense courage on her part. The guards, who knew the faces of the tenants of the house, would identify the girl they saw almost daily in the ghetto had the caught a glimpse of her. Through the window we saw her with the backpack on her back, holding Ghetta'leh in her hands. We accompanied her with our eyes and weeping hearts until she disappeared out of sight.

Yehudit passed through all of Kaunas with Ghetta'leh. She appeared to be walking with her daughter, and when Getta'leh got tired, she carried her in her arms. After a few hours, they arrived successfully at the nyanya's house. Both women cried bitterly. The kind nanny gave Ghetta'leh love and devoted care, just as she did with the other Kronzon children she raised.

That same day we sat in the ghetto, tense as a bundle of nerves—anxiously awaiting Yehudit's return to make sure that the operation had succeeded. We went out at dusk, when the work brigades were returning, and we waited near the gate of the ghetto. I ran to places along the fence where I would lurk when we would smuggle bags of food into the ghetto. When I spotted her brigade and saw her in line, I ran to inform the household waiting by the gate: "Yehudit is here!" Those few minutes seemed to us like an eternity. The entrance of Jews into the ghetto was not quick. You had to wait for the searches to be done, and standing at the gate was contrary to regulations and often involved beatings by the Germans. Yehudit was the heroine of the day and was received with hugs and kisses. The operation was a success; Ghetta'leh would survive. Yet the house became miserable, as if it had been stripped of its support pillar, the center of its life, its most precious soul. It was hard without her laughter.

On occasion, Yehudit would disappear from work with the help of good people who knew her secret, and she would visit Ghetta'leh. The nyanya would tell her that the girl sometimes cried, and she had a difficult relationship with her because Ghetta'leh spoke only Yiddish and did not understand Lithuanian or Russian.

Weeks passed. It seemed that all was going well. But one day Yehudit came back from the city with bitter news. The nanny's two sons, who were drafted into the German Wehrmacht and sent to the front, came home on furlough. When they returned, they found the girl. They gave their mother an ultimatum, that she had to get rid of Ghetta'leh. Whether it was an objection to saving Jews on principle or a genuine fear for their mother made no difference. The mother was ordered to get the child out of their home.

There was no choice. Yehudit had to once again go on the dangerous and sad journey—to return Ghetta'leh to the ghetto: again, with the backpack on her back, crossing the city and arriving at the Lithuanian woman's house near the ghetto fence and smuggling

Ghetta'leh across the fence to our house. When we opened the backpack and let her out, our joy was limitless. It was as though the light had returned to our house. For a moment, we forgot that she had actually returned to the condemned cell, and again the death penalty was hovering over her head.

Ghetta'leh remained in the ghetto until its last days. When the front was getting closer, the Germans started liquidating the ghetto. The few Jews who remained hoped that if they succeeded in hiding for a few days until the Soviet military arrived, they could possibly be saved. When the Germans ordered everyone to leave their homes so they could be taken to the camps, and likely to their deaths, Berta, her children, and the Pruzhans, perhaps with a few neighbors, climbed down into the shelter to the malina.

The advance of the Red Army from Vilnius to Kaunas was slow and even stopped. During the two-week standoff, the Germans were busy annihilating the ghetto. They searched from house to house; some of the people were murdered, and others were taken with them. On the loudspeakers, those who remained in hiding were ordered to leave, and all the houses, most of them wooden, were set on fire. When those trapped in the shelters realized that they were burning, it was impossible to get out; I will never know whether they died of suffocation or fire. Ghetta'lch was born on the day of the establishment of the ghetto and lost her life with its annihilation.

Immediately upon my liberation, in the first days of the month of August 1944, I decided to return to the ruins of the ghetto. I was advised not to do so since the city was full of armed gangs both in and out of uniform, and no one knew who they were and what they were doing. Anyone who valued their life was advised to keep their distance. But there was no power in the world that could have prevented me from returning to the ghetto, where I had spent three terrible years of my childhood. I expected the impossible, hoped to meet someone dear. When I reached Slobodka, I could not find the houses. I did not understand what was happening. Maybe I had made a mistake on the way. How could I be so confused? As I approached, my astonishment increased. I saw from afar the house of the Lithuanian woman outside the ghetto and the church tower I was so familiar with, but the ghetto was gone. And as I approached, I smelled a terrible, repulsive, suffocating odor. It was the smell of charred corpses. The ghetto was no more. The Germans had burned down the houses, and only the chimneys remained standing, looming up into the sky.

I recognized the foundation of our house, covered in ashes and remnants of burnt wood. The smell was unbearable, but my curiosity brought me to the entrance of the shelter. It is hard to describe what I saw. There were the charred corpses of my dear ones, the Kronzons and the Pruzhans. Opposite the door was my uncle Motel'eh Pruzhan. His white teeth protruded from his burned and twisted skull. Beside him was Ghetta'leh. It seemed that Motel'eh tried to climb up from the malina with his granddaughter, but that the ladder had collapsed. I couldn't stand what I was witnessing. I felt that my mind was becoming a blur, and it took everything I had not to fall into the pit. And then I lost consciousness.

Luckily, the Lithuanian neighbor returned home. She herself had left because of the stench of the rotting bodies. But every day she would come and check that no one had broken into her house or stolen something from there. Now, she saw a boy lying at the entrance to the shelter. She dragged me to her home and poured water on me. When I came to, she hugged me while crying bitter tears, as though she had reunited with her own family member. She crossed herself and called out to God because when she saw me lying there, she imagined that someone had climbed out of the pit alive.

She told me about the annihilation of the ghetto and how the Germans had burned the house. She had begged them not to do it because she thought the fire would spread to her house, but the Germans beat her and drove her away. She had heard the heartbreaking cries of the victims.

I went back to the Paulavičius' house. For a long time, I could not find peace.

13

THE MURDER OF CHILDREN

LET ME RETURN TO MY STORY.

At the beginning of 1944, the situation became desperate. My sister Yehudit and I decided that I should escape. We planned it down to the last detail. We were in touch with Jonas, and we set the date—April 20, 1944—and the place from which I would be taken to the Paulavičius' home. It was Hitler's birthday, and we assumed that the celebrations in honor of the "Führer" would lessen the German's alertness.

Everything seemed to be planned properly, but exact plans in the ghetto were impossible. Then, about three weeks before the planned date, the most horrific event in the history of the Kaunas Ghetto occurred: the Children's Action (Kinder Aktion). I came close to death that day.

During that time, I worked in a carpentry shop for youth. As explained previously, there was a belief in the ghetto that if you worked and were "productive," your chances of survival were greater. I worked several jobs in the ghetto, and the carpentry workshop was one of them. By this time, I had stopped playing the violin because we did not have the means for lessons, nor was there peace of mind. Most importantly, the household couldn't stand it. My farewell to my teacher, Stuppel, was playing Beethoven's Romances.

On March 27, 1944, when I arrived at the workshop, a messenger appeared and conferred with the mentors, the adult carpenters. It was evident that something unusual was happening. Indeed, they gathered us together, and one of the mentors explained that an

Action was taking place in the ghetto. He feared that such a large concentration of children in one place was dangerous. We were told to disperse and run home.

I ran in the direction of our house, to Bajorų Street, where we lived, but at that point I could no longer get home. The Germans had encircled section after section of the ghetto with a dense, armed chain of soldiers. A curfew was declared, and it was forbidden to leave the houses. I watched from a distance: the Germans went from house to house, from apartment to apartment. In most of the houses there were no adults because working-age people had left with the work brigades. So, they took the children and the elderly out of their homes.

I saw a boy of about ten carrying his two-year-old brother, kicks and strikes forcing them onto the bus. It was a public transport bus, but its windows were painted white. I saw how child after child was beaten and screamed at while being taken from their homes. Children who resisted were thrown into the bus as if they were packages. There were children in the arms of their mothers who refused to leave them, and the Nazis brutally tore them away. Dozens of soldiers attacked these miserable women. Whenever a mother fell unconscious, languishing in her own blood, her child would try to hold onto the fence, the pillar, the tree instead. They were dragged away by their arms and legs and thrown into the bus.

Because of the curfew, anyone found on the streets was doomed to die, yet there was nowhere to hide. I ran for my life. The encircling chain was getting closer and tighter. Anywhere I turned, there were Germans that encircled one house after another dragging out victim after victim. The horrific crying of the mothers and children was head splitting and heart wrenching.

I was already fourteen years old, but very skinny for my age. I understood that my life was in danger. The Nazis marked the entrances of every house with white chalk after they finished their murderous job. I decided to sneak into a house already marked with a white cross. In hiding, bent over and moving cautiously through yards, I got close to a house situated near the ghetto workshops. Two German officers were approaching the place at top speed. I moved aside and clung to the wall of the house. They passed me, and for a moment it seemed I had been saved, but at the last moment one of them turned his head back and noticed me. They came back toward me. I trembled with fear: my end was here. One of them showed no particular eagerness to catch me and left the job to his friend. "How old are you?" the other officer asked me.

"Sixteen," I said. He didn't believe me. I told him that I was a carpenter, and I pulled my professional tools out of the backpack that always hung on my shoulders: a hammer, pliers, and a chisel. Then I said, "Here are my tools."

"You are lying!"

I said, "No, I'm telling the truth," and I started to cry.

His friend said to him in German, *"Lass ihm gehen!"* ("Let him go!") but the crueler of the two insisted.

Unfortunately, a bus came crawling toward us to collect victims who they happened to have missed from areas where the search was over. The officer shouted at the driver to stop, but the driver apparently did not hear him and continued to drive, wondering whether to turn right or left. The officer ordered me to run and catch up to the bus. I asked for help from the "good officer" with my eyes, but he lowered his head. His friend raged, kicked me, and drew his pistol, pointing to the vehicle: "Run!" I ran, and it was clear to me that I was running to my death.

When I got there, the bus had stopped, but was about to start again. I turned to look back. The officers were still standing there, and the evil one had his gun pointed at me. I had no choice but to get on the bus, and then it moved.

The driver was speaking to a soldier standing near the front door of the bus. I moved a little inside, but decided that I would try to escape once the officers outside were distracted. When I saw that they had disappeared from the street, I decided I should try to jump off the bus. However, the soldier at the door noticed me and ordered me to go deeper inside. I hurried to the back door. The driver was speeding up. After a moment's hesitation, I jumped. I fell on the road and rolled over several times. Then I got up and ran to the marked, deserted house.

Looking back, I saw the soldier cock his rifle and point at me from the moving bus. Would I manage to get to the corner of the house that would hide me? Apparently, the movement of the bus was hampering the soldier's aim, and the driver stopped. I had already made it around the corner when the shot rang out. I was saved.

I entered the low, empty house, one floor high. A hallway cut it into two parts, with rooms on both sides. I went into the room furthest from the entrance. The contents of the house were strewn all over the floor. The Nazis had already been there. I hid in the furthest corner under the bed, and I dragged something in front of me to hide me. I laid there in silence, waiting for the murderer to come. Would he get off the bus? Would he come looking?

But no one came. Every minute that passed strengthened my belief that I had been saved and that my luck had held out once again. I decided not to leave until nightfall. When the sounds of footsteps and crying were heard, I came out.

The first day of the Children's Action had come to an end.

I stood near the ghetto workshops. When the Children's Action began, the workshops were heavily guarded so that the workers could not return to their homes and try to save their children. When the curfew was over and the guard was removed, the people broke out of the workshops and started running crazily, each to his own horror. Everyone wanted to believe that the disaster had spared them, and everyone was crying when they discovered they were wrong. Terrible cries hovered above the ghetto. The crowd was running and crying, and I ran and cried with them. People fell, got up, and fell again, and when they reached their homes and discovered that their children were gone . . . one tremendous cry rose to the heavens, but no one was there to hear it.

I ran home. Everything there was topsy-turvy. Yehudit was not yet done with forced labor for the day. But where was everyone else? I opened the closet and lifted up the bottom. The door to the hiding place was locked, a sign that they were inside. I knocked on the door, and there was no answer. I yelled, "It's me; open up! It's me." They opened the door, and compressed, poisoned air burst out. How had they been able to breathe in there? Too many people were crammed into the hiding place—while preparing it, no one had paid attention to the problem of ventilation. Those hiding inside were almost suffocated.

They started climbing the ladder: my sick uncle Motel'eh, breathing and gasping heavily; my aunt Chava lifting Ghetta'leh, who cried quietly—we had taught her not to cry out loud; and after them came Berta and the rest of the occupants of the house. These tenants knew of the shelter during its construction, but had refused to share in the expenses. However, at the critical moment they demanded to enter, and no one stopped them. Like sardines packed in a tin, they stood there clinging to each other. When they climbed out, their physical and mental condition was terrible. I told them there had been a Children's Action. Yehudit came home from work and was relieved to find me alive.

After the Action, the children who survived in the ghetto lived outside the law. Being found was a death sentence, one which any armed person was permitted to carry out. The next day, the Nazis came again to complete the Action and make sure no children were left. Once again, the members of the family went down into the malina; this time, I went down with them. We spent a whole day there and almost suffocated. When we could no longer hold on, we climbed out. The evening had already descended on the ghetto, and the Nazis had left. The entire ghetto mourned for its loved ones.

14

―⟨ঔ৩⟩―

MY ESCAPE FROM THE GHETTO

JUST A FEW DAYS AFTER THAT HORROR, WE DECIDED TO GO ahead with the plan for my escape. There were three active gates in the ghetto: the main gate from which the work brigades came and went and where the searches were performed; the second gate, also active, but much less so; and the third gate, which was locked and actually closed off the street that led to the Neris River (also called Villia or Vilija river) before the ghetto was established. One street connected the second gate to the third gate, and it was entirely within the ghetto.

For the purpose of my escape, my sister joined a brigade that, at the time, was working on the far shore of the river on the Aryan side. If the brigade had left through the main gate, it would have gone on for hours. The Germans, in their efficiency, decided that in this case it would be worthwhile to use the third gate to cross the Neris by boat and arrive right at the workplace. Since there were no registration and counting arrangements at this gate, the brigade would gather at the second gate, and after counting and registration, the brigade would pass under guard along the street that led to the third gate. Half of the brigade would board a boat with one or two German guards, and the other half would wait for the empty boat to return.

After the headcount by the second gate, the plan was for me to infiltrate the lines and join my sister as they walked through the ghetto. From there, we would both be taken outside the premises by boat with the first group. While the first group would be waiting on the shore for the second group, my sister would have to remove the yellow star from my clothes, and I was to head to a specific address close to that location, a rather isolated house of a Lithuanian woman. The little neighborhood was built on a hillside, and the houses were at quite a distance from each other. My sister was associated with this same woman in the trading business. She had coaxed her in advance, begging pity for me, and Yehudit must have also promised the woman payment so she would give me refuge for one day. I was to wait there until evening, when Kęstutis, the son of Jonas Paulavičius, would come to pick me up. I did not know where the Paulavičius' home was. As an experienced member of the underground, Jonas knew how to keep his secrets.

The night before I was to leave, no one in the house slept a wink. I was not yet fifteen years old, going off to a hostile city. Any mistake, any wrong move, would bring me to my end. The household was up before dawn, and they wept and wished me luck. The Kronzons and Pruzhans felt that this might be the final parting. Even my uncompromising Aunt Chava hugged me and asked forgiveness for all the wrongs she had done to me.

On the way, my sister instructed me and infused courage into my heart: "Don't be afraid! You look Lithuanian. No one knows who you are; nobody suspects you. Show confidence! They will not stop you and will not demand documents. Be brave!"

We got to the gate. I stood on the side. After the count and the registration, the brigade marched toward the third gate. I joined the lines. My heart was beating fast. The Germans did not suspect anything.

At first, everything went according to plan. The people and the head of the brigade knew and wished me success with their meaningful looks.

We arrived at the shore. The first group got into the boat. I was out of the ghetto for the first time in years! What thoughts and fears ... my sister was holding my hand, and we were already on the other side. We had about half an hour before the arrival of the second group. Several Lithuanians gathered around us as usual to trade with the Jews, and I passed myself off as a Lithuanian doing business with my sister. Therefore, when the Germans drove the Lithuanians away, I would also be among those who went freely to their businesses.

The first hitch happened when my sister removed the yellow stars from the front and back of my coat. Those spots were not as faded as the rest of my coat, and the shape of the star stuck out. What could I do? My sister told me to take my coat off. I folded it with the lining out and hung it on my arm like people do when they are warm. However, it did not seem natural that in the cold morning hours a person would not need a coat.

Time passed quickly. The second group arrived, and the Germans drove the Lithuanians away. We parted with a look, and I was on my way to my new destination. Fifteen minutes later, I got to the appointed house. I climbed the stairs and knocked on the door three times as agreed. The Lithuanian woman opened the door, pulled me inside, and locked the door with the dead bolt. When we were inside, she got down on her knees and crossed herself in front of a statue of the Crucifixion, gripped with fear. My fear grew when she asked me to accompany her on her way to the priest to receive his blessing. It seems that she had consulted with him beforehand, and he congratulated her on her willingness to save a Jewish child. He had also asked to see me.

From childhood, I was afraid of churches, of the black robes of priests and of the cross. Now I was suddenly facing my fear: the chapel and the black-clad priest with a big cross on his chest, who sat me on his knees and was surprised when he heard me speak Lithuanian so fluently. He asked me if I knew Lithuanian literature. When I recited portions of the poems of Maironis, one of the greatest poets of Lithuania, and "Anykščių šilelis," a classic Lithuanian work, he was very moved. He wished me success and sent me on my way.

In the evening, Kęstutis, Jonas's son, arrived. My sister warned me that if I didn't recognize the boy, it would be a sign that it was a trap, since the whole plan was based on the premise that Kęstutis and I knew each other and that he was the one who had influenced his parents to save me. If that happened, I would stay one more day with the Lithuanian woman, and my sister would take me back to the ghetto the same way we left.

Now a sturdy, older Lithuanian boy stood at the entrance to the house. "I'm Kęstutis," he said.

I replied, "I do not know you." It turned out that we studied at the same school, but not in the same class. After a short conversation, I decided to go with him. I said goodbye to the Lithuanian woman and set off.

We traveled through the city and walked across the Aleksotas Bridge on the way to the Panemunė suburb. Everything was familiar to me from my childhood. We were approaching the woods through which we could see Birman's sawmill, and we were already at the end house on the shore of the river.

Kęstutis told me to wait in the woods while he approached the house to make sure there were no strangers there. Every minute seemed like an eternity. Finally, I saw him coming out of the house leading a drunk somewhere. Then he came back to me and said, "Now we can go in." It was completely dark. No light came from any house.

We finally entered the Paulavičius home. Sitting across from me in the kitchen were the father, Jonas, his wife, Antanina, and their daughter, Danutė. Jonas smiled at me. They asked if I was hungry. Obviously I was starving, even though I had eaten at the Lithuanian woman's home. From that same meeting, I remember that they filled a clay bowl for me with a soup they called *zatzirka*: milk soup with chunks of dough, some kind of homemade noodles, all enriched with a spoon of butter. It was heavenly. Everyone stared at me as I quickly emptied my bowl. They asked if I wanted more, and I said, "Yes." I finished the second bowl as well. I was full, but I could not stop. When they asked if I wanted a third bowl, I was embarrassed to refuse, so I agreed. The household laughed and again filled my bowl. I was embarrassed to say I could eat no more, so I ate very slowly, forcing myself to take each bite. I suddenly remembered an ongoing argument between the children in the ghetto—could one eat to

Kęstutis (*right*) and Yochanan in Israel (1989).

satiation. I was one of those who said it was not possible . . . now, in the Paulavičius' home, I was proven wrong.

Even after the filling meal, they did not leave me alone. I was sweating from the hot soup and from nerves. Jonas said to bring the violin and told me, "Now play for us! I bought this violin for you." I took the violin. I played the well-known song "Dear Lithuania, Beautiful Homeland," a sad and sentimental song. Everyone listened and cried.

15

~⚬~

IN THE ATTIC AND
THE "TOMATO PATCH"

AND SO STARTED A NEW CHAPTER IN MY LIFE. I LIVED ON the top floor, in a small nook; it was a triangular shaped, a sort of storage room. The roof was slanted. During the day, I was permitted to go into the adjacent room, but I was forbidden to go near the window. I was not allowed to go down to the lower floor. They served my meals in my room and brought me a chamber pot in which to relieve myself, which they would empty daily. The person closest to me, who spent many hours with me in hiding, was Kęstutis. He was two years older than I was. I taught him how to play chess, and he would occasionally bring me a magazine that also had a chess section. He also procured a chess book for me, written by the Lithuanian chess champion Mikėnas.

On occasion, Jonas had me write a few words to my sister, and he would bring my letter to her brigade's place of work, a few kilometers from his house. These notes were written in Lithuanian because Jonas refused to carry a note in Yiddish. We had certain agreed upon codes between us so that I could let her know that everything was okay . . . and, in fact, these notes brought her comfort. She believed I would survive. Jonas cajoled her to join me. "Later, it will be too late," he would warn her. He was right. One day Jonas came to tell me, "I could no longer find your sister in the brigade." In fact, the entire brigade was gone. Jonas told me that the ghetto was about to be liquidated and that my sister had been taken to a concentration camp in Šančiai. This he found out from his sources.

I don't remember how long I was in the nook on the top floor. Hardly anyone would visit the house. Paulavičius was an unapproachable man who had something to hide from strangers. Young people sometimes came to visit Kęstutis and his sister. I was especially irritated by their cousin, Aldona, who would rummage in every corner of the house. Once she went up to the second floor and into the room next to my hideout. Kęstutis hurried after her, hugging her and pulling her out.

My stay in that hiding place came to an end due to an unexpected event. A uniformed neighbor was fishing illegally in the Nemunas. He intended to throw a grenade into the river and then collect the dead fish. Unfortunately, the grenade exploded in his hands. The neighbors gathered from near and far. Strangers invaded our house and began running around, searching every corner for a sheet or bandage for the wounded man. I was nearly discovered.

Jonas understood that having me stay in the attic was dangerous, so he moved me to a new hiding place. It was a deep pit with a visible opening, as if it were an underground storeroom or a shelter that the residents had been required to dig for the war. But it had an extension—a rather large room. The entire corridor and all of the walls of the room were covered with boards, and beams supported the ceiling. The whole little maze was covered with a thick layer of soil on which tomatoes were grown. To this day, I still think of that pit as "the tomato patch." In the summer, the tomatoes were watered, and the water would seep in through the cracks between the boards; there was permanent mildew there. The nights were terrible. I slept on a wet bench, and I would avoid straightening my feet to keep from getting wet. But I did not protest. I remembered my sister Yehudit's order: "Do not complain; suffer quietly!"

I got a sickly cough. Antanina noticed it. One night she dragged me to the house and laid me down in a bed on the top floor. Jonas and Antanina acquired medicine, pampered me, and fed me the best food they could get their hands on. Luckily, after a while, I got better.

16

~∾~

IN THE DEPTHS OF THE PIT

WHILE I LAY SICK ON THE SECOND FLOOR, I NOTICED THAT on Sundays a man in a German uniform came to the house. On one occasion, I even got a peek at him. I was lying in hiding upstairs when the sound of drunken song came from below. When the man left, Kęstutis told me that this man was a friend of his father, a Russian who had enlisted in the German Army. He did not tell me more.

On occasion, I would hear Jonas and his friend together downstairs, turning on the radio and listening to the Voice of Moscow. This was how the news of the General Staff of the Red Army came to me, and I came to know the voice of the famous announcer of Radio Moscow, the Jew, Levitan, who announced the liberation of cities and towns and progress in the various sectors of the front. The messages would always end with the words, "The eternal glory of heroes who fell for the freedom and independence of our homeland! Death to the German occupier!" And then there was the sound of artillery.

These messages strengthened my spirits as the front moved closer. I dared to believe that I would be liberated, but then doubt would creep in. I wanted it to be true, but a sinking feeling told me that my dreams would remain mere fantasies.

The front was approaching. We could clearly hear the sounds of artillery, and the area was swarming with German military. The roads trembled with the sound of the retreating truck motors and the tank chains, and the Gestapo performed searches. Jonas realized that my staying in the pit by the house was too dangerous. One night, he told me that I would have to change locations. He added, "Don't be afraid! The front is close, and salvation is close as well."

One dark night he took me out to his garden, where fruit trees and vegetable beds grew. There was also an open field, very close to Vaidoto Street, the town's main road. A somewhat steep slope led from the street to the field, and it was not easy to go down or climb it. At the edge of the field was a pit for storing potatoes or various tools. An awning covered the pit. From a distance it looked like a triangle whose top stood three-quarters of a meter above the ground. It was a typical awning for rural storage pits. The bottom of the pit was deepened, with an extra lower floor whose roof was supported on columns. No one would imagine that under the straw in the basement was a space where a Jewish boy was hiding. Jonas reassured me and promised to come every evening and bring food. The area was swarming with Germans, and bringing the food and removing the waste was fraught with danger, but there was no choice.

I carefully climbed into the pit, and Jonas came with me. We lifted a board, and Jonas instructed me to go down the ladder and replace the board from inside. "There's a mattress and blanket down there," he said, and then he left me. I sat on the edge of the ladder and thought about my bitter circumstances: spending my days in a pit. What scared me to death was not the noise coming from the street, the shouting of the German guards or the rattle of the truck engines, but the squeaking of the mice. There's no way to describe a more terrible fear. I recalled all kinds of horror stories; the mice turned into rats in my mind that would pounce on me and devour me. The Brothers Grimm stories I'd heard in my childhood resurfaced in my mind. So I decided not to go down into the pit, but to wait, grinding my teeth, for Jonas's next visit. And I resolved to tell him I could not bear the proximity of the mice.

Apparently, I fell asleep and fell off the ladder. I awoke from the fall and did not know where I was. My surroundings were pitch black. Remembering everything that had happened, I could not find the strength to get up. I may have fallen asleep again. In the morning, Kęstutis woke me. He whistled a tune we had agreed upon, and he found me immersed in a difficult mental state. I burst out crying and said I could not stand this. But he encouraged me, "Now, just as the front is closing in, you can't fall apart. At night the ground trembles, and the Red Army is near." The food he brought was meager. It was difficult to get food. I knew that the bowl of soup and slice of bread would have to suffice until evening or tomorrow morning.

Jonas came in the evening, stern looking, partially to strengthen my spirits and partially to scold me. His tone was severe: "You must tolerate your stay in the pit; your fate and mine are intertwined."

Days passed. What happens to a boy in a dark pit, where he can't even straighten his back? The imagination runs wild, as fear of the unknown escalates into thoughts of pain and suffering. Fortunately, Kęstutis brought me my beloved chess pieces, Mikėnas's chess book, and a book of poems by the Russian poet Lermontov. During the day, I would move the board a little, creating a small opening in the straw, and with a thin stick, I would move the straw from the crack and create a path of light. I immersed myself in the games of the greatest chess players, distracting myself a little from my predicament. Again and again I read Lermontov's poems, countless times. To this day, I remember some of the poems by heart.

My senses sharpened. I learned to differentiate the steps of an armed individual from an unarmed one. Hiding right by Vaidoto street, I could hear conversations from above.

The front was getting so much closer that it became dangerous to visit me. People avoided leaving their homes. Shots were heard from every direction. Kęstutis told me that he would no longer take out the bucket of waste. He brought me a little shovel and said that at night when everything was quiet, I should climb out of the pit, go to the bathroom in the bushes, and cover it with dirt, like the animals of the house. I had become a hunted animal.

The days and hours passed underground. I did not wash my face and body. The sores became like one big wound. The lice ate at my flesh, and the shirt that clung to my body was covered with dried blood.

17

FAREWELL FROM A DISTANCE

ONE DAY IN MID-JULY, JONAS CAME RUNNING IN BROAD DAY-
light and took me to the second floor of his house. He told me that
the Šančiai camp was being liquidated and the Jews were being led
on the Panemunė Bridge. The convoy would pass through our street,
and he would do everything in his power to save my sister Yehudit,
who was supposed to be among those who would be taken. During
the march, escape attempts were expected. If the escapees searched
for shelter on his ground, the Germans could, in pursuit, discover the
underground shelter. This drove Jonas to bring me back to the attic.

Through the cracks, I saw the Panemunė Bridge and those being brought from Šančiai; it was a large convoy of people. I knew
my sister was among them. Then I noticed a small figure leaping
from the bridge to the water like a stone falling. A volley of shots
followed the figure into the water. From time to time the unknown
swimmer would pick up their head, breathe again, and disappear.
The shots continued to miss their target. The shooters went down to
the beach, and from there they tried to hit the escapee. At the same
time, the lines loosened. As I was told afterward, there were more
escape attempts. In the end, the Germans decided to give up their
victim and reorganize the ranks. The unknown swimmer managed
to escape and, with the last of his strength, reached the house of Jonas Paulavičius. The swimmer did not notice a Nazi officer standing
on the beach. He drew his gun and shot the escapee. One shot was
fired, a second followed. The victim sank into the depths.

The author's brother and sister: Vera-Devorah (*right*); Zvi "Hirsch'ke" ob"m (*middle*); and Yochanan the boy, 1938.

For reasons I do not know—perhaps a problem with the transportation—everyone from the Šančiai camp was returned the same way they came. The following day, again they were brought over the bridge and then marched through Vaidoto Street, very close to the house. I watched them from my hiding place, and I transgressed the rule of not approaching the window. I then saw Yehudit walking in the convoy. She saw me in the window and waved. I waved my hand in farewell. Later on, she told me that on her horrible trek from camp to camp on German soil, she saw our mother from the fence at Stutthof, and with cries from afar she had let our mother know that I was alive and that she had seen me on the way. That raised my mother's spirits.

With nightfall, Jonas took me back to the pit. He told me that he had done everything in his power to save Yehudit. He walked next to the German guards and gave her a hint with a look toward the house, as though he meant to say, "If you manage to escape, that's the house you should go to." He accompanied the convoy until the train station to be able to help her if she managed to escape. He saw that she was looking for an opportunity to run away, but the guards were watching diligently to prevent any escapes.

18

THE RUSSIAN CAPTIVE AND RUBIN, THE JEW

ONE DAY, I HEARD HURRIED STEPS APPROACHING THE PIT. My senses told me that one of the sets of steps was Jonas, but who was the other man? I was gripped by fear. In my mind, the man accompanying Jonas was armed. Had he been caught? Was he bringing his captor to me? If so, it was the end. The steps turned into an urgent run. I heard people approaching the pit. I suddenly heard Jonas's voice: "It's me; don't be afraid!" He quickly moved the boards and said, "I brought you a visitor. He will explain."

We placed the board back, and Jonas spread the straw and left. In the dark, I could not see who had come, but I smelled the uniform and heard the weapon. He was a soldier in a German uniform, with his equipment, the folded blanket around his knapsack, the familiar, frightening steel cap, and the rifle. He turned to me in Russian, explaining that he would remain in my shelter until the arrival of the Red Army. And he declared, "They will not take me alive!"

His story begins in the summer of 1943, Kęstutis and his sister Danutė were in the yard, and suddenly, they noticed a German soldier riding a bike, leaving the main road on to the path directly to their house. The man asked in Russian if their parents were home. Jonas came out, and the Russian-speaking German soldier asked him if he remembered the Russian prisoner of war whose life Jonas had saved by giving him food in the winter of 1942. "It's me," he said. The man was brought inside, and the children were instructed to stay outside.

The soldier then explained to Jonas that, as a prisoner, there came a time when he could no longer stand the captivity. In the first winter, the prisoners were kept outside. In the morning, they would gather up the dead from that night. During the second winter, he understood that his end was near, and he had to choose between life and death. He knew that enlisting in the German Army would be a traitorous act that his homeland would never forgive, but his will to live won out. That was how, when the propagandists of General Vlasov came, the collaborator with the Nazis, he joined his army. He was released from captivity and taken to a sanatorium. He was cared for and fed. Afterward, he went through basic training and became a German soldier.

He was stationed as a guard in the concentration camp of the suburb of Šančiai, and during his leisure time he would visit Jonas nearby at Panemunė. In the past, Jonas had promised him shelter when necessary. There had been no point in running away and hiding, not when the front was still quite far away, and it was not yet clear when liberation would come, but now the soldier had come to remind Jonas of his promise. The two of them decided to keep in touch, and that as soon as the soldier's unit moved, the man would escape and go to the Paulavičius' house.

And now the time had come. The soldier told Jonas that in a few days the Šančiai camp, where my sister was imprisoned, would be liquidated.

After a day or two, I once again heard steps, and again the board was removed, and another person joined us. The new visitor was David Rubin, a religious Jew who told me he had been imprisoned at Šančiai, which had been liquidated, and the camp's inmates had been transported by train to Germany. When the inmates were marched via the main street of Panemunė, an opportunity arose to escape from the line. He hid for two days in the adjacent forest. Weak and hungry, he decided to go to Kaunas to find refuge in surroundings he was more familiar with, perhaps with one of his neighbors from days past.

However, the bridge over the river had been captured by the army, and the civilians were not allowed to cross. Opportunistic boat owners took advantage of this situation and transported people from shore to shore in their boats for a fee.

David's luck shone once again: the boat he had gotten on was Jonas's boat. To hide his broken Lithuanian accent, David held a pipe between his teeth as though he smoked. He was the last to get off the boat, and he told Jonas he did not have money to pay. Jonas said, "I know that you are a Jew." He tried to deny it, but Jonas stood his ground. "Your appearance gives you away. Come with me, and I will give you shelter in my home!"

David was concerned; he did not believe Jonas, and he thought that Jonas would give him up to the Germans because he couldn't pay. But David had no other choice. Jonas gave him words of encouragement and friendship, transported him back to the Panemunė shore, hid him during the day in his house, and at night, brought him to my hideout.

Now, in our small hideout, about two and a half square meters, we were three. The crowding was oppressive. During the hot July days, our breathing compressed the air. We were forced to place one board from the roof on its side to get some air because the suffocation was unbearable. We perspired, and our sores burned like fire. Still, I preferred this over loneliness. The Russian, who was from a village, captured two field mice who got into the pit and disturbed my rest. He released them outside the pit.

Around us almost no human voices were heard. The people locked themselves in their homes, understanding that the area was about to fall into Russian hands. From time to time, we would hear the sound of heavy machine guns and the echoes of mortar shells that shook the roof of the hiding place, and a thin hail of dirt would fall from it into the straw above our heads. Occasionally, military vehicles would pass by on the next street, and frightening German talk could be heard from soldiers who walked quickly past the pit.

We held whispered conversations. The Russian spoke of how he met Jonas and his family for the first time, the story told in the prologue.

Daytime hours were unbearable. We sat leaning on the hideout wall while our bent feet touched the opposite wall. Our limbs were numb. From time to time, we changed our sitting positions, knelt down, lay on our calves with our legs folded under us, and sat down again. We were perpetually exhausted, falling asleep on the floor of the hiding place, side by side, sometimes with our limbs intertwined, until evening.

At night, they brought us food; everyone got a slice of bread, and there was one bowl of soup for all of us from which we took turns eating, each with his own spoon. The food was meager, and we were starving. At night, when the quiet was disturbed only by gunfire and explosions, we would go out among the fruit trees, relieve ourselves, straighten our limbs, and breathe fresh air to fill our lungs. We could not stay outside for a long time. The fear of being spotted by a stranger immediately drove us underground. And so it went on, for many days and many nights.

On one of the last days in July, a massive explosion shook the hideout. The Germans had blown up the bridge over the Nemunas River. After a short while, we heard a tumult in the vicinity of the house, hustling and loud commands in German. My heart foretold evil; the blood froze in my veins. We were exposed, and that was the end. The Russian cocked his weapon.

In the blink of an eye, countless thoughts crossed my mind: What happened? How did they know? Who betrayed us? What would they do to me? Would they take me to the fort, or would they kill me here by the pit? It would hurt, but it would also be the end of my fear and suffering. What should I do? Should I look out? Maybe I could still escape. Or maybe looking out would bring them to the hiding place.

Silence permeated the pit. Then, we heard a massive explosion, then another, and another. Chunks of dirt started falling from the walls and the roof. The air smelled of gunpowder and smoke, there was a clatter of people again, and someone was running near the hideout. It was Kęstutis. "They're leaving," he said. "A sabotage unit blew up the sawmill in the yard next door. And now the neighbors

The Paulavičius home on the shore of the Nemunas River.

are trying to put out the fire, so that it doesn't spread to the vegetation and endanger the surroundings."

I needed a few minutes to calm down. David hugged and encouraged me. I was saved once more. We got back to the routine of the
hiding place. We continued to wait, but not for much longer.

The death sentence issued against me by the Third Reich was
about to expire.

19

ABOUT ANNA, OSCAR, AND OTTO

"Alle Menschen werden Brüder."

"All humans are brothers."

FROM BEETHOVEN'S NINTH SYMPHONY,
LYRICS BY SCHILLER

FROM THE MOMENT WE FIRST OPENED OUR EYES, ALL FOUR children of the family saw three figures: Mother, Father, and Frau Seitz. Since the roles of mother and father were already filled, the role left for Frau Seitz was that of grandmother. We, the children, called her Omama. We saw her as a combined grandmother (oma) and mother (mama) persona—our wonderful Omama.

The circumstances of her arrival to our home were a bit unclear. According to my sister Vera (Devorah), my father had brought her from Königsberg, where they happened to meet, and she agreed to follow him to Lithuania and run our household. My sister Yehudit maintained that my father brought her from a nearby village—Garliava, where she ran a farm of my father's—and then brought her to our house.

I have a different version, formed by the rumors and stories that I seem to have absorbed over time. Before marrying my mother, my father had been married to a woman named Chava (née Gurevich) for about ten years. That's when my father built the flour mill in Panemunė—an area where there were many farms—and the flour mill met the needs of the farmers. My father's house was built close to the flour mill. Chava developed a heart condition and was deteriorating. Managing the affairs of a large house weighed heavily upon her. It took another woman to look after her and run the household. World War I—like all wars—brought with it misery and deprivation; unemployed people were clustered in squares, and widows and children were crying for bread. Frau Seitz was one of them.

She was an educated woman and impressed my father with her gentility and patience. Frau Seitz had a daughter, little Anna, who had lost her father. We called her Anka. My kind father agreed that Frau Seitz's daughter could be raised in our home.

The common denominator between the versions regarding Omama coming to our house is the consensus that she came to our home before Father married my mother—Ronia (née Braude)—in 1919, after the death of his first wife Chava.

Omama was a pet name we children used, but the adults—my parents, relatives, and anyone who came to the house—called her Seitzova: Seitz with a Slavic ending. Her first name was Anna, like her daughter's name (which was why Anka's name was changed).

Seitzova created order in the home and demanded it be maintained. She enjoyed a special status. Even my mother, who tended to be controlling, could not tell her what to do, but could only ask her to do something. Although it was usually not necessary. Omama knew very well what was required for the household, and by her own initiative, she acted before any request was made.

There was mutual admiration and appreciation between her and my father. I cannot recall even an angry or loud conversation between her and my parents. Over the years, the production of the flour mill increased, and my father needed Seitzova's help more and more. When he would leave for his afternoon break, he would leave the cash box in her hands and sleep peacefully. And so, Seitzova became the second-most-important person in the house alongside my father. Assistants, who changed from time to time, were the ones hired to do household chores. Just before the Nazis arrived, destructive wave of biblical proportions, a young Russian girl named Fenka worked for us. She was the last assistant I can recall. In anticipation of the holidays and other gatherings at our home, one of the flour mill workers would join us to assist with the preparations, most often, a worker named Ona. At the end of her day at the mill, when Seitzova would retire to her room, no one dared call upon her—that was an unequivocal order from my father.

The farmers would leave their grain for grinding, continue on to the market square to sell their product, visit the taverns, and get drunk. At the end of the day, they would return to pick up their sacks of flour. Oftentimes they would come late, after nightfall, when the mill and the gates of the courtyard were already locked. The loud drunks would pound on the front door of the house and demand their bags. Seitzova would leave her room, and to save my father from leaving the house for the flour mill, she herself would go out and give them their bags. She did not fear their shouts and threats, and she would scold them and promise in a threatening tone that this was the last time she would give them their sacks after closing hours. When they were significantly late, she sent them home empty-handed. The farmers would mutter complaints under their breath, yet the next day they would calmly come in to receive their flour. "They have to get used to order," she said, the famous German order—*Ordnung*!

Seitzova was like a family member in our home in every regard, loved and respected. When she fell ill and needed an operation, my father did not agree to have the procedure performed by the national healthcare system and opted to pay for a private surgeon. To me, the youngest child in the family, she gave special affection. On winter nights, at bedtime, she would hold the ends of my down blanket, spread her hands up, and press them against the tiles of the huge fireplace. And when I got into bed, she would quickly cover me with the heated blanket.

I don't remember my mother reading me stories and fables. Omama did this: during our free time, on Saturdays and Sundays, and especially when I went to bed for the night. I loved those evenings. She would bring a thick book, printed in gothic letters to read from. I knew Snow White for the first time in its German name, "Die

Schneewittchen." And how sorry I felt for poor Hansel and Gretel, imprisoned by the wicked witch. She read us countless other stories.

Omama did not only give—she also demanded: "Did you do your homework? Did you practice playing enough today?" And if the answers were not affirmative, there would be no stories or fables.

Our Omama, as befits a grandmother, also knitted. For us, the children, she made wool hats and earmuffs, and for Father, she knitted especially warm gloves. And when we misbehaved and expected to be reprimanded or punished by our parents, she was always lenient. She interpreted every offense as youthful mischief that did not justify punishment.

As years went by, her daughter Anka reached adulthood, married Otto Müllerschkowski, left our home, and settled in an adjacent village, Garliava. But Omama stayed with us. Even when her grandchildren were born, she did not change her address—our home was, and remained, her home.

As the international situation became more serious and Hitler's Germany accumulated more military acquisitions, nationalistic feelings among the German minority in Lithuania grew. But Omama ignored it, as if this had nothing to do with her. All events were measured and weighed against one main criterion: whether it was good or bad for the Fein family.

However, there were two fateful events on which she could not help but take a stand: the first was the Soviet occupation of Lithuania and its implications and the Soviet-German treaty allowing Lithuanian citizens of German origin to immigrate to Germany.

Lithuania's becoming a Soviet Republic did not bode well for the Germans living there. No one believed that the Ribbentrop–Molotov Pact (the Soviet–Nazi nonaggression pact of August 1939) would last long. They feared for what would happen to them when war broke out. What was especially difficult for Omama, the second fateful event, was Anka and her husband's decision to emigrate to Germany with their children. The separation from her daughter and grandchildren was unbearable for her, especially because Anka pleaded with her to go with them.

Anna Seitz (the "Omama").

Her family was part of the first wave that left. Omama still hesitated, but when the first letters arrived, they played on her heartstrings, and she couldn't bear it. Omama decided to go.

With a heavy heart and tearful eyes, we parted. We had managed
to get a letter or two before the war broke out, and then it seemed
that this was the end of the tale of Omama, Frau Anna Seitz. Yet the
story was not complete. Sometimes, marvelous tales have a sequel.

In 1919, a young German man, twenty years of age, was looking for work and came to see my father. He introduced himself as a miller and a mechanic. The young man impressed my father with his maturity. Father needed a man of his expertise. And so, Oscar Stankoweit became an employee of our flour mill.

Oscar felt secure in his place of work and built his life around it. He made a home for himself in Panemunė, got married, fathered three daughters, and lived a calm and orderly life. Over the years, my father grew very fond of him, and the barriers between employee and employer disappeared. Oscar Stankoweit was a talented man with a unique technical understanding and hands of gold. There was no malfunction beyond his ability, no extraordinary solution he could not improvise. When the equipment was replaced in the 1930s and a new English-made diesel engine was introduced, Oscar surprised the importers and technicians with his ability to install and operate the engine.

The Stankoweit home was open to us just as our home was open to them. On Christmas, we would visit their home, wish our blessings for the New Year, and sing "O, Tannenbaum" ("O, Christmas Tree") with them. That was before the wave of destruction. Oscar had it good with my father. Otherwise, he would not have continued to work with us for twenty-two years—half his life.

In 1941, a year after the Russian conquest of Lithuania, when it became a Soviet Republic, the aforementioned mass emigration of Germans to Germany began. I don't know if the slogan a "home in the Reich" (*Heim ins Reich*) had aroused dormant nationalistic feelings in the Stankoweits or if this was them going with the flow in the overpowering wave of emigration, fearing what was to come under Russian rule. Regardless, the Stankoweits decided to emigrate to Germany as well.

And so, in February 1941, we parted sadly from the Stankoweits. Oscar's leaving symbolized the decline of the mill's power and prestige under Soviet rule. A few days before his departure, Oscar came to my father with a request: a letter of recommendation. "What is the value of a Jewish recommendation in Hitler's Germany?" my father asked.

But Oscar insisted, "The Germans love certificates and permits." Father took a sheet of paper torn from a notebook, without a company name, and wrote in German the following words:

> Certificate of Recommendation[1]
> I hereby confirm, that Mr. Oscar Stankoweit worked for me from 1919 until February 1st, 1941, as a miller-technician. He always fulfilled his position with exactness and devotion. Mr. Stankoweit is an excellent and talented man and will be an asset wherever he works.
>
> The Owner of the Flour Mill
> M. Fainas (M. Fein)
>
> Panemunė February 10, 1941

The journey to the "home in the Third Reich" was a sobering one: the Stankoweits did not arrive in Germany very quickly. For many months, they wandered among transit camps on Polish-occupied territory in the Łódź area. They slept on wooden bunk beds in crowded huts, their mattresses were sacks of straw, and their food was meager. The men were recruited to the Wehrmacht, the rest traveled to East Prussia and were again housed in camps. All of them were employed in various jobs, sometimes laborious, in the field and without payment. Sometimes the girls were sent away. Oscar's daughter, Liza, had to travel to Estonia. If there was a difference between their way of life and the lives of prisoners, it wasn't much.

In the summer of 1942, the camp residents were told that anyone who wished to do so could return to their former home within the German occupation.[2] It was a golden opportunity to get out of camp life, and Oscar grabbed it with both hands. At the end of the summer of 1942, he returned to Panemunė to see what was left of his house and to examine the possibility of returning with his family from "the house in the Reich" to their former home, which had once been warm and peaceful. He found his house empty of tenants, but also emptied by looters. Day and night, he slowly restored his home.

He also returned to my father's mill, where he had spent half his life. He did not find my good and kindhearted father. He was employed by a German who had purchased (or received) the mill from the occupying forces. For twenty-two years, Oscar had worked

The letter of recommendation that Yochanan's father wrote for Oscar in 1941, a short while before the German conquest.

for my father, but he lasted only a few months with his own compatriot. In his distress, he decided to purchase a small, neglected, half-destroyed mill from the authorities and restore it. This prewar mill was also owned by a Jewish family, the Vorobeys. For months, Oscar persisted day and night, stubbornly and skillfully, in restoring the mill and his house with his golden hands.

At the start of 1943, after two years in the camps, the rest of the Stankoweit family returned to their home in Panemunė, and with them our Omama, Anna Seitz. The Stankoweits met her in their wanderings in one of the camps and from then on never parted. She worked with Oscar in the small mill and lived in their home. Our house, which had been her home, where so many of her years had passed and where she raised her daughter with us, was occupied by a stranger. She was told that we had been deported to the ghetto. She mourned our fate and her heart grieved. She decided to do something.

One morning, at the start of July 1943, while the brigades were preparing to head out to work through the ghetto gates, Yehudit noticed a German looking at her. He stood outside the ghetto near the gate. She could not distinguish between ranks and insignias, but she had the impression that the man was an officer. Slowly, he walked toward the fence, to a place where he could better see what was happening, and did not take his eyes off her. Their eyes met. He then walked away from the fence.

Emotional and frightened, Yehudit began digging through her memory as to where she had seen that face. And then she remembered with certainty; the man in uniform was Otto, Omama's son-in-law, Anka's husband. He used to come to our home, and we used to go to his. He had been friendly—but who was he today?

There was danger embedded in every uniform, and Otto wore one. Yehudit's fear was heightened, when out of the corner of her eye, she saw that he was accompanying the brigade on its way to work.

When she arrived, the daily trade was being handled between the brigade and the Lithuanians. This custom, as has already been described, had become routine, and the guards did not do anything to stop it—on occasion even they benefitted by turning a blind eye. The whole time, Otto was standing and watching what was going on. Yehudit, who was terribly frightened, kept looking over at him and studying his face. When the crowd scattered at the orders of the guards and the work group reformed, Otto came over. While walking, he whispered, "Zaicienė [Mrs. Seitz in Lithuanian] is here. I will return." And then he left.

That morning, Yehudit felt continued unrest. Stunned by the intensity of the events, surprised and emotional, she tried in vain to make sense of her thoughts. What did all this mean? Should she hang her hopes on this meeting? Was this meeting with Otto coincidental, or was he perhaps looking for someone from our family? And even if the meeting was coincidental, he did say he promised to come back.

The return of Omama, who had lived with us for more than two decades, was like the return of a family member to his imprisoned brothers. Would Yehudit get to see her? But as the days passed and Otto did not return, expectations and hopes dimmed.

Yehudit returned to her routine. She again carried a few items on her back that she would offer to the Lithuanians in the factory yard in exchange for food, or she would leave without her star to her hiding places, where she transacted her small business to keep the family alive.

That was what she was doing on July 21, 1943, as well. When she removed her wares from her backpack and raised her head to look for a customer, in front of her was a man with a small parcel in his hand. It was Otto. Without a uniform, he looked just like any passerby. When he spoke, his fear was palpable. Yehudit suggested that he go around the corner, and she would try to remove the yellow patches and meet him. Soon the two of them were walking together as if they were father and daughter.

Where they went, where they sat, how long their conversation lasted—Yehudit vaguely remembers details; what she does remember is what was said in the conversation. From Oscar, Yehudit learned that everyone—Oscar, Otto, and their families—had returned from Germany to their homes in Lithuania and that our Omama also had returned and was living in the Stankoweits' house. Oscar also said that he had come on behalf of his mother-in-law, who for a long time had urged him to look for our family in the ghetto, and that he had finally succeeded in finding us after many attempts.

He continued telling Yehudit that Anna Seitz already knew that Otto had seen her. Excited and weeping, Omama had begged him to make contact. So, there he was, despite the danger. He also said that

Yehudit should not be afraid of the uniform he had been wearing; he had not volunteered—he was drafted despite his age.

Otto asked that Yehudit write a letter to Omama and gave her the pen and paper he had prepared in advance. I imagine that the rest of the meeting took place on a bench or in a café. It would have been impossible to write a letter while walking or standing.

Yehudit did in fact write a letter to Omama. The letter, dated July 21, 1943, is in my possession to this day. It is written in Lithuanian. The writing has faded with time but it is still legible:

Dear Mr. Stankoweit![3]

I didn't want to write to you, because perhaps you would be uncomfortable, but my conscience does not let me keep my silence.

When I found out that Seitzienna [Mrs. Seitz in Lithuanian] returned, I didn't sleep for many nights. I wanted to see her so badly. But perhaps she forgot me. Three years have passed—a very long time. But I never forgot you Seitzovinka, and I will never forget, because I loved you so much.

My dear, if you do in fact want to come to meet me, Stankoweit will tell you where. Write to me if you will come and when, and I will meet you.

Be good and come, I long to see you and talk to you.
Dear Mr. Stankoweit, Please send regards to your wife and children.

Stay healthy. Yehudit

Seitzovinka, I am waiting for you. Write to the following address:

To Miss Kliorytė
Jonavos Street, II Alley
Kaunas

The letter was actually written to both Oscar and Anna. It begins with a formal address to "Mr. Stankoweit," despite us having been on a first-name basis.

Perhaps Yehudit was unsure of who Oscar had become.

Yehudit's request to the Omama to contact Oscar for the receipt of the contact address, when it appears at the bottom of the letter, attests to Yehudit's confusion and agitation.

The meeting dragged on too long. Otto was already anxious to finish. It is horrifying to think about the price that these good people would have had to pay if they had been caught. Otto took the letter and read it. Then he folded it, stuck it in his pocket, and left.

Seitzova's response came immediately to Klioryte with two alternative dates set. Her letter was not posted but was brought by someone from the Stankoweit household. After making the first move, Otto retreated behind the scenes for a time. The dates set in the letter were committed to memory, the letter was destroyed, and on the predetermined date, Yehudit came to Klioryte's to meet Omama. Their meeting was one of soft cries, hugs and kisses, and heart-rendering sighs, like a mother reuniting with her daughter. Omama did not come empty-handed. She brought supplies and gave some to the woman of the house. They did not speak much because time was short. They set up a series of future meetings. As a precaution, they decided not to write, lest their communications were intercepted. A date was set for the next meeting.

That was how our relationship with our wonderful Omama was renewed. In the period between July 1943 and May 1944, to Yehudit's best recollection, there were five meetings. Once, Anna could not come, so Liza, Oscar's daughter, a girl two years younger than Yehudit, came instead. She, too, risked her life and was clearly given permission from her parents and their blessing. The meetings were short, sad meetings, in an atmosphere of fear and tension. Yehudit came out of each meeting with a precious package of food to feed our hungry mouths. The owner of the meeting place, Klioryte, received her share but did not settle for food alone. Yehudit had to complete the payment with a garment or some other object. Klioryte worked as a merchant, and Yehudit was not her only client; she carried on a small business from her home. Despite that, the meetings between Anna and Yehudit in her home were more than a mere business transaction for Klioryte, her willingness was an expression of human kindness.

Yehudit told Omama Ghetta'leh's story, how she was taken out of the ghetto in a backpack to be handed over to the Kronzon's Russian nanny and how she had to return her to the ghetto. That was how the topic of rescuing arose, according to Anna; it kept them busy all the time. Anna spoke with pain. She said she did not have her own home, and she was living in the Stankoweit's crowded house. The yard of their home bordered a military camp, and several of the officers had befriended the Stankoweits and spent their free time in their house, she explained. Our rescue, therefore, was beyond Omama's capability.

In another meeting, apparently in May 1944, Anna was told that I escaped the ghetto and was in a hiding place in the home of a Lithuanian. This time, at Omama's initiative, the topic of Yehudit's rescue once again came up. It turned out that the subject of our rescue was discussed between Anna and Otto, and my escape from the ghetto removed a great obstacle. Hiding two people was twice as difficult, especially for a boy, whose Jewishness was evident on his body. Now that Yehudit was on her own, the idea of the rescue had become possible.

Time was of the essence. The Germans' retreat from Kaunas and the evacuation of the German families was a question of a few months or even less. Before their escape to Germany, Anna was to leave the Stankoweit's house and join her family: her daughter, her son-in-law, and her grandchildren. Omama suggested an urgent meeting, within a few days, after discussing the matter with Otto. Both were to come to the meeting, and Yehudit was to be ready to leave with them. Where they would be going, she did not know. She would only be told after Otto had finalized his plan.

They had to convince Kliorytė to agree to Otto's coming, who would be presented as Omama's Lithuanian son-in-law. After much deliberation, she agreed. Her opposition had stemmed mainly from a desire not to expose her apartment to another person. In a gloomy, sad, emotional, and frightened atmosphere, Yehudit and Omama, Anna Seitz, parted as if they sensed that this could be their last meeting.

Yehudit returned to the ghetto with the package of groceries. She had intended to talk to Berta about her meeting with Seitzova and the plan to rescue her. She also knew how the conversation would end: she would not get Berta's blessing, and she would not be able to look her children in the eyes; her heart would break. She would have to give up even this last opportunity, just as she had given up Jonas's pleas to join me.

Yehudit remembered well her discussion with Berta months earlier before my escape. Berta had made every possible argument for Yehudit not to leave them. She mentioned our moral debt, that bitter day, February 6, 1942, after being separated from our parents, when we were gathered into her small house and given a roof over our heads.

Was the roof over our heads weighed against the price of Yehudit's life? Did the livelihood of the household for two and a half years in the ghetto, with innumerable risks, not reduce the debt somewhat? Did the heroic attempt to save Ghetta'leh not balance it out? I cannot answer; I can only understand: Berta was crushed under the burden of her life. The responsibility for her children's fate in the face of the coming end was unbearable. She went crazy; she could no longer bear her fate alone. She therefore pleaded, begged, and demanded that someone be by her side to help her overcome the torment in her soul. And so, the destinies of Berta and Yehudit were tied by a solid bond of moral debt.

As agreed upon earlier, Yehudit had to go one last time to see Omama. The departure from the ghetto in June 1944 was not the same as in the past. The ghetto was declared a "quarantined camp," and the brigades leaving for the city were diminishing. Berta was afraid that Yehudit would not resist the temptation to be rescued and would go to Omama. When Yehudit did not return that evening with the brigades, she felt sad and betrayed.

The events of that day are deeply engraved into Yehudit's heart. Early in the morning, she arrived at the field outside the exit gate of the ghetto and left for the city with one of the brigades. When the brigade arrived at a location unknown to her with guards she did not know and had not bribed, she realized that leaving would involve great risk. Yet she decided to leave no matter what.

She managed to slip away. Once she was convinced that no one had noticed her escape and that she was not being followed, she made her way to the meeting place, Klioryté's house. She was late, and

Otto, who had been waiting for her for a long time, was quite tense. "Anna," he said, "will not be coming." He did not bring any goods because he intended to take Yehudit with him. "We owe it to your father. My wife grew up and was educated in your home," he said.

Based on the previous meeting's discussion, she could have expected such an offer, but when it came, it struck her like a bolt of lightning. Now she was facing a fateful decision. She had come to thank them and refuse, but when she was actually at the crossroads of an opportunity to escape to freedom, her resolve was shaken. Yet she anguished over the thought of leaving Berta and the children, especially Ghetta'leh, for whom she had developed motherly feelings. Could she leave them without looking them in the eyes, without giving them hugs and kisses, without one last goodbye?

How does one deal with such dilemmas? Sometimes by running away, trying to put them off for another week. Otto pressed her for a decision. She didn't understand the significance of what he said at first. He spoke of time running out, of the German retreat from Kaunas, of his family's escape from Lithuania to Germany, which was imminent. "They are escaping?!" If so, where was he taking her? Where would he hide her? In whose hands would he be placing her? Were they reliable? She refused to understand the significance of what he was telling her.

He spoke of her "Aryan" looks, of her joining them as a family member, and of documents that he could possibly get for her. She now understood that he was talking about taking her to Germany.

Those who were shut in the ghetto dreamed of their liberation day and night, of the coming of the Red Army, of the German retreat and their defeat. The Germans would retreat along with the local collaborators, who had Jewish blood on their hands and for whom liberation day would be a day of judgment and accountability for their actions. Anyone who was not German and retreated with them would be perceived as a Nazi, as someone who had strong reasons to abandon their homes with everything they had, to flee their country.

In her mind's eye, Yehudit could visualize the convoy of retreating troops, her ears echoing with the bloodcurdling orders in

German—could she sit among them and escape with them from her liberators? Her indecision was over; her refusal was no longer tentative. She would not go to Germany.

They hugged and parted, wished for each other's survival, and hoped for better days. Her bitter cries brought him to tears. She promised never to forget what they had done for her, that her memories of Omama would stay with her forever. She asked him to pass this message on, and he promised to do so. He left first. Klioryté, who was worried about Yehudit, brought her water to drink and to wash her face. It took her quite a while to get back to herself.

Now she would have to go out into the hostile streets. Yehudit was asked never to come back. The house would be locked up; Klioryté would leave to stay with her relatives in the village "until this is all over" so as not to get caught so close to the end. And so this shelter, too, was lost.

When she got back to where she had slipped away from the brigade, there was no one there. Two sentries stood in the courtyard, and everyone else had disappeared. Perhaps they were swallowed up inside the building or taken elsewhere. This created a huge problem: How would she rejoin them? How would she return to the ghetto? With no alternative, she decided to activate an emergency plan that she had formulated in case of such an incident: she would burn some hours in the streets, walk toward the ghetto, and there, on the street leading to the gate, she would infiltrate the lines of one of the brigades that would gather there before reentering the ghetto. Obviously, it was better not to wander the streets and return with the original brigade with which she had left.

But this horrible day had not yet come to an end. A young man walked toward her, and as he approached, his eyes lit up. His face had a cheerful smile, as if he had met a longtime friend. "Hello, Miss, aren't you by any chance Fein's daughter?" he said loudly, too loudly, totally inconsiderate of her situation. She realized she was in deep trouble. What would she answer? With a forced smile and fake good-naturedness, she said she did not know him. With a diabolical sneer, he started to elaborate on all of our family's sins.

Yes, he understood, he said, that she would not recognize him. How would this wealthy daughter recognize a poor young man like him? After all, we wealthy Jews paid no attention to the poor, especially if they were Lithuanians. It was beneath our dignity. He later said that he had studied with our sister Vera at university, but while he had to stop because he lacked the money, she continued to study with the support of her rich father. It was clear that he knew our family, and his hostility was growing. "I knew your brother too—he was a Bolshevik, wasn't he?"

Thus, in a few sentences, he summed up all of our shortcomings: we were Jews, arrogant, bourgeois, but also Bolshevik, and haters of Lithuanians. Yehudit was at a loss—what could she do? She attempted to say goodbye and tried to get away, but he took her arm and said, with a poisonous smile, that it would be very hard for him to part with her so quickly.

A Nazi officer passed in front of them. The young man called out, yelling, and pointed at her, "*Jude, Jude!*"—"Jew, Jew!" The officer approached and asked Yehudit if she was a Jew, and she answered yes. He ordered her to accompany him. The Lithuanian was satisfied and revealed that he knew another word in German, which he pronounced in broken syllables: "*Auf Wiedersehen*"—"See you."

Yehudit was brought to the Gestapo. Now she knew that her good luck had turned, and she no longer had any hope of being rescued. She had taken too many risks, and, therefore, it had to end this way. After a while, she was brought out of her cell to stand in front of the Gestapo officer. In answer to his question, she said that she lived in the ghetto and had no family. The implication was, of course, that she had no additional names to provide for punishment. He asked if she understood the enormity of her crime, and she did not answer. He raised his voice and demanded an answer. "I'm hungry. I was looking for food," she replied.

After a few moments of silence, he asked, "Should I kill you or beat you—what do you choose?" She did not reply. He raised his voice and demanded she respond.

"Do as you wish," she replied.

"You're lucky you met me and not someone more strict," he said. He rang, and a soldier entered the room. "Deal with her and take her back to the ghetto," he ordered.

Could it be that she understood correctly that she would be returned to the ghetto? In fact, she was returned to the ghetto, beaten and bleeding. First, she was taken into one of the rooms, where the Nazi struck her in the face, knocking her to the ground, bleeding and out cold. He kicked her in the back and started whipping her. She screamed. How long he continued to beat her after her screams stopped, she had no idea. One assumes even a Nazi would tire, eventually.

After she was dealt with, she was dragged and thrown in a car and was brought to the ghetto guards, where she was dumped onto the prison floor. That evening, an officer of the ghetto guard arrived—apparently, he had been told of the incident. He looked at her and ordered her to be released. The policemen laid her on a cart and brought her home.

And so ended that horrible day in June 1944, the day she parted from Otto, and through him, Omama and Oscar. She never saw them again.

I know that the Stankoweits fled Lithuania on July 6, 1944, twenty-four days before the Russians arrived, and after many hardships and wanderings, they settled in a place where the wheels of their wagon had collapsed hopelessly. Oscar died in 1963, and close to that date, probably in 1964, Anna Seitz, our unforgettable Omama, died. I do not know Otto's fate.[4]

When Berta saw Yehudit wounded and bleeding, she tugged at the hairs of her head sorrowfully and blamed herself for everything that had happened. "I should have let you go," she murmured.

Yehudit tried to quiet Berta's conscience and said, "There was nowhere to go. Escape to Germany was impossible for me."

Berta took care of her devotedly. She had extensive medical knowledge, and there was still a stockpile of medicine at the time of the establishment of the ghetto from Dr. Kronzon's clinic. After a long painful period, Yehudit returned to herself. Now, at the end of June 1944, they practiced going down into the malina. In spite of the starvation, they lowered critical supplies into the pit—crackers, water, and blankets. Every night, everyone expected the arrival of the murderers, so they slept in the hiding place. Berta kept urging Yehudit to flee because no one could help her in her distress. "Whatever will be, will be," she said. But the guarding was tight, the brigades stopped going out, and there was nowhere to run.

The days and nights in the malina increased Yehudit's fears, so much so that she considered giving up on the hideout. She felt as though she was buried alive. Berta believed that the malina was their only chance for survival. The malina had already stood up to challenges, and it was difficult to spot. Nobody imagined that the Germans would burn an entire city with its inhabitants. There was still a measure of innocence in the hearts of many that characterized those who yearned for life. Perhaps Berta had also been strengthened by her belief that there was no other option. Waiting for the Germans upstairs in the house was suicide. Her elderly parents and her three children lost the right to live after the Children's Action, and anyone carrying a weapon was allowed to kill them.

Yehudit decided that she would not go down into the malina and would await her fate. Every evening, the family would part from her when they climbed down into the hideout, and the next day, when nothing had happened, they blessed their survival for one more day.

On the day of their separation, there was no time for farewells. The soldiers showed up, and everyone hurried down to the hideout. Yehudit placed the closet floor back, opened its doors wide, scattered things, and dropped objects so that the Germans would think their friends had already been there, and she went out to meet them. She was placed in a group of people who had also surrendered themselves, as she had, and was taken to the Šančiai camp, where she stayed until the camp was liquidated in mid-July 1944. Berta's fate,

Oscar Stankoweit, 1961–1962, about a year
before his passing.

and that of her parents and her children, has already been told. They
were burned alive.

<center>~~~</center>

Twenty-one years later. In 1965, Yehudit traveled to Germany to
a small village near the city of Verden/Aller to search for her past.
Some of it, she found. She met Frieda, Oscar's oldest daughter, and
heard about Oscar's passing from her. It was an emotional meeting.
Frieda had heard little of the past from her parents, and the rest—
Yehudit filled her in during a conversation that went into the night.
She received Yehudit warmly and with love.

As a parting gift, Frieda gave Yehudit the letter of recommendation our father had given Oscar on February 10, 1941, and her letter to
Oscar and Seitzova from July 21, 1943. Pictures of them are included
in this book.

Otto and Anka Müllerschkowski at their wedding, 1930.

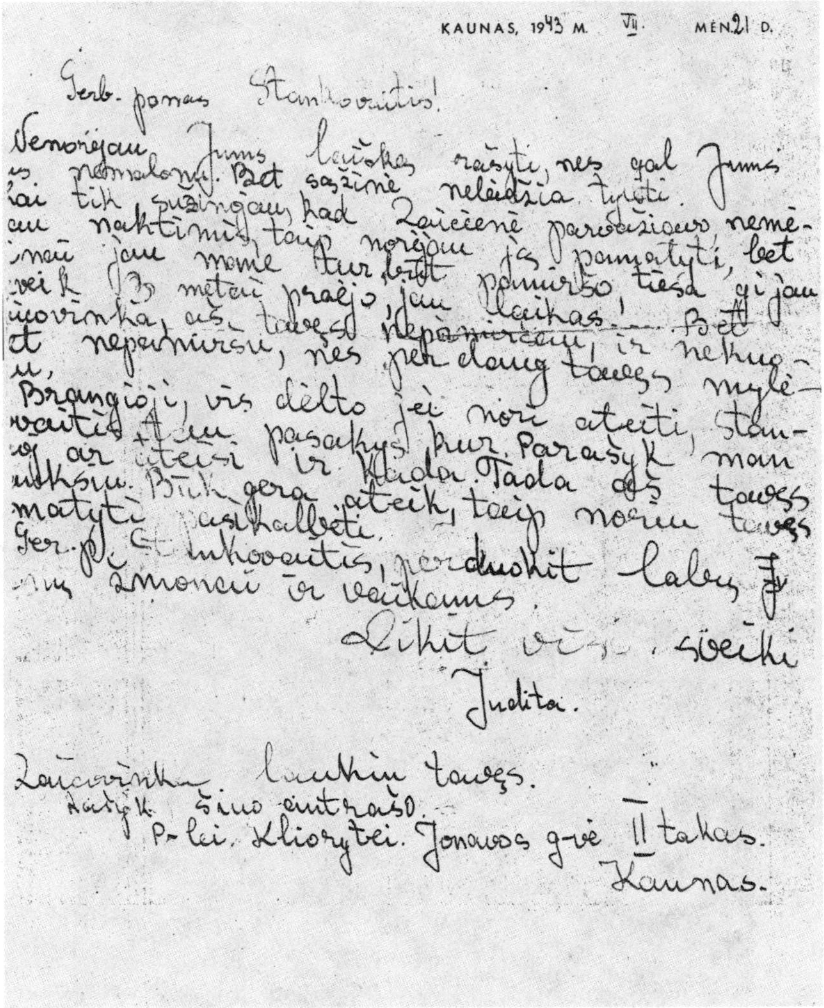

KAUNAS, 1943 M. VII. MĖN 21 D.

Gerb. ponas Stankevičius!

[handwritten letter in Lithuanian]

Judita.

Yehudit's letter to Oscar and Anna, given to Otto
to pass on to them, July 21, 1943.

20

THE SIXTEEN SURVIVORS

THE LONG-AWAITED DAY CAME AT THE BEGINNING OF AU-
gust. That morning, I once again heard quick footsteps. Jonas led
armed men to the pit. "The Russians have come!" he yelled in Russian. He scattered the straw, lifted the boards, and instructed us to
get out. The first out was David Rubin. I could hardly walk, paralyzed
by weakness and fear, but also from the excitement.

A Russian soldier grabbed my hand and pulled me up out of the
pit. I will never forget his words: "My brother, you are free!"

I was told that on that same night, at the break of dawn, Jonas went
out to greet the Red Army. He waited for them near a small-mined
bridge in order to warn them of the mines. When he met the first
scouts and brought them to his home, he told them how he had saved
people from death as a sign of solidarity with the Red Army and
as resistance against the Nazi occupiers. The soldiers who came to
meet me in the pit were those same scouts. I was told that Antanina
had begged Jonas to act with caution to make sure that the Russian
advance was final and that the area wouldn't be handed back and
forth between the Russians and the Germans. Antanina had said
that Jonas should wait until the firing stopped. But Jonas could not
control himself. He went out to meet the scouts and brought them
home while all the other houses around were still locked from the
inside. No one dared go outside.

When my two friends from the pit and I got to the house, we saw
an unbelievable sight: in addition to the Russian scouts sitting there,

there were thirteen more people, all of whom Jonas had saved. Including us three, sixteen people had found refuge in the Paulavičius home. The people looked dreadful—unwashed, unshaved, their clothes filthy and stained with blood. Their bodies were one big wound, covered in open sores. I didn't know that I looked exactly the same way.

Among the sixteen were twelve Jews, two Russians, and two Lithuanians. I don't remember the names of the Russians and the Lithuanian partisans, but I can name the Jewish survivors: the four members of the Schames family, the boy, Shima'leh, his parents, and grandmother, Mrs. Feinsilber; Dr. Chaim Ipp and his wife, Dr. Tanya Ipp; and the engineer Aaron Neumark and his wife, Mania.

I was ninth in the group that Jonas had decided to save. The other three Jews escaped from the convoy that had left the concentration camp at Šančiai when they were led to the Panemunė bridge. They told us their stories: When their group was led to the bridge, a convoy of German tanks had passed in the opposite direction. The place was narrow, and the lines loosened slightly. Some people managed to cross the bridge, and some remained behind. During the confusion, an eighteen-year-old girl, Miriam Schumacher (later Krakinowski), managed to escape from the line. When the Nazi soldier caught her and tried to return her, she objected that she was Lithuanian. He led her to the line and asked the people if they recognized her. They all denied it unanimously, and he therefore sent her off.

At that time, Jonas was in his boat, sailing parallel to the path Miriam followed. He expressed his willingness to save her, but she vehemently denied being Jewish. When they ended up in front of the Paulavičius house, he got out of his boat, came ashore and blocked her path. "Luckily for you," he said to her, "you've found a friend, and anyway, you don't have many options. A few hundred meters from here, Gestapo men are checking documents." Pointing to the house on the side of the river, he said firmly, "This is my home, and I will save you!" After some hesitation, Miriam followed him. He took her down to the cellar, opened the secret door, and let her into the hiding place.

David Rubin, whose story has already been told, was the eleventh survivor. Riva Katavushnik was the twelfth. She had also managed to escape from the convoy. Jonas had identified her as a Jew and persuaded her to come to his house. Actually, because of her refusal and her fear, he had pulled her forcibly to the "tomato patch."

Those were the twelve Jews who found refuge with Jonas. The others were two Russian prisoners. Both had served as guards in the Šančiai concentration camp. They fled the camp before its liquidation and had arrived at the Paulavičius' separately, dressed in German uniforms. The last two were Lithuanian, anti-Nazi partisans who were captured but escaped from the line of people being led to their deaths at the Fourth Fort.

I must add that the troubles were just starting for the two Russian captives who had served in the German Army and were now hiding at the Paulavičius's. The attitude of the Soviet Union toward people of this type was very severe. Oftentimes they were executed on the spot as traitors. The scouts Jonas had brought to the house threatened to kill them, but Jonas shielded them with his body. He made a feast for the scouts, placed a bottle of vodka on the table, removed the red flag from its hiding place, and ordered me to play "The Internationale."[1] This scene seemed like something from a surrealistic play. The scouts contributed their American food cans to the celebration. When the alcohol softened the hard hearts of the fighters, Jonas approached them and asked for forgiveness and mercy on behalf of the prisoners. Even the survivors of the Šančiai camp, who had taken refuge with Jonas, testified that they were easy guards, merciful, and helped the inmates as best they could.

The scouts left them alone, but the matter of the two prisoners did not end there. A few days later, when the first military government institutions were established in Kaunas, Jonas and the two Russians went to the commandant's office for a trial. The trial lasted a whole day. Jonas found witnesses to testify on their behalf, and his efforts bore fruit.

It was perhaps one of the lightest verdicts ever handed down in the trial against the people of Vlasov. They were attached to the penal battalion together with various criminals who would buy their freedom from prison by volunteering for such a regiment. These battalions were stationed on the most dangerous fronts and sent on the most daring missions. From what I know, one of the Russians fell in battle, and the other was seriously injured and lost a lung. For some time, he kept in touch with Jonas through letters from his village in Russia.

21

ABOUT HIDEOUTS AND PEOPLE

THERE WERE THREE HIDING PLACES ON THE PAULAVIČIUS'
property that I knew well because I had stayed in them: the first—
under the tomato patch; the second—the pit with the double floor
close to the main street; and the third—in the attic, in the triangular
nook that formed between the wall of the room and the sloping roof.
But there was a fourth, large, central hiding place under the house
in which I did not stay and whose secrets I learned only years later.

For three years after my liberation, I lived in Panemunė, at first in
Jonas's house and then in my family's nearby former home, but I did
not visit the hideouts even once, and I did not return to the ghetto
to see it again and search among the smoking embers for a souvenir,
testimony, or documentation.

The mechanism of repression, the irrational resistance to returning to these horrible places, and the desire to erase everything from
memory are explanations for my escape from my past. Yet as the
years went on, the memories arose forcefully. At every meeting with
my friends who had taken refuge in the Paulavičius house—and
there were many of these over the years—we recounted and described what had been there. From these recollections I hope to create a faithful picture of the secrets of the large hideout.

The area of the hideout was about nine square meters, similar to a
railroad sleeper car, built underground. Jonas, as you may remember,
worked in the railroad factory, and the building plans were taken
from there: a compartment of a railroad car, four and a half meters

long and two meters wide. On one side, next to the wall and along the length of it, were four bunks made out of boards, arranged on two levels, with two bunks on each level. Between the bunks and the opposite wall there was a narrow walkway along the entire length of the hideout. At the end, a small corner was closed off with a curtain—the bathroom. The walls and ceiling were covered with boards and supported by wooden beams. I was told there was a ventilation pipe that did not stand up to the test, but not everyone in the hideout remembered it.

People lived in this underground box, suffered quietly, and survived. The first of those in the hideout, Lena and Itzhak Schames, their son, Shima'leh, and the grandmother, Lena's mother, Mrs. Feinsilber, lived in the hideout for five months, from the beginning of March until the end of July 1944. Initially there were four people underground, crowded, without the ability to move more than four meters. Yet this was still luxurious compared to what the future held.

The older Schameses arrived in a hurry, because their son, as you may recall, could not acclimate, and Jonas had to bring him his parents as quickly as possible. Their belongings had been left in their house at the ghetto because they could not take much with them when they escaped. Their house was left to Aaron Neumark and his wife, Mania, who was a relative of the Schameses. Neumark continued to remove objects from the Schames's house, carrying them on his back and in his knapsack and bringing them to Jonas, who came to Neumark's place of work for that purpose.

That was how Neumark became Jonas's contact and his emissary in his search for rescue candidates, according to his own criteria. Neumark found me and similarly the Ipps, and he became the key man in making first contact between the escapees and Jonas. Jonas became very fond of Aaron Neumark, who became a natural candidate to be saved, since he too was an engineer and therefore fit Jonas's criteria.

My arrival at Jonas's house did not burden the people in the hiding place because I was hidden elsewhere, and no one but the Paulavičiuses knew about my existence. But the addition of the Ipps in the hideout abruptly changed the living conditions of its inhabitants. After Mania and Aaron's arrival, eight people were crammed into a nine-square-meter hideout. At the request of those survivors who are still with us, and in honor of the memory of those who are gone, I will describe their lives in the large hideout. But first—how did they escape from the ghetto?

The escape itself was not necessarily the hardest part. The biggest problem was finding somewhere to escape to. To find, in the surrounding sea of hostility, someone who would agree to risk saving a persecuted Jew was a real challenge.

Dr. Chaim Ipp's method of escape became a model for other escapes. Ipp left the ghetto with one of the brigades that went every morning for forced labor, mostly to the airport, which employed thousands of workers. The escapees had to join the brigade after its people were counted and registered. This was only possible with the knowledge of the head of the brigade and with his full cooperation. Acquaintances and connections, along with mutual help and solidarity, enabled the escapees to find the appropriate brigade.

That is what Chaim Ipp did. At the right moment, he deserted the thousands of workers and was swallowed up by a crowd of Lithuanians who came to trade objects for food. Jonas arrived on the appointed day and milled about in the crowd. After a while, he left the place surrounded by others, and with a nod of his head, he motioned to Chaim Ipp to follow him. Thus began a journey, with many dangers involved. Jonas went first and a bit further behind him, Chaim Ipp. After a few hours' march, he was collected and swallowed underground. In the same way, his wife, Tania Ipp, and Mania and Aaron Neumark arrived one by one. According to Mania's memory, all this happened in May 1944.

Eight people in an area of nine square meters. They slept two by two on shabby, straw-lined bunks, narrow and hard, hearing the breath of the other. Horrible nights, as long as an eternity. Even when dawn arose, they did not know it. In the hideout, in the darkness, it was an eternal night. During the day, they lit a small electric lamp, but when they finished making the necessary arrangements, they quickly turned it off. The heat in the hiding place was unbearable, and the warmth of the lamp added to it. They sat half naked on the bunks and wiped their sweat with a damp cloth. Their wounds burned like fire; the plague of lice preyed on their bodies and minds. And so nights were as days, and days were as nights, over and over.

Chaim Ipp's situation was the hardest of all. An infectious eczema exhausted his strength. He was depressed. He spoke of futility, of his imminent death, of an injection that would end his life. He always kept poison with him. In the corner bathroom, hidden by a curtain, stood a bucket that served everyone in turn. It was deeply degrading. How the remnant of human dignity for those in hiding was crushed. Did one have to pay such a heavy price for the chance to live? Behind the curtain was a water tank for washing—a quasi-washing, moistening the body to cool it a little, for a few moments.

But there were moments when there was a spark of hope: when Jonas made his nightly visits. They waited for him as a man awaits salvation. He would only come at night because any mistake or lack of caution of the smallest kind could condemn them all to death. He explained that if he were to come during the day, a neighbor could ask, "Where is Jonas?"

They would answer, "He is not home."

And then the neighbor might say, "How is he not home? I just saw him a minute ago!" It is frightening to think of the consequences of such a thing. Therefore, Jonas came at night, to listen and to be heard, to encourage and to impart strength. He knew how distressed they were.

This man had a wonderful wisdom about him. His visits had a pattern. First—empty the waste bucket, rinse it, and put it back. Those in the hideout had already gotten used to relieving themselves before Jonas's arrival. Then—remove the bucket of dirty water and add clean water to the container. The whole time it took for these jobs, the door of the hiding place was open and cool fresh air poured in. The people breathed fresh air into their lungs and inhaled and inhaled, as if it were possible to store healthy air for the choking hours of the night.

Afterward, Jonas would have conversations with them. Sitting on one of the boards, he spoke, encouraged, and answered their questions even before they were asked. The food was meager, he knew, but it was hard to get. The shortage was great; everyone was hungry. "The little you get will keep you alive," he said, "since you do not expend any energy. You have to hold up a little longer. The front is getting closer; the Red Army is dealing the Nazis great blows. At night, we already hear the sound of artillery."

This gave them some encouragement. The noise of the artillery became the noise of the rising dawn. The words "the Red Army" meant not just their literal definition, the name of the Soviet Russian military; they were lofty words, a symbol of heroism, an object of admiration. For the local population, the Red Army was the conqueror, but to us, who were betrayed and killed by many of the locals—it was the Liberation Army. Jonas knew how much those trapped in the hideout needed encouragement and comforting. He brought a map, hung it on the wall in front of the beds, and in the light of the little lamp marked the approaching lines of the front with pins. The words of encouragement strengthened their spirits, and the pins that were updated daily were the backup for the words.

Every pin punctured into the map was like a knife stabbing the Third Reich. They believed that the day of liberation would come. And as that day approached, Jonas made a red flag and hid it under one of the bunks in the hideout. Not only a flag—he brought a rifle as well, but everyone hoped there would be no need for it.

At first, when the front was still far away, meals were served three times a day and met the minimum standards for sustenance. The main problem was acquiring the food. As the war dragged on, the shortages of food worsened, all the more so near the front. The battles were drawing closer. Sometimes, the events in the surrounding areas did not even make it possible to go down into the hideout to bring the little that there was. In those instances, a loaf of bread and a pitcher full of coffee substitute were lowered for the entire day, and the people inside starved.

On regular days, bread was lowered in with some kind of accompaniment: jam or cheese, on occasion an egg, once in a while butter, but mostly lard and some kind of drink. Lunch was one course: a thick soup with barley, pieces of meat and potatoes, or milk soup with homemade noodles, and some accompaniments. Dinner was similar to breakfast. Late at night, when he came down for a heart-to-heart talk and updates on the front lines, Jonas would bring a pitcher of coffee.

The thickness of the soup and its quality were indicators of the developments along the front. In the last weeks before liberation, the thick soup disappeared and was replaced with hot water with bits floating in it that were hard to identify. The manner in which they sat to eat, the dishes and their removal, worrying about a minimal standard of cleanliness under the conditions of the crowded hide-out—I cannot describe this because I did not experience it myself. Therefore, I leave those to the imagination of the reader.

What caused them the most suffering? What were the sources of friction between them? How did they handle the collective fate forced upon them? Were they bothered by each other's behavior? Were some stronger than others? Did they agree or was there conflict?

There were no arguments between them. There were also no statements that expressed criticism, nor a desire to change things. Common fate and forced living conditions prompted them to hold grievances and bear their suffering in silence. When freedom would come and everyone would go their separate ways, then everything would be said, but all would also be forgiven.

The Schameses came to the hideout because of their son and not because they met the criteria set forth by Jonas for being saved. As you may recall, they first turned to their neighbor offering money and other items of value in exchange for saving their son. They may have actually paid a sum—this I don't know. When that same neighbor made the connection between the Schameses and Jonas, the same monetary offer was presented. Under the circumstances, when Jonas agreed to collect all the family members, the amount also increased. Years later, when stories were told of the old days, Jonas did not hide the matter of the payment. He explained that he did not demand more than the amount needed to feed the people.

The Schameses have a different version. According to them, they paid Jonas more than was necessary for food, and the surplus was payment for the rescue itself. Moreover, according to them, they sustained the rest of the survivors with their money. None of this was said outright while they were trapped in the hideout, but it was expressed, the survivors told us, in passing statements and especially in their behavior and their attempt to determine the arrangements in the hiding place.

The Schameses were the first to be holed up in the hideout, though they were there by themselves a mere two months. At the time they felt that the hiding place with the four berths—a bunk for each— was theirs. But Jonas thought differently. His plan was to save more Jewish intellectuals—doctors, engineers, future leaders who could restore the Jewish people. And indeed, one after the other, Tania and Chaim Ipp and Mania and Aaron Neumark joined the hiding place. The arrival of this group, of course, greatly reduced the living space. Everyone now had to sleep in pairs—a couple in each bunk—and breathe in the stuffy, compressed air.

The senior hideout residents determined that the newcomers would get the upper bunks. It was a demonstration of authority and protection of seniority rights. An additional expression of their authority was given in the matter of food distribution arrangements. Every time food was brought down by a member of the Paulavičius family, the Schameses would take it from them and distribute it among the people in the hideout. They spread the bread and poured the soup.

At the time, nine people were hiding at the Paulavičius's: eight in the large hideout and me. The two Russian captives were also promised refuge when the day came. But saving eleven people was not enough for Jonas.

After Aaron Neumark came to the hideout, Jonas made contact with Dr. Greenberg and his wife, from the ghetto, who were also supposed to come to the Paulavičius's. Mania knew they were supposed to be coming, and she pleaded with Jonas that he allow her mother, who had remained behind in the ghetto, to join them. He agreed to this as well. Another group of three people was therefore supposed to arrive. The timetable, the arrangements for escape, and the transportation were set, but the plan went wrong and the attempt was unsuccessful. Jonas did not give up. He worked hard, used every resource at his disposal, took risks, and set another date for the rescue of the three.

When Jonas arrived at the designated place, no one was there to meet him. The rescue operation was too late. The liquidation of the ghetto had already begun. The Greenbergs and Mania's mother were trapped and could no longer escape. Jonas returned crestfallen. When he came to the hideout for his nightly discussion, he talked about the failed operation. That was how the Schameses learned of Jonas's plan to rescue another three people.

The Schameses were very angry, and Lena decided to express it. When Jonas left the hideout, she went up after him, which was against protocol, and she carried on a conversation with him that could be heard by all.

Because she felt that her family was in hiding because of her money and not by grace, Lena demanded that no more people be brought in because the poisoned air was already suffocating the people in the hideout. She claimed that her little son and her mother would not be able to cope. The conversation between the two could have ended differently had Jonas revealed that there were other hiding places in his house where he would hide other survivors. But revealing this was impossible for a man as secretive as himself. And when he replied that he did not need anyone's approval for the rescue operation to which he was so dedicated, the conversation ended bitterly. It defined his relationship with the Schameses even after their liberation.

The stain on Jonas's reputation and the insinuations that he rescued people for the money make me angry. Were it true, he would have only rescued those who could pay—the Schameses—giving them the whole hiding place to themselves, and he would have parted ways the moment the Russians returned. And what did Jonas do with the extra money beyond the living expenses, if there was such a surplus? He brought more and more survivors. He went wherever people were led to their deaths to pick up the fugitives and hide them in his home. Sixteen people found refuge in his home—twelve who had no money to pay in addition to the Schameses. He hid them, fed them, and risked his life for them. Moreover, after the liberation, he even gave a survivor a considerable sum of money to escape from Lithuania. Is this how a greedy man behaves? Is this what a greedy man does? No; these acts characterize the Righteous Among the Nations,[1] among whom Jonas was one of the most prominent.

My relatives, the Pruzhans and the Kronzons, had the means to pay. They took the risk of not handing over any possessions when the Nazis had confiscated all valuables, and their money remained with them. Yet they met their horrible death in the basement of their house because they did not meet our Jonas or any other Jonas to whom they could pay everything they had to be rescued and survive. They had no one to pay.

Over the decades, my thoughts have often returned to those days, to the hideouts and to those who were trapped. The matter of their relations among themselves and the opposing views of Jonas's actions haunt me even now as I write about it. Can human reason guide our actions in such inhuman circumstances? Can these questions be dealt with in hindsight?

We all know how a literary hero must behave. He must fight valiantly for his just war and not be captured; he must endure every interrogation and torture and not betray his friends; he must be the last one off a sinking ship into the lifeboat—if he is the captain, perhaps he must even sink with his ship into the depths—and so on and so forth in heroic sagas. But people of honor and heroes are few; the rest are ordinary people who just want to live. That was true of the people trapped in Jonas's hideout. They lived in unbearably difficult conditions, and they never fought. There was no obvious friction, and even in moments of weakness and breaking, no one raised their voice to the other. Only after liberation, when they parted ways, did they express their views regarding the motives that guided Jonas and expressed out loud what they had kept in their hearts.

22

THE PAULAVIČIUSES

I've reared a monument not built by human hand.

A. S. PUSHKIN, "THE MONUMENT"

JONAS

To this day, I am still amazed at the riddle that is Jonas Paulavičius and his family. To this day, I do not fully understand their motives for saving sixteen people, risking their own lives.

Jonas followed every condemned group driven by his house, on the main street of the suburb, to the Fourth Fort (an execution site), or to the trains. With his sharp eye, he kept watch for someone who might run away, whom he would then be able to pick up. An obsessive internal dictate led him to wherever he could pick up escapees and give them a hiding place in his house and in the pits in his field.

There were some who saved Jews for money, but that wasn't the case with Jonas. Of the sixteen, only one group, the four-person Schames family, had any money to pay. The others made it clear that they had no money and no other property worth money, and yet it was no obstacle. The shelter was provided free of charge. And lest we forget—it took a lot of money to get food to feed so many mouths.

It is difficult to find one decisive factor to explain Jonas's lofty deeds—rather, a combination of several interconnected factors may better explain how this remarkable story took place.

Jonas was a simple man, a laborer, uneducated, but with a complicated personality; often his words and actions seemed contradictory.

Jonas Paulavičius, 1923.

His communist worldview was undoubtedly a significant factor in his actions, but it was not decisive and certainly not the only one. His communist outlook was emotional and devoid of ideological roots. His loyalty to some of the members of the then-illegal Communist Party, whom he knew personally, was greater than his allegiance to ideology. His loyalty to his fellow man as individual human beings who should be treated with respect was never broken. As for ideology—this was set aside and its corners were rounded when it conflicted with other, more practical needs.

―⁓―

From 1945 to 1946, a repatriation movement began for Polish emigrants, who arrived as refugees to the Soviet Union from regions conquered by the Germans in the years 1939 to 1941. The repatriation certificate was a simple typewritten form, without a picture. It showed the name of the certificate holder as well as the place and year of birth, which were written by hand. In addition, the letter bore the all-powerful "round stamp," in Russian: *kruglaya pechat*!

Like an open call to a thief, these primitive documents invited counterfeiters. A document forging movement developed. The forgers learned the process of bringing Polish citizens back to Poland, where Zionism and other movements that specialized in transferring people to the West could be found. After the war, they did not even need *machers*[1] because Polish citizens of Jewish origin could submit applications for immigration, and in most cases, their request was approved. The role of the macher, the mediator, was limited to expediting the process of receiving a passport—all of it, of course, for money. Armies were coming and going, regimes were falling and rising, and only corruption remained: when everything else withers and shrivels—corruption flourishes.

This was the background to Mania and Aaron Neumark's decision to leave Soviet Lithuania. However, they did not have the money. Jonas, who was managing my father's mill at the time and had the flour "faucet" at his disposal, was a wealthy man for his time. Mania hesitated: Should she ask Jonas for his advice and help? How would this communist react when the people he saved decided to flee from communism? When Jonas heard from Mania that they wanted to run away, he was saddened. There was silence, but after a moment's thought, he said, "Why does a mother love her children?" He continued, "Because she birthed them through agony." That was the parable, but what was the lesson? "In the hideout, I gave you life. You are like my children, and now you are leaving me. The army that liberated you will become your enemy? Life works in strange ways. Have you thought it all through? Are you aware of the dangers? It will sadden and pain me if after all that you've been through, you were to be captured and sent to the land of the polar bears [Siberia]. Please reconsider and come back to me in three days."

This is what Jonas said, as was told to me by Mania many years later. With a few simple words, formulated with the wisdom of life's experiences, he said so much.

Mania and Aaron's decision to leave was final. When Mania came back to Jonas after three days, he knew what she had decided before she even opened her mouth. "Take it," he said and handed her a small, well-wrapped package. The package had in it the amount of money required for Mania and Aaron to purchase a travel document to Poland; ten thousand rubles—an amount that at that time equaled twenty-five monthly wages. They parted with hugs and kisses, and Jonas—the iron man—cried!

Regarding Jonas's communism: Near the end of the war, after Lithuania's liberation, as the battles on German soil were still underway, Kęstutis received a draft notice. Yet Jonas, the man whose communist outlook motivated him to save Jews and other persecuted people, and who saw himself as an anti-Nazi fighter, refused to send his son to fight the Nazis. He had already risked his family's lives; he did not intend to risk his son's life yet again. In his war against the Nazis, he thought he had done enough. The war was about to end, the Third Reich had collapsed. The front was far away, somewhere on German soil, and the victory, he thought, would be achieved without Kęstutis taking part in it. Kęstutis fought alongside his father in his personal war against the Nazis, and he had risked his life every day and night. Jonas thought that was enough. He loved his son more than his political views.

The doctors, Tania and Chaim Ipp, had found refuge, as you remember, in Jonas's house. The Ipps owed their lives to Jonas, and now in his distress, he came to Dr. Chaim Ipp to collect a small part of his debt.

Dr. Ipp was then the director of internal medicine at one of Kaunas's hospitals. Jonas asked to have Kęstutis hospitalized in his department as a typhus patient, thus postponing his enlistment by a year. Could Dr. Ipp have refused? Could he have explained that the fear was too great? The punishment would be ten years' imprisonment in the gulags and the loss of his license to practice medicine, were he caught. What was the weight of these risks compared to the risks Jonas and his family had taken in saving the Ipps? Sometimes it seems that nothing is easier than distinguishing between good and evil, legal and illegal, moral and immoral, permissible and forbidden.

But life presents us with complex tests, creating circumstances in which the forbidden is permitted and the illegal is the supreme law of morality.

Dr. Chaim Ipp, of blessed memory, a trustworthy and honest man, innocent and pure of heart, proceeded illegally. He agreed.

Kęstutis was hospitalized, and his supposed illness was documented and treated—everything was done as though it were truly real. No doubt this could not have been accomplished by only one doctor, even if he was the head of the department. It was reasonable to assume that Dr. Ipp had collaborators who were included in the secret. In the meantime, the Health Department came to the Paulavičius' home, thoroughly disinfected the entire house, and pasted placards on the door and on the walls of the house warning the public against entering the house, lest they become infected. I was forbidden to go to school, since I lived in the patient's house. After a while, Kęstutis "recovered" completely, the hospital reported to the conscription office about the "illness" of the conscript, his conscription was postponed a year. At the end of the war, the draft order was canceled altogether.

It is impossible to simply explain Jonas's actions as being dictated by his views, since they were flexible when necessary. His views influenced him, but did not always prevail.

Greater weight was given to his devotion to his friends, especially one who was mentioned previously: Balys Baranauskas. The man, a veteran communist, knew Jonas back in the thirties and lived for a while in the Paulavičius' home in the village of Birutė, even before Jonas set up his home in Panemunė. His connection with this educated man, who had status in the underground movement, was very flattering for Jonas. When the war broke out, Baranauskas fled to the Soviet Union and later, as previously mentioned, he began to broadcast in the Lithuanian language, calling on the Lithuanians to fight the German occupier in every way possible, including saving Jews and the persecuted. These broadcasts, to which Jonas listened intently, were for him a command of sorts. His senior friend ordered, and he had to carry the order out.

Did he want honor and glory? Perhaps something of that flattered him too. The desire to show his senior friend the living monument he had built for himself was burning in his bones. I remember his happy face and his tearful eyes when Baranauskas came to visit him sometime after the return of the Russians, sitting in an army jeep in the uniform of a colonel, accompanied by a junior officer, and Jonas presented me as if to say, "Here is living proof of my actions."

Baranauskas told his confidants about Jonas and even wrote about him in his memoir, published in 1965 in his book *Nineteen Years in the Underground*. All of these, in my opinion, were important factors, which, in addition to Jonas's views, explain his actions to a large extent.

But another factor that influenced him heavily, and in my opinion guided him above all else, was Jonas's good heart—his sensitivity despite his rough exterior. He found it hard to bear the mass murder of the Jews, and it was particularly painful to him that it was perpetrated by his Lithuanian brethren. I know this: that was what he said; that was how he spoke.

———

Jonas also had enemies. He was withdrawn from society, for he had something to hide. Even before the war, when the hated Communist Party activists, whose ranks numbered about seven hundred members in all of Lithuania, found refuge in his home, he had to keep his tongue and guard his secrets.

The act of saving the Jews—an exceptional thing that speaks for itself—was seen by many as an act that also endangered the lives of one's neighbors. "How could he take on such a responsibility?" They were friendly to his face, kindly referring to him as "*Žydų tėvas*"— "the father of the Jews." Yet behind his back they said the same words with a different intonation, without a smile and with grinding teeth. The crowd did not like nonconformity. Some thought and whispered that the man became rich from his business with the Jews. "They're rich. The Jews probably paid him a lot of money." Jealousy increased even more when Jonas began running the flour mill. Flour is bread, and bread during times of hunger is gold. The wicked imagination knows no bounds.

"Tell the truth—how much did you pay him?" Kids my age asked me this many times.

And when I said, "Nothing," they refused to believe it.

"Did you give him the mill in exchange for your rescue?" they continued asking. And if children thought like that—what did their parents think?

Jonas, the ordinary man, the laborer, the human, the brave anti-Nazi fighter, met his death on his own battlefield. When we parted in 1947, he was at his full strength. I was told about his end many years later.

On May 1, 1952, the Soviet's big holiday—which was celebrated by drinking to the point of drunkenness, both by supporters and enemies of the regime alike—Jonas returned home drunk and fell into a deep sleep. The assassin stalked him in the vegetation near his house. Seemingly knowing his routine, he climbed to the height of the window, shot the sleeping man, and killed him. That was how Jonas met his fate.

Those who were saved by Jonas told and continue to tell their children and grandchildren about this wonderful man, the Lithuanian, Jonas Paulavičius. If my book contributes to the perpetuation of his name—that would be a proper reward for my labor.

Who killed Jonas?

Antanina revealed that Jonas had an enemy from his youth. In the past, they had lived as neighbors, but their paths parted: Jonas turned left, the other one—right. During the war, that same man collaborated with the Nazis and took part in their crimes. When the Russians returned to Lithuania (1944), the man disappeared. One day, Jonas met him in the street and identified him, despite the outward change in the man's appearance: he had grown a beard and mustache. He had even changed his name. This meeting bothered Jonas very much, and he was concerned that Jonas would expose him. According to Antanina, he was the man who killed Jonas. She told us that the man was caught, tried, and sentenced to two life sentences: one for collaborating with the Nazis and the second for murdering Jonas. Antanina's story ends here.

Kęstutis rejected his mother's story completely. True, he confirmed, there was such a man, but at his trial, it was neither proven nor even alleged that he had murdered Jonas. Why, then, did Antanina tell a story that was not true? I will express Kęstutis's answer to this question: my mother wanted revenge; my mother wanted justice; my mother wanted punishment. The man and his end matched her wishes. With deep conviction, she continued to live with the belief that her husband's murderer had been punished.

In the book by Balys Baranauskas, which I mentioned earlier, the author states that Jonas was murdered by "bourgeois nationalists," a standard Soviet statement that clarifies very little.

I have thought a lot about Jonas's death.

Jonas did not die in an accident, nor in a drunken brawl, and not from a stray bullet. Jonas was murdered, and it was premeditated. The murderer chose a holiday, waited for nightfall, followed him, and ambushed him. Fear for the worst punishment—if he were to get caught—did not stop him from carrying out his plan. Lack of sympathy, enmity, jealousy, and envy are insufficient to push a person to commit murder. Only a very deep reason—fear of Jonas, the need to silence him—could have led to such careful planning of the murder and the determination to carry it out. Perhaps there is truth in Antanina's assumption of the identity of the murderer, of which she had so thoroughly convinced herself, even if it was not proven in the trial. Maybe. Yet with no solid proof, we must side with Kęstutis: the murder of his father was never solved.

DANUTĖ

Jonas's eldest daughter was his favorite—beautiful, delicate, and fragile. The thought of her being caught, tortured, or executed terrified him. He was driven mad with fear. Jonas decided to send her away from home. If she would live separately, he thought, if the rest of the family were caught, maybe she would have time to escape.

Danutė Paulavičius.

They found her a place to rent, and she rarely visited the family's home. I saw her very few times during my stay at the Paulavičius's. The precautionary measures Jonas used to save his beloved daughter did not always help. Baranauskas wrote in his book that during one of the raids the Germans occasionally conducted on the streets to kidnap passersby for forced labor in Germany, Danutė was caught, but she managed to escape by jumping off the train.

Danutė only returned home after the war. Because I continued to live in the home of the Paulavičiuses, I grew to know her. As the danger passed, the house was opened. Guests began to visit, especially young people, friends of Danutė and Kęstutis. During these joyous gatherings, I took an active role, and my violin accompanied their songs and dances. Happiness and youthful joy compensated for the period of suffering, fear, and seclusion. Danutė became like a sister to me. In my reflections, she was even more than that.

She had a shy smile. Even when she was close to death, she did not stop smiling. It started with a constant, stubborn cough. When it worsened, she was examined and hospitalized. The doctors determined that it was tuberculosis. Treatments, injections, hospitalization—nothing helped. Danutė continued to fade. I was in Moscow at that time. As I will explain, I had contracted another disease that seemed incurable. A specialist managed to halt my illness, and my chances of recovery seemed promising. Jonas was told about my recovery. In desperation, he decided to bring his daughter to Moscow. Perhaps there, in the big city, salvation would be found for Danutė. Substantial financial means were required, but nothing was too expensive or too difficult where Danutė's well-being was concerned.

Danutė was accompanied to Moscow by Kęstutis and Jonas. They used all of the introductions and connections they had in an effort to get her the best possible treatment. Danutė was hospitalized and given the best that Soviet medicine had to offer in those days, but to no avail.

At that time, before the era of antibiotics, tuberculosis was in most cases a death sentence, and there was no one to appeal to. In 1947, she was picked as a flower at the peak of her youth. She was twenty-one years old when she died.

KĘSTUTIS

In one of my conversations with Kęstutis regarding those days, I asked if his parents had asked his opinion when they decided to save Jews and hide them in their house. He smiled and answered with a question: "Do you think my father's house was a democratic parliament? My father told me what he was going to do. I had to help with everything, to act as an underground activist, and to keep my mouth shut."

Even if Kęstutis had only followed orders devotedly and nothing more—he would have still earned a place on the list of Righteous Among the Nations along with his parents—which in fact did

Kęstutis Paulavičius, 1950.

happen. But he did more than follow orders. As in my case: if not for him, how would my name have ever gotten to his parents?

Kęstutis, then seventeen years old, gave my name to his parents and asked them to save my life. And how would I meet the criteria according to which the candidates for rescue were chosen, how would a fourteen-year-old boy be regarded as educated and intellectual? Kęstutis found the reason: the boy played the violin well, he said, and he exaggerated and added compliments, over and above my skills. Jonas agreed. I came to the Paulavičius house, and the rest you already know: I lived—and it is not an exaggeration to say that it was thanks to him.

That fateful evening, Kęstutis, still a teenager, went to the house on the shore of the Vilija (Neris) River, where I had temporarily been given refuge, and brought me to his home. We passed through the streets of the hostile city, passed guarded bridges; my fate and the fate of many lay in his hands. Kęstutis was responsible for me on behalf of his parents. Once I was hidden, he brought me my food, emptied the waste bucket, and relieved my loneliness. Kęstutis brought me a chess set, a chess book, and a selection of Maironis poems, one of the greatest poets of Lithuania, purchased especially for me. Kęstutis understood my distress and devoted much of his time to me. He talked to me, recounted films he had seen, and brought me books to read. I devoured the books by Karl May, and sometimes I forgot reality and imagined in my mind the places in those books.

I was told that one day Jonas and Antanina went out to take care of a few errands, and Kęstutis was left alone at home. The military police were searching for a deserter. On their path, they met a woman and asked her if she had seen the escapee. She, in fact, had seen him but pointed in the opposite direction, which led them to the Paulavičius' home. The military police stormed in and searched room after room. They opened the closets, looked under the beds, searched every corner, and reached the basement, which served as a workshop for Jonas. There was a carpentry table there, work tools, shovels, all sorts of things, and the floor was covered with wood shavings. All of this made it difficult to spot the small door that led to the hideout.

At the time, there were eight people in the hideout. Kęstutis managed to get to the basement ahead of military police. With an agreed upon knock, he informed those hiding—"Danger!" They held their breath and kept total silence. He covered the little door with his body, leaned on the wall, and spread his arms out as though saying, "You can see, there is nothing here." The soldiers left in a hurry and continued their chase. Not many withstood such tests, and those who did will understand the stress Kęstutis was under, how his heart pounded.

I have Kęstutis's testimony from a 1998 filmed interview for the Holocaust archive in Lithuania. The first part of the interview took place in Kęstutis's home, the second at the Fourth Fort. In his testimony, Kęstutis points out the locations and describes the murders that he was a witness to as a boy. Children, and he was among them, hid behind a hill covered with mounds of stones. They watched those unfortunate people, men and women, partially in the nude or even fully exposed. Group by group, they were led into the great pit and shot to death. The murdered were covered with dirt in a mass grave. It is a dreadful thought, those wounded who were buried alive among the dead.

No great effort was made to hide the crime. In answer to the interviewer's question, Kęstutis said that in the street that passed right next to the location of the murder stood an armed guard, ordering any cart that came close to turn around and go back where they came from. Everyone knew why: the echoes of the shots told it all. In answer to the question of the interviewer, Saulius Beržinis, director of the archives: "Were the shooters German?"

Kęstutis answered, "No. That job they left for the Lithuanians." The Germans just filmed the atrocity. Kęstutis told of how he couldn't sleep on the nights after he witnessed those events.

Fate was not good to the Paulavičius family—further witness to the fact that there is no heavenly mercy. In 1947, Danutė died in the prime of her life. In the same year, during the thawing of the snow, the ice sheet was broken on the Nemunas, and the area was flooded in a manner that had never been seen before. The rising waters rose to a high altitude, and the Paulavičius' house, near the shore, was lifted from its concrete foundations, floated between the ice blocks, and became stranded on the beach, some distance from its original location. Their house was like Noah's ark. Everything that had been in the courtyard of the house and in the cellar was destroyed and lost. The family continued to live there for about ten years. The need to build a new house on their plot of land was unavoidable.

After Jonas's death in 1952, the economic base of the family was greatly undermined. If all this were not enough, Kęstutis, like his sister, contracted tuberculosis, and his recovery process was slow and prolonged. He was hospitalized for two years, and his higher education was interrupted. In the absence of sufficient funds, construction of the house continued for many years, and when construction ended, the house was far from complete. Years later, an electrical short caused a fire that destroyed the top floor of the house. As I write these lines, Kęstutis is approaching his seventy-fifth year. In this autumn of his life, he is still working on rebuilding his house and has not yet achieved rest and prosperity.[2]

ANTANINA

She was the woman behind the scenes without whom the saving of so many lives would not have come to fruition. Even though Jonas ruled the roost and forced his will on the household, without Antanina's consent, he would have been helpless. With her consent, she took upon herself, not only the risk, but the daily labor involved in feeding the refugees and taking care of their needs.

At the end of May 1944, nine people were hiding in the Paulavičius home, and the cooking and needs of all the extra people had to be taken care of. Antanina also had to ensure that unexpected visitors would not notice the size of the pots. The main difficulty was acquiring food. How do you explain buying such large quantities of food for a family of four, in a suburb where everyone knows everyone? It was therefore necessary to travel to remote, rural areas to shop for food in larger quantities and at lower prices than in the cities in order to sell part of it and save the rest for household expenses. In time, the courtyard of the Paulavičius home became a small rural farm. The cow provided fresh milk, the chickens laid eggs, and the journeys to remote villages and the hauling of the groceries were done with the help of a horse harnessed to a wagon. All livestock was purchased and spread out in the yard of the house and in the nearby field.

These tasks were not done solely by Antanina. All the members of the household were recruited to help out, but the principal burden fell on the shoulders of this wonderful woman. Kęstutis went to school, Jonas on occasion went to Kaunas, to meet his contacts in the forced labor brigades in order to deliver and receive messages, and Antanina worked and worked from morning to night, day after day. Physical and mental forces and the belief that the nightmare would be over soon enabled her to function and not be crushed by the heavy burden.

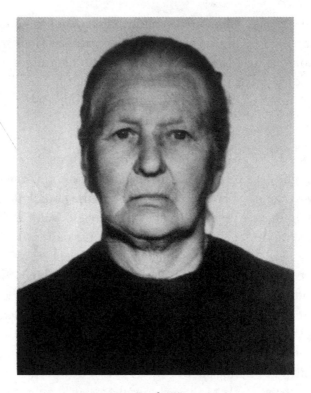

Antanina Paulavičius, 1970.

At one point, I must have contracted pneumonia, and my cough got worse. Antanina removed me from my dank shelter to the top floor of her house. She washed my body, treated my wounds, cleaned my head soothingly, like a mother caring lovingly for her son. She also managed to get me medication. Now I know that Dr. Chaim Ipp guided her from his hiding place regarding the treatment and medication needed for an anonymous patient.

The survivors of the Paulavičius' hiding places scattered to the four corners of the earth. Fourteen of the sixteen left Lithuania, and their connections with the Paulavičiuses were severed. Letters we wrote went unanswered and perhaps didn't even reach their destination. It was not convenient to write letters from communist Lithuania to the West, and especially not to Israel. My sister Vera kept in constant touch with Antanina and Kęstutis until she immigrated to Israel in 1971. In the 1980s, the connection was renewed. Antanina, by then a sick old woman, expressed her desire to see her children before she died; that's how she referred to us, the survivors. In 1988, we brought her to Israel. Her visit renewed her relationship with the survivors, and before her arrival, we gathered and were like family members who had not seen each other for years. Miriam and Moshe Krakinowski, who came especially from the United States, joined the Israeli survivors and their family members, and only the Schames family, who had settled in Peru, was absent from the meeting.

In an impressive ceremony at Yad Vashem, Antanina and Jonas were granted a certificate as Righteous Among the Nations, and a tree was planted in their name. In a hall packed with Lithuanian immigrants in Israel, the wonderful, silver-haired woman unfolded her story in simple and moving words. The question was raised from all directions: "Why did you do it? What made you risk your life and you dear ones' lives?"

I will quote her answer from memory, as closely as possible: "I saw them being led—men, women and children; I saw their suffering; I saw their death. It broke my heart. I knew that anyone who would find shelter in my house would not end up suffering to their deaths in the fortress [in the Fourth Fort]." The audience rose to their feet and applauded. Many tears were shed.

The ceremony was reported in the news, and the story of the Paulavičius family spread widely. Under pressure from the editors of *A New Evening* (a reality show in Israel), I agreed to appear with Antanina on live television (March 9, 1988). The joint show with Antanina aroused emotions, and dozens of strangers phoned me. People wanted to hear more details, and some wanted to meet her up close. When they came, they brought her presents. Thus, a story that was preserved in the hearts of few became public domain. When we wheeled her through the streets—she had trouble walking—people recognized her and hugged her. She responded, "This is a reward I did not expect."

We worried about her. At night, we stayed near her bed to listen to her breathing. The time came to part ways. Loaded down with

Antanina in Israel.

luggage—no one thought of excess weight—we brought her to the airport. When she had difficulty maneuvering the plane's gangway, we arranged for accommodations. They allowed us to accompany her to the plane. Before she left, Antanina said, "Those were the best days of my life!" She had to spend one night in Bucharest and the next day had to report to the airport for a flight to Moscow. How would she do it? How would she manage? Where would she spend the night? How would she move about without a wheelchair? But many hearts had opened to Antanina. We turned to the Foreign Ministry, and they turned to the Israeli Embassy in Bucharest. The wife of the ambassador, in an official embassy car accompanied by an assistant, located Antanina, and to the amazement of the other passengers—who were

Righteous *Among the Nations award*.

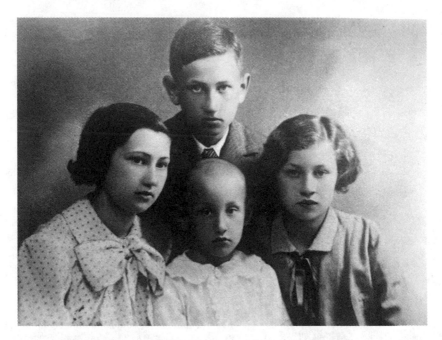

Yochanan's two sisters, Yehudit (*right*) and Devorah (Vera);
his brother Zvi (Hirsch'ke) (*top*); and Yochanan.

about to spend the night in the terminal—she was taken for a good
night's sleep, and the next day was brought to the plane.

After Antanina saw "her children," whom she had saved and adopted, she had no more wishes to fulfill. Very few months after her
return from Israel, she passed away. Jonas's and Antanina's deaths
left an emptiness in this world.

PART

II

23

※

THERE IS NO LAW AND
THERE IS NO JUDGE

"Homo homini lupus est."
"Man is wolf to man."

A ROMAN EXPRESSION

SLOWLY, LIFE WENT BACK TO NORMAL. EACH SURVIVOR WENT
their own way and started to rebuild the ruins of their pasts. As for
me—I was about fourteen, alone, and without a place to go to. As
such, the Paulavičius' house remained my home.

The period between the return of the Russians to Lithuania during the months of July–August 1944 and the end of the war in May
1945 was a time of poverty and hardship, characterized by political
tension and resistance against the new-old Soviet rulers. This was
especially true at the beginning of this period. The Lithuanian public didn't accept the return of its country into the lap of the Soviet
Union, and an uncompromising, nationalist core fought against the
regime both politically and militarily in an attempt to turn back the
clock, but it was unclear how this would happen and from where
their salvation would come.

The war, the approaching and retreating armies, destroyed in-
frastructure, and the ineffectiveness of the authorities in supplying
basic needs to the public gave rise to substitutes, whose all-inclusive
name was the black market. In the eyes of the Soviet authorities,
there was no crime more serious and despicable than dealing in the
black market, yet it was the Soviet economy itself and its conduct that

gave rise to it. The black market, which may be more aptly called the free market, fulfilled economic functions that the government found difficult to carry out.

Since there were shortages in the city and the surrounding area, Jonas acted resourcefully, reactivating my father's flour mill—near our home in Panemunė—before the Soviet authorities took over. With my help, he found the former mill workers, mechanics, and other professionals, and the mill began operating at full capacity. For efficiency's sake and to shorten the distance they had to travel, Jonas and Antanina moved into my father's house.

The flow of flour into the market—to bakeries and ordinary citizens—was a basic necessity. However, Jonas found that the fuel, oil, and spare parts required to operate the mill were in low supply, and most farmers had no money with which to pay him for the milling of the grain. It was therefore necessary for the farmers to barter a portion of the flour as payment. This flour was then sent to the market and traded for money or for homemade vodka, "samogon." The proceeds from the sold flour helped Jonas pay for original or counterfeited supplies for the mill. Corrupt military salesmen from various supply units provided the market with what the authorities could not.

Once I had to travel from Kaunas to Vilnius and back. I needed to go, but there was no transportation between the two cities. The solution to the problem was the creation of unofficial stops where people would wait for a ride on a military truck. It would arrive, the crowd would get on, the driver-soldier would collect the fee—a known price, as if it had been determined by the authorities—and a torturous ride would begin. At even the smallest downhill stretch of the road, the driver would turn off the engine and let the vehicle roll almost to a stop before turning the engine on again. Again and again, the engine would be turned on and then off again. The passengers who sat on the floor of the truck were thrown from side to side while conducting small talk—mostly bad-mouthing the government. The fuel saved in these maneuvers reached the market, and in exchange, alcohol went to the soldiers.

This process encompassed a multitude of crimes and offenses. The transportation of civilians in a military truck was forbidden, and charging for such a trip was doubly so. Moreover, stealing petrol and selling it in exchange for alcohol was a serious crime. It was done in the light of day, as an open and publicly known secret. Military drivers provided only small quantities of fuel to the black market. For operating large machines, like the mill, it was necessary to turn to bigger and more "professional" suppliers. The bigger amounts of fuel came in barrels, as if it were supplied by the government.

As time went on, the methods used by the black market's suppliers became more sophisticated. Porters and drivers would bring truckloads of grain stolen from barns in East Prussia using forged documents (such documents were easily obtained). As more grain was brought to the mill and bartered as payment, the mill's supply of flour increased. In the absence of enough money, the flour also served to supplement the salaries of the workers. And the workers— who could not live on flour alone—bartered their flour as well. That was how a vicious cycle was created that became a general pattern of behavior that was difficult to stop. Jonas became a rich man, relative to the time and place.

Mania, a friend from my hiding place in the Paulavičius house, told me how she lived after the liberation. She had lived in poverty until she managed to get a job at a beer factory. At the end of the month, the government plant did not have the money to pay its workers' salaries. Instead, the factory paid her and the rest of the workers two cases of beer, along with a few liters of spirits and yeast. Of course, the plant managers did not assume that the workers could live on beer, spirits, and yeast alone. They knew that merchants would buy these products for the black market, and in return Mania and her coworkers could buy the basic necessities.

The shortages and the hardships intensified the anger and disdain for the useless authorities created fertile ground for clandestine forces that instigated secret political propaganda, spread by worth of mouth. As happens with secrets, the more quietly they are whispered, the louder they become.

At first, it was claimed that Germany had not yet lost. With the front approaching the German border, the Germans would evoke unprecedented war tactics, yet unknown, and even employ secret weapons that were saved for these moments of truth. There were whispers: "The Germans will still come back." While unrealistic, this slogan had an impact, casting doubt on the stability of the Soviet regime. Many concluded that it made more sense to wait for what was coming and not to rush into merging into the Soviet economic and political system. But how long could one wait for the return of the Germans, when the entire war was being waged on German soil, its armed forces were trapped between two fronts, and its total defeat was no longer in doubt? Therefore, the whispering of "The Germans will still come back" was replaced by another whisper: "The Americans will come!"

The belief in America's unparalleled strength was resolute and unwavering. Its economic strength was self-evident and required no proof beyond what could be seen in daily life. The Red Army ate American canned goods and wore American military boots, and even the officers' uniforms and the plastic buttons sewn on them, with the Soviet insignia—a pentagram with a hammer and sickle in the center—were made in America. All kinds of American products, especially a pork dish—*svinnaya tushonka*—and clothing items, mainly shoes, were stolen from the army's warehouses and supplied by corrupt quartermaster clerks to the black market. In lieu of money, vodka was occasionally used as currency with considerable success.

Not only food and clothing, but also the American equipment that served the Red Army were apparent to all. Visually, it was clear that the equipment exceeded the level of what was made in the Soviet Union. It was a common occurrence for the motor to die in a Soviet truck. Sweating soldiers had to twist and turn the manual crank back and forth in an attempt to bring it back to life, while the US-made Ford and Studebaker trucks never stopped running. A Soviet tractor dragging a cannon crawled slowly down the suburban street, while an American tractor raced by, as if it were on a pleasure trip.

The public believed their eyes and at times expressed their opinion as to America's superiority over its Soviet ally. Not only the civilian public, but also the soldiers secretly believed in the technological supremacy of the United States. I remember that for a long time the authorities could not restore the municipal electric grid, and most of the area was in darkness. The suburbs of Panemunė and Šančiai were overrun with barracks. During this period, a large Soviet army was stationed there, with camps that were like a state within a state. In the nearby camp there was lighting supplied by generators for certain buildings. They made sure to provide electricity to the officers' club and to the hall where military bands occasionally performed, and once a week films were screened—most of them war movies.

I made sure to be available on any the day that a film was screened and to accompany the officer, Captain Dima Kuznetsov, who lived in our house (and whom we will discuss later), to get to see the show for free. The next day during recess, I would tell my friends about the movie; that was how I became a sought-out storyteller. Sometimes I managed to have a friend join me at the movies, which further elevated my social status. But there were cases when the projection of the film, from which the soldiers expected so much, was unreliable. The Soviet generator, brought to the vicinity of the hall, would refuse to operate. Hundreds of soldiers stood around the clumsy machine, with a number of tough men turning the crank over and over again. After much effort, they managed to get it going. It would cough and gasp until it started running regularly, although noisily, and convinced the soldiers that it would work. The soldiers would run into the cinema to find the best view for the screening. They would then inform the commander of the place, Colonel Shtulberg, that the film would indeed be screened, and he would appear and step toward his reserved spot. All the soldiers would rise when he entered. In reply to his greeting, they would answer in unison, "Good health to Comrade Colonel."

However, on the occasions when the hundreds of soldiers who were crowded in front of the movie theater would note that the generator was manufactured in the United States, they would immediately run into the theater to take their places before the screening, without waiting for the motor to start; they knew it would start and keep working. Instead of the decrepit crank, there was a string around the motor's gear. With one strong pull, the generator would come to life instantly and would run quietly, not disturbing the sound of the movie.

The public believed, therefore, that the United States was far superior to the Soviet Union in everything. Despite the war, which demanded huge resources, America was capable of flooding Russia with its products. Wishful thinking, in this atmosphere, led to a desperate belief in the slogan, "The Americans will come." And how would they come? The explanation was catchy: at the end of the war and the fall of the Reich, new political arrangements would be established in Europe, and, like the rebirth of many countries following World War I, independence would be restored to the nations of Europe, including the Baltic states, as it once had been, between the two world wars.

Along with political propaganda—regarding the regime's instability and transience—the opponents of the communist regime resorted to guerilla warfare. As night fell, control of the rural areas and remote suburbs transferred to the hands of murderous gangs. These gangs emerged from the forest at night, burst onto the roads and into villages, and sought revenge against anyone who was identified as having collaborated with the regime. At the top of the list of assassinations stood the Communist Party activists whose emissaries were active in the rural areas as propagandists. They were murdered mercilessly. Additionally, some villagers who had saved Jews paid for it with their lives, immediately after the German retreat.

The mill's mechanic, a very honest man who lived in a rural area, was visited one night by armed men from the forest. When he realized that the windows of his house were being guarded and that there was no escape, he opened the door at their demand. The night's guests warned him that if he continued to work in a mill that strengthened the regime by providing them flour, he would pay for it with his life, and they left. The man reported the events of the night to Jonas and his coworkers, but there was no one to complain to. There was no law, and there was no judge. Who could protect him? He continued working hard to support his family. A short time later, the mechanic received another visit. This time they did not speak, but knocked him to the ground with blows, and in front of his sobbing wife and children, they shot him.

This was the gloomy atmosphere surrounding my life, the life of the only Jewish child throughout the region, alone, living in the arms of a loving Lithuanian family who locked themselves up at night, behind closed windows and bolted doors. Talk about the "situation" that usually took place at home, during family discourse, also spread to my school in the suburbs. Here, the boys were able to talk about the nighttime events and to give their imagination and thoughts free rein. I seemed to be like them in everything, one of their own, but at the same time it was understood that the heroes of the night were not my heroes. Even a hint of sympathy for their actions left a bitter taste in my mouth. In the political conversations among the boys, I was perceived as identifying with the government, and as soon as I got close, the conversation stopped abruptly. There were also those who slapped me on the shoulders and pretended to be friends and companions, promising me personally that there was nothing to fear: if things changed, I could find refuge with them. I, unlike the rest of my kind, was a "good Jew." Thank God I never had to take them up on these promises.

The government could no longer let things go on as they were. It was clear that if they did not take action, what was left of their influence on public opinion would go up in smoke, and no one would ever trust the government's ability to stabilize daily life and embark on a path of rehabilitation and normalization.

The sign for what was to come was indicated in a pointed political article published in the party's newspaper *Tiesa* (*The Truth*), written by the editor, a prominent and influential party man. Titled, "The Sky Is Falling" ("*Dangus griūva*"), the article was based on the popular fable that tells of a small, scared rabbit, who, while skipping between the garden beds, felt a smack on his back. It was a cabbage leaf that fell on him, but because of its sky-blue color, and because of his foolishness and cowardice, the rabbit thought the sky had landed on his back.

The author of the article (whose name has since slipped my mind) made sure to remind readers of the details of the famous story: the rabbit started running amok to save himself from the end of the world, and to every animal that came his way and asked why he was running, he replied that the sky was falling. The animals joined him, running in a desperate attempt to save their lives. And so the stampede of fleeing animals grew, trampling every good plot. Needless to say, the donkey, the symbol of stupidity in the fables, is also among those running away. The herd ran and panted until they encountered a wise animal, as I remember a bear, who advised them to lift their heads and to see that the bright, beautiful sky had not fallen, but continued to dwell up above in confidence and peace.

So that was the parable—and what was the analogy? The vicious, political propaganda being waged by word of mouth about the return of the Germans or the arrival of the Americans with the approaching end of the Soviet regime was tantamount to spreading nonsense about the sky falling; those who were ignorant lacked understanding and, placing their faith in these rumors and passing them on to others, were like to the herd of animals running amok, who failed to understand the lie in these venomous words.

The author of the article styled himself as the wise bear in the story, who intended to enlighten the people. The Germans had been defeated, the Americans were very far away, and the Soviet regime was alive, strong, and stable. The article ended with a warning: although nothing was falling and everything was stable, it was possible that something would fall on the back of some donkey (in Hebrew, the word *donkey* can refer to either the animal or a fool). It would not be the sky falling, but a painful landing—the government crushing the fool.

The article had great influence, and its threatening tone was taken seriously. In those days, I did not read newspapers and certainly not editorials or political articles. Several boys at school told me about the publication of the piece, and if the boys were talking about it, it was surely a part of their family conversations. When I told Jonas about the article, he smiled, pulled out the paper he had kept in his drawer and let me read it.

As promised in the editorial, an ongoing military campaign against the armed gangs began. Army units raided villages and forests to locate the hiding places of the Lithuanian nationalists and eliminate them. This campaign showed no mercy. One morning, the residents of the suburb found three bodies thrown at night into the market square—murderers from the forest. Their faces were covered with stubble, their clothes were thin and patched, and belts of rope were tied around their waists. Their bodies were riddled with bullets. It was a less-than-subtle hint of what to expect for those fighting against the regime. But the fear of the night did not pass quickly. Those who feared for their lives locked themselves in their homes and wished for better days. But better days were yet to come.

Rumors spread that soldiers were raiding homes at night on the pretext of looking for suspects and while doing so were stealing and looting. I was distressed to hear that the soldiers of an army that had liberated me were described as thieves and robbers. Yet even if the descriptions were exaggerated, deep inside, I knew they were true. I could sense it.

———

At that time, Kęstutis and I lived in the Paulavičius home, while Jonas and Antanina lived in my father's home near the mill. The division was necessary to guard the houses and the property. Leaving a house locked and empty meant abandonment. One evening, when darkness fell, Kęstutis and I blacked out the windows, as required by the local "commandant," so that no light would come through. We locked the two entrances, and in the light of a small kerosene lamp in the corner of the kitchen, we read and prepared our homework. Suddenly we heard footsteps in the yard, which did not bode well in the dark during the curfew. The Paulavičius house, as we recall, was isolated from the other houses. This location helped to make it a refuge for the persecuted, but also a target for schemers.

There was banging on the door. To the question, "Who's there?" we got an answer in Russian. The nighttime visitors said they were the commandant's patrolmen (*komendantskij patrul*), who came to check the cause of the noise and the light, which had supposedly come from inside the house. I replied that it was not true, that there was no one else in the house. This was a big mistake on my part, since I had now confirmed to the thieves that there were no adults in the house and only two teenagers inside. They demanded we open the door so that they could search for people hiding. Again we made a mistake and opened the door.

Two armed soldiers entered with a flashlight and began a search. They moved from room to room and from corner to corner. Their eyes lit up. They had noticed a large bolt of flannel cloth that Jonas had purchased in one of his deals for the purpose of selling it. Flannel was very much in demand at the time. It was used to make puttees, which were preferred over socks for wearing boots. Immediately, the search stopped, the "suspicious" fabric was lifted onto the shoulder of one of the soldiers, and both of them turned to leave. I was so angry—why would a Soviet soldier do such a thing? Despite my life's bitter experience, I was still a terribly innocent boy. I blocked their way, cursing and ordering them to return the flannel! I was brutally pushed to the ground, and the two left.

Disappointed in myself and being unreasonable, I followed the bandits. They did not return to the main street lest they bump into anyone, but walked along the river, and I followed some distance behind them. It was a wintry month, and the white of the snow made the figures stand out. I saw them clearly, but they saw me as well. They stopped, and so did I. One removed his rifle from his shoulder and held it in his hand—a hint that I should not keep following. They walked on, and I continued to follow them.

They took the path that led to the Jewish cemetery. The one with the cloth on his shoulder continued to walk, and the other one hid and ambushed me. When I approached, he came out of his hiding place, took hold of his rifle, and ordered, "Go back, or I will shoot to kill!" I went back. Anger and shame gripped me. A big crack opened in my wall of innocence. I felt guilty. I was the one who had convinced Kęstutis to open the door to "our" soldiers, who would for sure leave after the search proved that nobody was home. What would I say to Jonas? How would I explain my foolish innocence, opening the door to robbers? For many days, my heart was bitter, and I thought about what I could have done differently.

It was not long before the story repeated itself: footsteps in the courtyard, banging on the door, "commandant patrolmen." "We heard noise, light shining through—open up!"

"That's not true," I yelled. "There is no noise here and no light—we will not open up!"

And they continued, "Open up, or we will break down the door."

According to our plan, prepared in advance, I escaped through the other door to call for help. At the late hour of the curfew, the streets were deserted. There was no living soul there. What was I to do? I ran as fast as I could toward the military camp. After a few hundred meters, I noticed two uniformed men leaving the camp gate. They noticed me and pulled out their weapons. Puffing and panting, I cried out, "Help, they are robbing our house!"

One of the two who was an officer asked, "Where? Who?"

I described the situation and urged them to help.

"Who's home?" asked the officer.

How was I to explain who Kęstutis was, what kind of relationship we had? How could I cut short the questions and idle talk? "My brother is home. I ran to call for help. They'll kill him!" I cried out. "Come quickly, I beg you!"

Looting was a known problem, and the local commanders tried to put a stop to it to improve the image of the army in the eyes of the civilians. My trembling body and my frightened face left no doubt that in fact a robbery was taking place.

"Run!" ordered the officer, and the three of us took off with me in the lead. As we approached the house, the looters heard our steps in the snow.

One of them was standing by the shattered door, his rifle in his hand and yelling, "Stop! Who is walking at night during curfew?"

"The Commander of the Guard," answered the officer, indicating his rank as captain and his name.

And that was how the two looters found themselves facing the Commander of the Guard. In response to his assertive question as to what they were doing in this house instead of being out on their patrols, they claimed that there was "noise" and "light shining through." Even though he did not believe them, he went through the motions of questioning me: "Who is in the house?"

"My brother and I, no one else," I answered.

"Where is your brother?" he asked. When Kęstutis realized the door was being smashed, he had escaped to the second floor, where he was hiding in one of the attic rooms. I called out to him loudly, and he came out of his hiding place and down to the ground floor. The officer removed the looters from the house, stood them with their backs against the wall, and ordered the sergeant to disarm them. "You are humiliating our army," he hissed and led them away.

The local governor, the commandant, was a man who enjoyed the pleasures of life. More than once, he drank bitter vodka at Jonas's table. He told Jonas that the looters were tried, and their harsh punishment was made known to the rest of the soldiers.

That was what the times were like. During the day, my fear was swallowed up in the clamor of boys' games in the schoolyard, but when night came, I could not be at peace. I was very lonely in that empty house, which was running itself without a guiding hand. From time to time, Kęstutis and I washed the floors. On occasion, Antanina would come to do the bare minimum, washing and hanging our clothes to dry. On weekends we would eat at the Paulavičius' and leave the mill and the house in the hands of a guard, but for the most part, Kęstutis and I conducted our lives alone. From time to time, Danutė would come from her apartment in Kaunas, usually on weekends, and a group of young people would visit the house and sing songs and dance to the music as I played. Mostly, however, the days were sad and lonely.

I continued to live with the Paulavičiuses for six more months; I had no one else, and I had nowhere to go. They treated me like one of their own children. Sometimes I even received preferential treatment, to ensure I would not feel like an orphan. I was given new clothes and generous allowances of pocket money. I was just like one of the family. But there were nights when I could not sleep, and I was gripped by a crushing sorrow. On nights like this, my mood fell into an abyss. What did the future hold for me? Would I grow up to become one of the locals, or would I return to the customs of my father's house and the traditions of my people? At times I was flooded by memories and longings for distant days, for my friends who spoke Yiddish and Hebrew, for the warm and loving family nest, for all things that were no longer and would never return. I repressed to cope with my sorrow, distracting myself from my orphanhood with the humdrum of everyday life. I refused to look directly at the tragedy that had befallen my life.

24

GRAŽINA

"Life is no walk in the park."

A TRANSLATION OF A RUSSIAN SAYING,
"LIVING LIFE IS NOT LIKE CROSSING A FIELD."

WITH THE RETURN OF THE RUSSIANS, REFUGEE FAMILIES began moving back to Lithuania, especially party members and senior officials who had escaped to Russia at the start of the war. With them came their children, who lacked a regular education during the war. They did not have any report cards indicating their grade level or academic achievements.

It was publicized that any youth who did not have documentation or other proof of their studies and achievements may be tested to determine their grade level before being placed in appropriate classes. I cannot recall whether these were national exams or if each school tested those students coming to them. I had several weeks to prepare, and I was to make an effort to demonstrate a respectable level of knowledge so that I would not lose all the years spent in the ghetto and in hiding. I skimmed through Kęstutis's schoolbooks, and I was horrified. There was no way I could read even a fraction of the material. My absence from school for the three years in the ghetto had greatly impacted my education.

With a heavy heart, Jonas and I went to one of the high schools to register and get details about the materials needed for the exams and how they were being run. On the way, we saw a woman walking

150

toward us who looked exhausted and pale. When she came closer, I immediately recognized her: Dr. Rabinowitz, our family's prewar dentist, a resident of Šančiai. In the past, such encounters had begun with a greeting and ended with brief pleasantries, but now, after the deluge, every such encounter moved us to tears. Every stranger became close.

She kissed me, inquired about what had happened to us, and when she heard that I was alone and that the man beside me, Jonas, had saved me, she began to cry again. She shook his hand warmly and thought aloud, "Why weren't there more like you?" When we told her where we were going, she advised me to get help from a teacher with an impressive ability in her field, who had once been her patient. Dr. Rabinowitz gave us the woman's address, noting that she was friendly to "us"—after liberation, she had gone immediately to her to cry in her arms. We parted, though not before she peered at my teeth and found them in better condition than would have been expected, though she cautioned that it was only a superficial exam.

When we finished our business in the school, we went to the legendary teacher, Gražina Jagorskienė, whom Dr. Rabinowitz had praised so highly. The door was opened by a very attractive woman, about fifty-five years old, simply and meticulously dressed. Her hair was pulled back taut in a bun, as was the custom of good grandmothers. Cleanliness and order dominated everything in her home. In a corner, on a small table, she placed a jug of water on a glass tray, with three glasses. Shelves and cabinets were crammed with many books. We were in awe. We were asked why we had come, and Jonas muttered, "This boy needs your help, the dentist sent us to you . . ."

"Rabinowitz," I added.

We were invited in. Jonas stood awkwardly in front of the woman and spoke briefly about what he'd done for me and about the responsibility he felt for my education and my future. He stressed that I was a talented boy who played the violin, chess, and other exaggerations so that she would be willing to prepare me for the exams.

Surprisingly, she hesitated. She might, she said, return to her childhood region in the area of Vilnius, where many of her family lived, so she couldn't commit. Jonas tried to get her to tell us why she was alone. Her face grew serious and sad. After some silence, she evaded the answer, saying, "It's a long story." Even after, when I was in her company for many hours, days, and weeks, she did not shed light on her situation. Although she refused to speak about it, I guessed that a great tragedy had befallen her home.

Jonas returned to the subject of my studies. His reasoning and logic were simple and sound. The war was still being waged in Lithuania, he explained, and the roads were not safe. In his opinion, there was no way for her to return safely to Vilnius. Moreover, she would need a special permit. Even if she could leave Kaunas, this could only happen in a few weeks or months. By then, he said, the boy would be way past his exams. In the end, she agreed to take me on. I felt a tremendous relief, as if all responsibility had been removed from me. Someone would take care of me and settle my affairs.

We were invited to sit. She turned mostly to me and spread out a plan according to which we would proceed and progress. She inquired as to what I had learned so far. I had five years of study behind me: I completed my first four grades at the Hebrew school in Kaunas—the Schwabe Gymnasium[1]—and fifth grade at the local school in Panemunė during the Soviet period. Gražina said that, as far as she knew, the examiners did not have the authority to skip an examinee two grade levels without studying, so I would have to reconcile myself with the loss of two years of schooling of the three years in the ghetto. "It's for your own good," she encouraged me. "You will be more mature, and you will not fail your studies."

At the same time, she advised me to consider the possibility of attending night school, which would certainly begin to operate because many youngsters would not be able to attend regular schools after a few years of absence from the classroom. Indeed, abandoned, orphaned, and homeless youth were a problem that the authorities had to take into account. But I rejected the possibility. I was afraid I would get into the company of older boys. I wanted to be among my peers. Jonas asked me to wait, and he went to another room to speak to her privately. He must have promised her a suitable payment for her efforts.

We said goodbye. My mood was improved beyond recognition. I was to start the next morning.

On my first visit, I brought Gražina a large loaf of peasant bread, whose taste did not fade even after many days, and in the crockery, I carried molten pork fat and a piece of smoked ham. I could tell she was happy. Over time, I came to realize that these generous payments by Jonas were an important and essential source for her hard-pressed existence.

She was well rounded with extensive knowledge in many fields and had a clear educational approach. I typically had three lessons with her each week, though sometimes even more. As the exam approached, I began to visit her daily. These were not lessons in the usual sense, like a long school day. Gražina could tell when I was tired and was no longer absorbing. She would then stop me, push me to do exercises with her so that I would wake up, and then discuss topics with me that I cared about. My enthusiasm for explaining music and chess to her energized me further, achieving her purpose. During these breaks, she inquired about my experiences and thus learned the story of my rescue and details about my rescuer.

Gražina, a teacher of stature, knew all the arrangements, procedures, and instructions given to examiners. She explained to me that there was no way I could possibly absorb all of the material that had been taught for years in school. The examiners did not intend to demand precision but to examine general intelligence and to insist on the candidate's ability to integrate into a class of his peers, even if his knowledge were less than theirs.

So, in addition to learning as many facts as possible, I needed to speak clearly and articulate correctly. My Lithuanian had always been excellent. Jewish children often struggled when prompted with the *kukurūzai* test ("corn" in Lithuanian); the challenge being to pronounce the sharp Lithuanian R in the word. I passed this test without difficulty. Gražina and I read stories, and I had to summarize them. I was asked to verbalize what I had done from the moment I got up in the morning until I arrived. In the mornings, when I went to Gražina, I had already practiced and formulated a description of my day up to the moment I came to her since I knew she would demand it.

These exercises actually drew my interest. When she realized that I could memorize poetry, Gražina recommended that I learn several important poems in Lithuanian literature and create an opportunity to quote them on the exam. She taught me testing strategies to impress and string along the examiner. "You can trick them," she said, smiling. She was an expert at shortcuts and created a schematic for me to memorize and remember details. Geography was the story of nations and peoples, and history a legend of kings, palaces, fortresses, and heroic battles. Using a story of forbidden love of a beautiful Lithuanian girl and a handsome Teutonic captive, Gražina described the Battle of Grunwald (1410), emphasizing the Lithuanian dominance in the victory achieved by Vytautas the Great.

The language and literature of Lithuania were central to our discussions. Once she caught on to the fact that my writing was often full of errors, I had to write dictations of poetry that I knew by heart. As part of my homework, I also I had to write from memory and look for spelling errors by comparing what I had written to the original text.

This wonderful woman made me love learning and even enjoy doing homework. Coming to her unprepared would have been a crime.

My meetings with Gražina were unforgettable. Soon the barriers between student and teacher came down, and we had conversations about everything, especially about my past, my home, my parents. At the same time she would correct my characterizations, formulations, and expressions. And so, she found out about Mrs. Seitz who had lived in our house and about the stories she read to me in the evenings. When I mentioned, among the stories, Snow White—Snieguolė in Lithuanian—she remarked to me, "Why don't you say that in German?" And she pronounced the name of the story in German with an unmistakable accent. I guessed that Gražina knew German. In fact, I should have known this sooner, given the German books that were arranged on her shelves. To my question of whether she knew German, she replied with a blunt yes. The expression on my face was of wonder. "Do not be afraid," she said. "You already know I don't bite!"

All my attempts to learn about her life were futile. She knew how to milk everything out of me, but everything about her she kept to herself. She was a mystery to me. Time passed quickly, and I felt confident as the test date approached, the test that might affect the course of my future.

———

The exams were conducted in one of the city's high schools. After the registration and paperwork, the youth gathered in the hall. A few were accompanied by parents. Everyone whose name was called out went to an adjacent classroom, where they were examined by a committee of three or four teachers.

When my first name was called with the Lithuanian suffix of "-as"—"Yochananas Fainas"—there was giggling in the hall. It was not only the unusual sound of the name that caused the audience to giggle, but the heritage implied by it. Here, a Jewish boy—"Are there still any of them left?" From the moment I came to stay with the Paulavičiuses, they attempted to come up with a more reasonable pronunciation for my name. The Lithuanian equivalent for Yochanan is Jonas, but this name already belonged to the head of the family, and Kęstutis's second name was also Jonas. It would have been quite ridiculous to have a third Jonas in the house. So the name given to me was Juozas, Joseph, and affectionately Juozukas, like Joey. My original name was reserved for formal registration in offices and with the authorities.

And so I stood before three examiners—one woman and two men. A form with my personal information lay in front of them. First, they inquired about me and asked who the Paulavičius family was, whose address I gave as my place of residence. I explained that I was a boy left alone and lived in the home of my Lithuanian rescuers. I sensed that the examiners had sympathy and understood my situation. I was asked if I had studied during my years in the ghetto, whether I had been assisted by teachers for the exam, and how many grades I had completed before the outbreak of the war. I answered that in the ghetto I had studied irregularly, which was not exactly accurate, and that for this exam I was assisted by a teacher. Her name was familiar to the examiners, and they exchanged looks between them. The conversation was long, and I felt I was formulating my words well and in a mature manner.

The exam began. I was asked to name the capital cities of several countries in Europe. My answers were correct. I was asked to describe the war between the Lithuanians and the Teutonic Order. Here I stumbled, but I redeemed my stumble with a thorough description of the collapse of the Teutonics in Grunwald. The emphasis of the exam was placed on Lithuanian language and literature, in which I excelled. Following Gražina's advice, I recited Maironis's poem about the Trakai Castle and "Anykščių šilelis," and my recitation rendered them speechless. I am sure that none of the examinees knew this classical work by heart. This was not what they had expected from a Jewish boy. Finally, a short text was dictated to me, which I wrote in chalk on the board, without any spelling errors.

The exam ended successfully, and I was to be placed in seventh grade at the school where I was tested. I requested to be placed in Panemunė instead, so that I would not have to walk eight kilometers to school and back daily. They promised that after the start of the school year, the office would arrange the necessary permit.

I secretly thought I would skip another grade the next year with Gražina's help. I couldn't wait to tell Gražina. When I did, she welcomed me with a hug and kisses.

For three months I studied at the school in Kaunas. Occasionally, on my way home, I would visit Gražina, who always welcomed me warmly and with love. I felt like a wanted visitor, and I was convinced that her warmth and love were not dependent on the food packages that Jonas would send her periodically. Her conversations with me enriched my spirit and broadened my mind. She knew how to help me with my studies without it feeling like a continuation of my school day.

I could talk to her about anything and ask her anything, but I never crossed the line regarding her privacy. The mystery added to the magic of her persona. A deep friendship formed between the boy and the older woman—an aging woman, according to the concepts of that time—though sometimes I imagined her as girl my own age.

I suffered greatly during my time at the school in Kaunas. The long daily walk from Panemunė was the least of my problems. It was the anti-Semitic incidents that weighed heavily on my life. Every school day was a battle. I got pushed "by mistake" and knocked down "by accident," and the nickname "Jew Boy" was heard daily, more than once. During breaks, I was rarely included in the games and would remain in the classroom. Yet here, too, I was disturbed and harassed more than once.

I was likely the only Jewish boy in the entire school, and boys from other classes would come to see the Jewish exhibit. When they realized that I had no horns and that I didn't look any different than other Lithuanian boys, I was made to take the R test of the *kukurūzai*. From time to time, I talked to Gražina about my troubles, and she advised me to try to ignore the other boys until they tired of bullying me and became used to my presence.

But they did not get tired of it.

Truth be told, most of my classmates were not bothered by my presence. There were even a few who liked and accepted me. The bullying campaign against me was led by a group of three or four thuggish teenage boys. The boys' language was rude and crass. They would roll *machorka* (low-grade tobacco that was crumbled into coarse crumbs and distributed to the soldiers) in newspaper; they smoked and encouraged others to smoke. They invested their energy in planning ways to harass me, and they managed to attract other boys to their cause.

My standing rose slightly when I reached a draw in a simultaneous game against Chukayev, a chess master who played against twenty kids at the school. It was not clear whether he was a soldier or a civilian because he wore a uniform without any insignia, and there were no medals of distinction on his chest. He was said to have been wounded at the front. Following his recovery, he was not fit for military service and made his home in Kaunas.

After we met, he invited me to the chess club he had started to organize. I willingly agreed. The club was located in the former Lithuanian president Antanas Smetona's home, where I met many young chess enthusiasts. I felt comfortable with them, and there was no divisiveness based on ethnicity. I later became one of the group of boys who hung around Chukayev, who guided us.

Yet my life was still centered around the school, where my circumstances were still less than ideal. They had not yet responded to my request to be transferred to another school in Panemunė. For this to happen, I had to have a certificate attesting to my current grade level and my academic achievements. My homeroom teacher promised me that at the end of the trimester, I would receive a trimester report card which would serve as the certificate that I required. I doubt he understood the importance of my transfer.

In the meantime—there was an incident.

One day, the vice principal came into our class with a young woman who was obviously Jewish. He introduced her to the students, telling them that she would be our English teacher. Wishing her and all of us productive studies, he left. Right from the start, the boys ran wild. The teacher's requests for silence were met with disparagement, and the disturbances grew louder. The same group of bullies who made my life a living hell were the same ones who led the campaign against the Jewish teacher. A girl stood up and demanded that they stop interrupting because she wanted to learn, but her voice was silenced. She was immediately accused of sympathizing with Jews—not just Jews, but "stinking Jews." The frenzy became a chorus of yelling and screaming that could no longer be subdued. The teacher took her planner and left the classroom in tears.

An argument burst out among the students. Some condemned the incident, saying that the event had gone too far, and that it would not end well. The instigators, on the other hand, were proud of their success: they drove out the "Jewess." I gathered my books and note-books into my bag and got up to leave. I was shaking with anger. On my way to the door, one of the bullies tried to stop me by grabbing my sleeve and pulling me back inside. I clenched my hand into a fist and struck his face. After he recovered, the thug grabbed a point-ing stick and ran toward me, but another boy, decent and strong, grabbed him and motioned for me to get out.

The bully and a few of his friends caught up to me in the street, and a brawl broke out. My chances of my getting out of it intact were slim. Blood was already running from my nose, and the bully con-tinued beating me while his friends encouraged him and prevented me from running away. Luckily, a large man came by the scene, and when he saw what was happening, he leapt into the battlefield and separated us. He pulled the bully hard and asked, "Why are you hitting him?"

The boy replied, "Because he's a smelly Jew!" The bully did not finish what he was saying, as the man punched him in the face, and he fell helplessly. His friends retreated around the corner. The man looked at me, winked, and ordered me to leave quickly. I wiped my face with my sleeve and ran away, while I still could. I went to Gražina, but she was not home, so I started walking toward Panemunė, pensive and sad. It was clear to me that my time at this school had come to an end.

In the evening, I told Jonas what happened. He couldn't believe his ears and was furious. He demanded that I go to Gražina to ask her advice the following day. He said he would do whatever she said; he would even use his connections in the Communist Party if he had to. I could not sleep that night. How could I live here? What would my future look like? How could I go on?

The next day, as Jonas ordered, I went straight to Gražina in-stead of school. She was surprised by my early visit. Even before she opened the door, she could hear from the way I said my name ("Juozukas") that something had happened. She opened the door while she was still tying her robe. I told her every detail. She asked if I was accurate in my description and whether a teacher intervened. I confirmed that everything was absolutely true and that no teacher had intervened—there had been no time for it since I ran out of the school.

Gražina was livid. The anger made her face sharp. She was even more beautiful to me then. She quickly poured herself a cup of tea, spread a slice of bread, and offered me some. I accepted. "We'll eat quickly," she said. "We're going to school; I still have some say there." Unlike her usual self, today she was silent. She got dressed quickly, and we set out toward our destination in a hurry.

Everyone was already seated in my classroom, and we went into the teachers' room, where there were a few teachers, the principal, and the vice principal. The principal stood up to greet Gražina and took her hand warmly—evidence that he knew her. After the greetings and a few polite words, the smile disappeared from her face. She asked to speak to him alone.

We went into his room, and he asked us to sit down. Gražina spoke on my behalf, resolutely and furiously, occasionally dropping to a near whisper that added strength to her words. It was a different Gražina, different from the one I knew: a fighting Gražina. "They're ruining the boy's life," she said. "Not a day goes by without some verbal incident and physical violence."

She described a few cases that stood out. For example, that I had once complained to the homeroom teacher about being called "Jew" (*Žydas*). She asked the principal if he could guess the teacher's response. The principal did not even try. She then recited the homeroom teacher's response, with his feigned innocence: "I don't see it as an insult—aren't you a Jew? Anyone who tells you that you are Jewish—you should respond with, 'You are a Lithuanian!'"

"Do you understand the meaning of that response?" Gražina asked.

"Yes, I understand everything," the principal said. "Yesterday and today, there have been frantic discussions regarding both the English teacher and the boy's case," he said, pointing to me and continuing. "Everything will be handled with a strong hand."

"You don't know everything," said Gražina. "Yesterday there was a real danger of serious bodily injury—or worse." The principal claimed she was exaggerating. He had been told, he said, that it was I who had started the fight.

Hearing this, Gražina brought her face up to his. With a venomous whisper, she hissed, "Are you an arena judge counting points? Whoever held him"—pointing at me—"to prevent him from leaving the classroom—he started it!"

"My friend," she said in a low voice, barely more than a whisper, "they will not come back; times have changed forever! The boy's rescuer is linked to the authorities—do you have any idea of the danger you risk if this matter goes beyond the school? They drove a teacher out of the classroom because they refused to learn English from a Jewish woman. She might still file a complaint."

I did not understand Gražina's words. Was she threatening him with external intervention, or warning him that he must act in order to prevent it? What did she mean when she said, "they will not come back"? Was she referring to the whispering of the Germans' return to Lithuania? "You must put an end to this!" she had said. Whether it was a request or a demand, I was not certain.

The principal stirred and shifted, glanced in my direction, and uttered, "Gražina," as if to say, "How could you speak this way in the presence of a student?" He then asked me to leave, and she motioned for me to do so. I exited the office and stood in the teachers' room. One teacher indicated to me that I may sit. Behind the door, the conversation was being held in a whisper, and I could not hear it. In the room, the teachers continued talking quietly among themselves so that I could not hear them either. A few minutes later, the vice principal was invited to join the discussion with Gražina. The ringing of the bell announced the end of the lesson, and another bell signaled the beginning of a new lesson.

After a time, I was again invited into the principal's office. Gražina was serious but calm. I was asked if I still wanted to leave the school. Without any hesitation, I said yes. I was told that the school was prepared to give me the required certificate that would enable my transfer, but the principal asked me not to leave. He turned to me softly and pleasantly. "What happened will never happen again," he said.

His vice principal supported his words and begged me not to leave, adding, "A small group of bullies are ruining the reputation of our school. They do not represent our spirit: your departure will be construed as submission; we need you to stay in order to subdue them." I considered the matter and decided to leave the school. More than I wanted to subdue, I wanted to survive. My mental state was painful. There were hours when I felt terribly lonely.

Gražina spoke on my behalf. "He will consider it," she said.

"Now, let's go," said the principal. The three adults got up and asked that I accompany them. We went down one floor to the classroom where I usually learned. There was a class in session. When we entered, the students' faces grew serious. There was silence in the classroom, a fearful, tense silence. It was obvious that something out of the ordinary had happened.

The principal took a note out of his pocket and called the name of the leader of the gang, but he was not there. The principal called out the names of his three friends, and they got up. The principal said, "You are to leave immediately and return tomorrow with your parents. I have not yet decided if I will speak to them myself or someone in uniform will!" Everyone was in shock at what he said. Nothing like this had ever happened.

The three of them turned to leave. One of them played dumb and asked, "What did I do?"

"Out!" ordered the principal. "Tomorrow, you will find out." They left. It was doubtful whether the principal wanted to involve the authorities and if such an issue would even interest the "uniformed," as he put it. But the threat made a strong impression on the students, and it was clear that they would have to pass the message on to their parents.

The principal pointed to me and said, "This boy—he's an orphan. His family was murdered. I expected his friends to help him live, not to make his life more difficult." I wanted to stand up to the test like a "man," but against my will, my eyes got damp. Gražina placed her hand on my shoulder.

One girl raised her hand, and the principal gave her permission to speak. "Not everyone behaved that way," she said. "There are a few, but the whole class is not to blame." Other students raised their hands after her. Their words touched me. They spoke cautiously, gaining confidence as they went on. They said that the gang was a problem for everyone and disrupted their learning. One girl said that they harassed her on her way from school, and they spoke obscenities that she was ashamed to repeat. I wondered if I was in the same class or whether I was dreaming. I did not understand how things had changed so quickly from one day to another.

The principal continued to describe me as a good and positive boy and said that I was a chess player and violinist who could contribute to the cultural life of the school. "But unfortunately," he said, "he's going to leave, and you know why," he added. There were whispers. "So, what do you say?" he asked.

There were those who called out that I should not leave, that they wanted to be my friend. One girl suggested that the "hooligans," as she called them, should be removed from the classroom. The principal quieted the speakers and, with an expression of satisfaction, turned to me. "Do you see how much you are wanted here?"

Was it really true? Were they to be believed? The principal suggested a fresh start for the class and asked me to return to my seat. I was emotional and confused. I remained standing. After a few moments, I managed to regain my composure and asked that I not stay at school that day because I did not have my schoolbag. Gražina signaled to the principal not to overwhelm me.

That was how that day's drama ended. I walked with Gražina to her home. She placed her arm around my shoulder and hugged me strongly. We walked silently. After a while, she asked me if I understood the great victory and its importance. What I did not understand—she explained thoroughly. In those moments, I loved that woman more than any other person on earth.

The next day, I went to school. In the days that followed, an atmosphere of reconciliation enveloped the whole class. Many sought to be near me. I was invited to play in the schoolyard; some even invited me after school to their homes. One girl was interested in how I lived without parents and who took care of me. There were many signs of affection, and while sometimes I felt embarrassed,

I was happy. Humans are strange beings. Such a sharp transition took place within just a few days. I did not question the sincerity of the change in attitude that the other students showed toward me. When it comes to human behavior, I tend to choose a positive interpretation. Even then, that was my view. It was easy to accept things this way.

A few days later, toward the beginning of the class, when all the students were already seated, a teacher entered the classroom and asked me to accompany him. I did not understand why, and I was curious. The entire class was expecting something.

In the corridor, a short distance from the classroom, stood one of the boys from the gang. Next to him stood his father, dressed in work clothes, his skin rough and wrinkled. The teacher introduced me to him, and the man began to apologize. "My son," he said, "is not a bad boy, but his friends' influence on him is devastating." He asked me to forgive his son. I was embarrassed. I was not accustomed to adults asking me for forgiveness. I felt uncomfortable, as if it were my fault that the boy's father had been put in such a situation. I forgave everything, so I could be released from this embarrassment. The boy's father shook my limp hand and left. We entered the classroom. I returned to my place, but the boy remained standing next to the teacher. Everyone was asked to sit down. From the boy's bruises, it was evident that his father probably did not spare him the rod. The boy spoke to the class, admitted that he had made a mistake, expressed regret for his actions, and asked me and the other students to forgive him. The pace of his speech indicated that what he said had been well practiced.

The school's response was thorough. The head of the gang did not return to study there, and his friends were dispersed into various classes.

In the following days, I thought a lot about continuing my studies at the school in Kaunas. Things were going well in class. I already had a few friends: one, a chess enthusiast, the other a boy two years older than me who played the violin and was interested in my musical skill. On occasion, I visited them and even brought my violin with me, to play small pieces for two violins. The other musician suggested that we prepare Bach's Concerto for Two Violins for the upcoming school event. With the sheet music I received from him, I began working on the first part of the piece and realized how severely I had neglected my violin for so long. I played the scales to ease my stiff fingers, and finally got back to playing reasonably well. I hadn't known Bach's double violin concerto before, and I was mesmerized by its beauty. The dialogue between the two violins, which I practiced for hours, raised my spirits, and the joy of music gave me a satisfaction I had never known before.

I thought about my musical future. Even before the war, my teacher, Mr. Solonoitz, had come to my parents and suggested that I take the entrance exams for the conservatory, where besides studying the violin I could learn other musical subjects, and without which I would not succeed long term. And so, I had taken those exams and had passed them successfully. Studying at the conservatory meant my beloved teacher would be replaced by the violinist Matiukas, a well-known music teacher in Kaunas. That was a difficult year for me. In the afternoons, after school, I had to take a bus to Kaunas, and after several hours of study at the conservatory, I returned home in the evening. Study, music, conservatory—a heavy load for a child.

Likewise, my load was heavy now. I had added not only music and chess to my load—I had been exposed to the charms of chess in the ghetto—but I also had to contend with the draining, daily walk from Panemunė to Kaunas, to school and back. It was hard for me to manage it all, and my new home at the Paulavičius' was not built to support all my whims.

Gražina was the only one who understood me. I often went to see her straight after school, and her house was like a second home to me. I would quickly finish my homework with her help. I don't remember ever needing more than an hour for it, and sometimes even less. Her opinion was that I should stay at the school in Kaunas, as she had held the school in high regard, rather than the school in the "remote suburb," as she called Panemunė. The matter of the difficult, long walk she resolved with the assumption that the authorities

would have to resume public transportation over time. So, after pre-
senting solutions to some of the difficulties, she recommended that
I concentrate on two things that I should take seriously: general
studies and music. "Chess, you'll play," she said, "only in your spare
time." Contrary to her advice, I still felt the temptation to attend a
school within walking distance of the house, and I was influenced
by the requests of some of the children in Panemunė, with whom I
played in my free time, to switch to their school.

Considerations, deliberations, and so many thoughts weighed on
my mind during those walks from Panemunė to Kaunas, and in a
sense, they shortened the walk. Gražina and her pleasant home carried a great deal of weight in my considerations.

Though I postponed the decision—circumstances decided for me.

One day, when I came to Gražina's after school, I found her upset and emotional, and though she tried, she couldn't hide it. She
apologized that she would not be able to host me this time because
she was hurrying to pack a few things for a trip to Vilnius, and that
she would be away for three weeks. The house wasn't as it usually
was. The impeccable order had been replaced with objects tossed
everywhere. One packed suitcase was ready in the corner, where a
small table with a pitcher of water and glasses had previously stood.
Another suitcase lay in the middle of the room and had all kinds of
items strewn in it. Several shelves were empty, and the books were
stacked on the floor for packing. Through the doorway I saw in the
other room a wooden crate full of objects, and to my surprise, I
noticed a man wearing an undershirt full of holes trying to close it.

"A three-week trip?" I wondered. Gražina put her hand around my
shoulder as usual and led me to the door. It was clear that I could not
stay and that I could not ask what was really going on. We parted.
When I left, she kissed me warmly, hard. There was something special about our parting this time. I left confused, and I foresaw bad
things happening.

When Jonas asked me what was bothering me, I told him what
I had seen. To my astonishment, Jonas was not surprised by what

I had to say. He listened to my story calmly, but I could tell he was pretending. I felt that he knew something but was keeping it to himself. There was no reason, he said, not to believe Gražina, and he suggested I go visit her in three weeks, when she returned from her trip. But the packing of her things and the books that were removed from the shelves made me doubt that I would ever see her again.

I waited, I counted the days, but after two weeks I lost patience, and after school I went to Gražina's. I knocked on the door, and the steps from inside were unfamiliar. The door opened, and there stood a young man wearing a torn undershirt, drunk, the smell of alcohol on his breath and the remnants of his last meal hanging from the corner of his mouth. The entrance to the room was full of belongings, and unopened packages were strewn all over.

He asked what I was doing there. I was stunned, and the only word I could get out of my mouth was "Gražina." From the depths of the apartment, I could hear a woman's nervous voice: "Who is it?"

The man turned to her and answered, "Another young fan looking for Berta."

"Not Berta—Gražina." I insisted on correcting his mistake, but my objection was not accepted.

"Gražina, Berta, same difference! She went away—left." And in a drunken, merry voice he added two words in an attempt to mimic German speech: "Gražina *fahren Berlin!*" "Gražina go Berlin." He spoke little—and said much. Gražina was Berta? And why was her trip described in German—"*fahren*"? Was that a hint of a German connection? How did one go to Berlin from Soviet Lithuania? The war was still raging in full force on German soil.

I was still standing there stunned when a woman stepped out briskly from the apartment and leapt at the drunk. Her push almost knocked him over. "Shut up, you fool; close your mouth," she yelled at him and then, in a quick, tense tone, turned to me. "My husband is drunk and has no idea what he's talking about. Gražina left for Vilnius, and now we live here." I had not yet finished asking for Gražina's new address when she already answered that she had no idea. Perhaps she didn't know, or she did know and would not tell. The door slammed shut, and I stood for a long time frozen in place. The sound of the argument behind the door stirred something within me.

I walked home slowly, aching with grief, my thoughts chasing one another. I couldn't make sense out of anything. What had happened to Gražina? What had become of her? I felt a tremendous loss, as if my entire world had been destroyed. I went home. Jonas was still busy with the mill, and when he came up, I told him what had happened. He listened, and once again no signs of surprise registered on his face. I inquired about Gražina's sudden trip and especially emphasized the strange words that the new, drunk tenant had uttered: "Gražina *fahren Berlin*." Jonas carefully considered his words and said that in a while he might know something and would not hide anything from me. Until then, he had asked me to hold my tongue and not talk to anyone about her. My curiosity increased and ignited my imagination. I understood that Jonas knew something, but I also knew that he would not utter a word until he was ready to tell me.

Days went by. It took me a long time to realize the depth of this woman's influence on me and the significance of the change in my life after she disappeared.

I mourned her loss for a very long time.

One day my classmate invited me to his home to play chess. We would have a few hours until his parents came home from work, during which time he was free from his studies. There were in fact still some normal homes, where order, discipline, and education remained intact. As for me, I created my own daily order. I was free to do as I pleased and did not understand the shortcomings of freedom. As we walked, we approached Gražina's house, and I thought of her. When we passed the house, I told my friend, "My former teacher lives there." I said it in the present tense because I did not want to admit that she had left Kaunas permanently. "What, Gražina was your teacher?" he asked. I was surprised at his question—how did he know her name? It turned out that she was known to the neighbors as a teacher who gave private lessons, and her name was well known in the community.

Our conversation about Gražina could have ended there, but a few words that were said casually struck me with amazement: "Of all people, you chose a German teacher?" And later, as though whispering a secret, he added, "She ran away from here, probably hiding in some hole!" I answered blankly in an attempt to keep my cool, as though I had no interest in the story. In reality I was surprised and could hardly hide it. My chess game was a bust; my mind was elsewhere.

I walked home quickly so I could tell Jonas what I had learned about Gražina. My mind absorbed the story, and her frightened flight seemed to confirm its truth, but my heart refused to believe it. I could not accept that this good and beloved woman, who had loved me so much, had done unspeakable things, for which she would have to hide in "some hole." I told Jonas, and he listened to me earnestly, but again he showed no signs of surprise. Finally, he said he wanted to talk to me about it privately. What did he know? How did he know?

I accompanied him on the way from the mill to his house. We walked down the path from my father's house to the Nemunas River, and while walking slowly along the shore, he spoke to me as if I were an adult, not a boy. In simple and clear language, he presented some life lessons, the truths from which he did not stray.

A man needed to know how to keep a secret, he said. We need not tell others everything we knew. "Where would we be today," he went on, "if my household and I had not held our tongues?" His message was clear: what he would now tell me, I would have to keep to myself. I promised that I would. Jonas continued. "Man," he said, "is sometimes caught up in circumstances in which he is compelled to act contrary to his views, and this contradiction should not be seen as a betrayal of ideals. Life is very complicated, and it is better not to get into situations where the heart struggles with the head."

Jonas revealed to me that he had visited Gražina a number of times on his way to talk to the authorities about the mill and would bring her food. He didn't tell me this—in part because I couldn't carry such heavy loads—but mainly because he felt Gražina was in trouble, and he, Jonas, typically ran toward others' problems.

She was a withdrawn and frightened woman, who kept her secrets and lived according to the rule: "Your tongue—your enemy." But Jonas convinced her that he was looking out for her best interests. He explained that he had helped people in trouble at the risk of his own life before, and if he could help her, he would do it willingly. In her despair, she put her fate in his hands and told him her story.

This is her story, in short.

Gražina and her husband were Germans from the Vilnius region. Her original name was Berta Jagorski—originally Jäger. They moved to Kaunas during World War I, when Lithuania gained its independence from Germany but as a protectorate (1917). Vilnius soon became part of Poland and remained so until World War II. Were Gražina and her husband Poles,[2] Germans, Lithuanians?—no one knew how to define them.

They had two sons born to them in Kaunas. Gražina worked as a teacher, and private tutoring took up a large portion of her time. Her husband was sickly and did not work for long periods, so the burden of sustaining the family fell mainly on her. Between the two world wars, life was peaceful. They did not especially mind when the Russians entered Lithuania in 1940 because they were leftists.

In 1941, when there was a mass emigration of German Lithuanians from Lithuania to Germany, they decided to stay put. They knew a thing or two about Hitler's Germany, and the euphoria of his victories did not tempt them. The recruitment of their sons to the military, if they emigrated, was certain, and this factor was also an important consideration.

Gražina and her husband imagined that their decision to stay would be interpreted as a demonstration of sympathy toward the Soviet regime. On the contrary: their decision made the regime suspicious of them. According to Soviet logic, it was inconceivable that a person who had been given permission to emigrate from the Soviet Union would willingly choose to remain. This logic led to the arrest of Gražina's husband on charges of spying for Germany several months before the war, and the sickly man never returned from the interrogation room.

In February 1941, Gražina did not travel to Germany, but in June
of that same year, Germany came to her. She had been concerned
about her sons' recruitment if they went to Germany, and now, with
the occupation of Lithuania by the Germans, she had to accept their
conscription. What she had dreaded most had happened.

The occupying authorities recognized her, against her will, as one
of them. In fact, for all outward appearances this was the case: a German woman whose husband had been arrested by the Communists
as a German spy, her sons serving in the Nazi army—who could be
better suited to their needs?

Gražina was offered a senior role in the administration. When
she rejected the offer, she was offered another senior position, which
she also rejected on various grounds, none of which were entirely
convincing The highly ranked man sitting opposite her raised an
eyebrow. Another refusal would be interpreted as political hostility.
When she was finally offered an administrative role in the field she
had worked in all her life, education, she could no longer refuse.
She did not have the strength to stand up to the mighty occupation
machine. So, begrudgingly she agreed and served as a supervisor.

Now I understood the meaning of the parable at the beginning
of Jonas's story and its lesson: "Sometimes man finds himself in circumstances where he is forced to act contrary to his views, and this
should not be seen as a betrayal of ideals."

The tide of war turned once again. Gražina's sons did not return
from the battlefield in Russia. The Russians returned to Lithuania.
She tried to escape with the retreating Germans, but whoever promised to take her did not keep his word, and she was left to her own
fate. Gražina remained lonely, broken, economically devastated, and
politically under suspicion. A German who cooperated with the occupier, the mother of two Wehrmacht soldiers, and, no less serious,
the wife of a spy. Anyone who knows anything about Soviet life to
a certain extent knows the status of members of the families of political prisoners. They were marginalized as lepers. Even those who
took pity on them were afraid to approach them socially, lest it be
to their detriment. They were not given proper jobs, they were not

admitted to universities, and they were forced to mark in question-naires (and such questionnaires were presented to citizens wherever they turned) whether a member of their family was imprisoned in the camps. And she, Gražina, embodied all that was bad: a German cooperating with the occupier, whose sons fought in the Wehrmacht and whose husband was a spy.

It was clear that sooner or later, more likely sooner, Gražina would be imprisoned in Siberia. There were those who even hinted to her that her days of freedom were numbered. What could she do? Without saying goodbye to her loved ones, she quietly left for the Vilnius region of her youth in an attempt to be swallowed up with a bor-rowed identity in a Polish community with the help of her family connections.

And perhaps another possibility would come her way.

Persistent rumors were circulating that residents of the Soviet Union who were Polish citizens in 1939 would be able to return to Po-land in accordance with the repatriation agreement that was decided upon between the two countries. When the time came, she would have to choose between living under an assumed identity, with all the dangers involved, and emigrating to Poland and from there, in the twilight of her life, to join her ancestors in Germany.

That was the whole story. Jonas knew enough to tell me that she loved me, and that she had not told me she was German because she thought I would reject her. She knew what her people had done to me. He added that I was like a son to her, but there was no need to say it; I felt her love deep down, and it was mutual. "As advocates for her," he said, "let's wish for her to arrive safely at her destination. Life is complicated, and one does not always know how to make the right choice." He concluded with a proverb: "Life is no walk in the park."

25

THE RETURN HOME

MY MOTHER WAS LIBERATED BY THE RED ARMY FROM THE Stutthof death camp on January 19, 1945, and in February she returned to what had once been her home. How had she survived as a woman in her fifties? How had she survived starvation and deprivation in the ghettos? How did she survive the transports and the death marches? How did she endure the hard labor, the torture, and the abuse? How did she survive the lice infestation, the filth, and the typhus that killed thousands of women younger than her? There is only one plausible explanation: it was a miracle.

My mother—in whom pessimism had always been ingrained—was stronger physically than she was mentally. Her life was saved, but her soul was destroyed. She was never her old self again; bitterness and dissatisfaction with everything around her accompanied her for the rest of her life. When she returned from the camps, the pessimism in her character intensified: the good places were always those that were out of reach, the good people were those who were far away or dead, and the good days were the ones that were long gone.

My mother knew that I had survived. From glimpses between the fences within the Stutthof concentration camp, my sister Yehudit recognized her from a distance. She had cried out to her that I was hidden in a Lithuanian's house and presumably had been saved. My reunion with my mother was emotional, but soon her presence became normal, almost routine. We had been separated for three years. I had grown up away from her and developed a different way of thinking and behaving, creating a distance and unfamiliarity between us. A lot of warmth and understanding was needed to bridge the emotional distance between us, both of which we seemed to lack.

We immersed ourselves in long conversations where she told me about what had happened to her. Today, after reading and delving further, I know that she did not exaggerate anything—it could not have been exaggerated: she experienced hell on earth. I told her of my experiences as well, but mine were less impressive since my suffering paled in comparison—and I had to make it up to her. She asked me to be by her side whenever I was free, not to play with my friends without her permission "because they hate us," not to ride my bike because I might fall and get hurt, and to go to bed early and sleep in her room. After having gotten used to independence and being as free as the wind to determine my own daily routine, I found it difficult to meet her demands.

I realized that staying at the Paulavičius' house at night, where Kęstutis was now living alone, was no longer an option. I would have to be at my mother's side at our house. But I refused her demand that I go to bed early. At first, I tried to please her. I would lie awake in bed for a long time in the dark, and when her breathing indicated she was in a deep sleep, I would arise, get dressed, and go back to the kitchen where Jonas and Antanina sat. In the light of a small lamp attached to a battery, we would talk or eagerly read Karl May's books and other suspense novels. One evening, I got caught. My mother woke up, and when she did not find me in my bed, she came out into the kitchen and ordered me back to the bedroom. When I refused, an argument ensued. Jonas intervened on my behalf but was reprimanded for interfering in matters that were none of his business. I stood by my refusal. For the first time in my life, I defied her. From that night on, the cracks in our relationship deepened.

One afternoon, when it was drizzling outside and I could not find anything to busy myself with, I went looking for someone to keep me company. I was a restless boy, troubled by memories, lonely. I walked through the empty streets, and on my way back from the main road toward the Nemunas, I saw a group of German prisoners close to the house digging a drainage ditch for the rains. Two Soviet soldiers were watching over them. They were the Wehrmacht soldiers who had frightened me so much before. Where was their spark? Where were their weapons and helmets? They were dressed in torn clothes, unshaven and dirty.

I was still standing there when one of them asked if I spoke German. I did not answer. He asked that I bring them bread. I again ignored him. I stared at them reflectively. Hate, vengeance, but also pity ran through me. *"Er ist dumm"*—"He's stupid," said one prisoner to another when they did not understand the meaning of my silence. In the meantime, the Russian soldier, the guard, approached us. Since the rain had gotten stronger, the soldier asked if they could take shelter in our home. Hardly aware of what I was doing—perhaps out of weakness or perhaps in response to the request of the Russian soldier—I led them home. Bent over and shivering from the cold and wet, they went inside and sat on the floor in our big kitchen, leaning against the wall. Just then, Jonas returned home from the mill and asked what was going on. I looked down and explained that I had brought a group of German prisoners to our house.

Surprised, he came over to me, hugged me in a fatherly manner, and said, "You did well!" Then he went to the big baking oven and took out two large round loaves of bread. The eldest prisoner came over to the table, carefully sliced portions with German detail and precision, and distributed the bread to his friends. Jonas took a bowl of butter out of the pantry. There was a variety of food in the house because the farmers who came to grind their grain would sell their produce in the mill yard.

Suddenly something happened. At the height of the festivities, the bedroom door opened, and my mother came out agitated and frightened. She had heard German being spoken through the door and could not believe her ears. What were these Germans doing in her house? When she saw her son and Jonas feeding German prisoners, she could not believe her eyes. She immediately burst out screaming, *"Raus! Raus von hier!"* ("Out! Get out of here!") The prisoners stood up in embarrassment.

Their looks sought pity from me and Jonas. Jonas tried to calm my mother, explaining, "Yesterday," he said, "they were enemies, but today they are as persecuted and hungry as we were, and people in trouble need help. That's what I've done all my life, and thanks to me your son survived. And that is how I will always act."

My mother gave up, but before she left, she made a speech: "Just know that we are Jews! Know that you are murderers! Know that my husband was murdered by the Nazis, my beloved son was murdered by the Nazis, our entire family was exterminated in the camps! I want you to choke on this bread that a Jewish woman gave you! This is my revenge." She said what she had to say and went back to her room.

There was a deathly silence in the room. The Germans did not touch the food until Jonas encouraged them to resume eating.

Feeding the prisoners, in my mother's eyes, was an extremely grave act. The violation of her authority especially hurt her. Previously, her consent was required for me to bring a group of my friends home, and now, without her permission, I had brought in a group of German prisoners. God only knew who they were and what they had done in their heyday. Furthermore, my actions were supported and encouraged by Jonas, toward whom my mother felt ambivalence: he had saved her son's life but sat in her husband's place. When I did not express remorse for what I had done, the rift in our relationship deepened.

⁓

The circumstances in which my mother was trapped upon her return intensified her pain. She remembered the past and could not accept its loss. Before the war, our home was always full of life. We never ate our meals alone—there was always a guest sitting with us at the table or a friend of my father's named Stenstein, from the town of Kėdainiai, who would stay with us for days when he came to see his doctors in Kaunas. Our close-knit group of neighbors: the Zilbermans; the Leibcziks; the Sonkins; the Bergsteins; my father's sister, Bluma, and her family—the Lifshitzes, who lived within walking distance from us, and their older children—Michael'eh and Reizel'eh—who were friends with my brother and sisters, and their youngest son, Chaim'ke, who was my friend.

Groups of boys and girls, friends of my brother and sisters, and my friends as well, who lived in the crowded city and loved to visit our house in the rural suburb on weekends to go swimming in the waters of the Nemunas, wallowing in the golden sand and eating fruit straight from the trees in our garden. Youthful laughter and joy filled our home.

Now, everything stood silent, a valley of death. My mother had returned to an empty house, dark and abandoned. Of all of her loved ones, only I remained. She felt that a total stranger was taking Father's place, managing the mill and getting rich from our property, and his wife behaved in our house as though it were hers. Jonas did, in fact, save her son's life—a noble act of the highest degree—she agreed, but as far as she was concerned, it was material incentives that guided his actions: saving a Jewish boy from a wealthy family would pay off in one way or another someday—and, in her mind, this is exactly what had happened. Even in our poverty, we remained rich in my mother's imagination, even more so than we had been before the disaster.

We fought, we made up, we fought again, and we threw insults at each other. I hurt my mother badly when I said that it was hard for her to understand Jonas's actions because it was doubtful that she would do the same. Other harsh things were said that would have been better left unspoken, and I regretted them, unfortunately, too late. My closeness to Jonas and my desire to protect his honor made me threaten to leave the house if she did not stop speaking against him. That was how I won her silence, though not for long.

One day, my mother spoke about my rescuers with strangers. These words reached the ears of the Paulavičiuses and were exaggerated and twisted, as often happens with gossip. The tension between my mother and the Paulavičiuses, especially Antanina, grew daily. My mother scorned everything she did. Antanina's food did not meet her expectations. The sarcastic remarks she threw at Antanina became more vicious. The antagonism between my mother and the Paulavičiuses was unavoidable, and I was stuck in the middle. My heart broke seeing my mother's attitude toward them, and this made it impossible for me to function. I could not find a way out.

Antanina held back her irritation. When my mother insulted her cooking, she suggested that my mother could cook for everyone—or even just for herself and me—in other words, to separate the kitchens. But my mother was not satisfied with any suggestion: while she felt that Antanina's meals were inedible, she refused to be the helper and cook for simple people, and she had neither the conditions nor the means to cook just for us. While she was critical of her situation, she was often equally critical when it was suggested that her situation could be reversed. No solution pleased her. Our quarrels intensified, and I was accused of favoring strangers over her. I was supposed to back her in all quarrels, even if I did not agree with her position at all.

Jonas decided to put an end to all of this. He invited me to meet with him. He was always friendly to me when we had conversations, imparting on me his life's wisdom, accompanying his thoughts with sayings and fables to complete them. Not this time. He was angry. Perhaps he was angry at me as well because I had unsuccessfully tried to take both sides, and I did not prevent things from reaching this state. He understood more than I could imagine about what my mother had been through in the camps, but he was not going to pay the price for the Nazis' sins. "I am not guilty for having lived," he said, "but I can be held responsible for your being alive, and I accept that responsibility!" These were painfully accurate words. Perhaps he meant to remind me of my debt to him, but it was not necessary. I remembered and will always remember Jonas until the day I die. My eyes were tearing, but he did not ease up. "You are mature enough," he said, "to understand what I am saying."

I had to relay to my mother what he had said. He did not want to conduct a direct conversation with her lest it become a quarrel, and then things would be said that could never be taken back. They also didn't share fluency in a common language. Jonas was not fluent in Russian—my mother's main language—and her Lithuanian was abysmal. I found out that Jonas knew my mother's opinions and her way of thinking from people to whom she had poured out her heart. As a result, a great rift opened between me and these good people who saved my life, who were family to me, and who were my protectors in my days of distress.

Jonas spoke. He had come into our house, he said, by virtue of the circumstances, out of necessity to keep an eye on the property. At night, he listened to what was going on in the mill and in the courtyard and sometimes even patrolled the area. He was not there as a successor to my father. However, he realized that my mother no longer wanted him there, and he had no problem leaving. Within a few days, he would find a night watchman, and then he and Antanina would return to their home, where their lives would be more comfortable and Kęstutis would not be abandoned at night. He also told me that I needed to understand that my mother's motives for her demand that I go to bed early was due to her fear of the night. If they, Jonas and Antanina, left, would her nights be quieter and safer?

I was speechless. All at once, I suddenly realized that I did not understand my mother. What I saw as an irrational obsession for control was in fact emotional distress. As far as the mill was concerned, he continued, it had been a long time since it belonged to the Fein family; the authorities controlled it. His work in its operation was appreciated, and its management was approved by the head of the supervisory authority, a man named Borstein. If he, Jonas, were to leave upon the wishes of my mother, and indeed he would do so if she so demanded, another man would be appointed without any relation or bond to our family.

Perhaps the new manager would require another room from the house, which would serve, for example, as a dining room for the workers. Why should they eat their dry sandwiches in the dusty mill? Perhaps the new manager would complain to the authorities that my mother was a nuisance and disturbed the operation of the mill. Since she was a bourgeois and former owner, it would be believable. Finally, Jonas blurted out a notion that struck me like thunder: "The new manager will not give your mother money, as I do. What will

you eat? How will you survive without me?" I stood there embarrassed. I did not know anything about the money he gave my mother,
and he understood that immediately. I was very upset that she had
hidden this from me.

Our conversation ended. I had to go to my mother and tell her
what Jonas had said. My conversation with Jonas was a big step in my
growing up. I suddenly became aware that life was not only studies,
playing music, chess, and games, but that the bread and butter that
were plentiful at our table could not simply be expected. My mother's
whims could easily destroy our economic base. I panicked. If the
time came, and the government became organized, it might come to
see the mill and the structure next to it—our home—as one business
unit, and we would then be homeless. I remembered that even before
the war, in the year of Soviet rule, it was said that large private houses
beyond the permitted size would be nationalized. Our house was not
this excessive, but in my panic and confusion, I feared every possible
evil. Now, at the gates of my maturity, an inner voice hissed: "Wake
up, kid; the privileges of youth are slipping away!"

Haunted, I went to my mother. I intended to tell her important
things, but she refused to listen. I was not worthy because I was Jonas's emissary and had sided with him. My mother was entrenched
in her positions and her logic, and she could not be convinced otherwise. I was furious. I raised my voice and addressed her fears. "Jonas
and Antanina are moving to their house and leaving us alone," I
shouted, "and it will be your fault." My words acted like thunder.

After a few seconds of silence, she burst into a bitter tirade. "They
can't do that to us. How could they abandon an old woman and her
son, the only Jews in this hostile environment, to the thieves, robbers, plunderers, and murderers who swarm here at night!" That
was a sign that her self-confidence was lost and her stances were
breached. I hurried to seize the opportunity. I told her that with her
behavior, the insults and stings that she hurled at the Paulavičiuses,
and especially the gossip about them, she was making them leave.
I also said that Jonas was considering leaving the management of
the mill. I reminded her angrily that she was connecting with every

other Russian-speaking person without knowing who or what they were, and she was pouring out her heart to them, all of her suspicions and fantasies. Over and over, I asked her how she could treat the people who had saved her son's life this way—an act for which, at the time, she would have given up her mill and her house as well as her entire world.

My mother defended herself: "What did I say?" or "Here and there I said things," or "They would not have known what I was thinking had you not told them and spoken ill of your mother!"

I was appalled at how she could be so self-righteous. I rejected her accusations. "I'm not the one who told them things," I said, "it was the people in whose ears you pour out your bitter heart and your delusions, as though the mill is still ours and Jonas is taking over. Jonas told me." My mother's face turned red with grief and anger.

There was silence. My mother reviewed in her memory what she had told people and found that nothing was particularly "terrible" unless the "gossipmongers"—as she called them—distorted her words and added vicious interpretations. I knew that in such conversations my mother could not control her feelings. I interrupted the awkward silence. "Do you think that Jonas's replacement will be so kind to you? Will he feel obligated to give you money that he doesn't have to? And why didn't you tell me you had all this money?" At this point, my mother broke into bitter tears. I immediately regretted my words, but they were already said and could not be taken back.

First, she denied getting money, but in the same breath she added that it was not that much. She was especially hurt by the implication that she was being miserly with her own son. She immediately rushed to the hiding place where she kept her money, opened the iron door of the huge furnace in the wall, and rummaged through it until she reached her wallet that she had hidden there. The things she rummaged through, dear God. There were bags of food: flour, grits, and canned food, which she had collected and hidden. The years of terror and hunger hadn't waned from her heart—they were crammed into the furnace. Now she wanted to please me with money and handed me a few bills, but I refused to take them. As she cried harder, I felt sorry for her and hugged her. "I have enough money," I said.

"From where?"—from Jonas.

"You should be ashamed of yourself," she said, that a stranger should give a boy pocket money and not his mother. I promised her that in the future, if I needed money, I would come to her. Now I spoke to her softly. The atmosphere calmed down, but the problems raised during our conversation—our quarrel—remained. I could not expect my mother to offer a creative solution to our complicated situation. I understood that I had to look for ways into the embittered hearts of the Paulavičiuses. And, in fact, I had an idea. I felt that I had the power to stop the inferno and, to some extent, to heal the rift between me and my rescuers. I was confident of myself and felt a sense of maturity.

I formulated for myself the main points that I wanted to bring to Jonas. I introduced them to my mother first—to inform her, not for her approval. She was miserable but agreed to all that I suggested.

At that point, we already knew that my oldest sister, Vera, had survived and was on her way home from deep in the Soviet Union. Her return was central to my plan. I wanted to minimize what was brought to Jonas's attention and place the primary blame on the gossipmongers. As far as management of the mill went, I wanted to postpone things until Vera returned and to turn the matter over to her. With these ideas I returned to Jonas.

We sat opposite one another as adults would do, and we talked. I explained to him that my mother was devastated and one could no longer find any logic in her actions or her words. In addition, her words had been distorted, and not everything repeated to him had actually been said. I asked him to believe me. My mother's hostility, I continued, was not directed at him. It was directed at any man who would take my father's place—no matter his name. "My mother begs your forgiveness," I added. "She is very sorry about everything that has happened." But my most important point I kept for the end. "As you know, my sister Vera is on her way. She is a mature and educated woman. With her here, the situation will resolve amicably."

I knew I had hit the nail on the head when Vera's letters arrived. She showered praises on Jonas for his bravery; she was so thankful for him having saved me. He immediately offered to have her join him in the management of the mill. Although the mill was no longer owned by the family, Jonas placed a great deal of importance on having a family representative involved in its management. He was sure that this would stop the gossip that he had taken the mill from a minor. This way, his management of it, which was recognized by the authorities, would also be recognized ethically by the previous owners.

At the end of our conversation, I asked that he not leave our house and certainly not his position in the mill. "This," I continued, "is my mother's request as well." I don't know whether Jonas was convinced by what I said, and I doubt he believed it was my mother's request, but the air was cleared and calmed. The sharp edges were rounded. Regardless, there was still a bitter aftertaste left behind. A few days later, Jonas found a nice elderly gentleman who lived in the neighborhood and hired him as a night watchman. Jonas and Antanina then left for their own home.

It was clear that after my mother's return and Vera's expected arrival, we would part with the Paulavičiuses, as did all of those rescued, each of whom went their own way. But I, unlike the others, had continued to live with the Paulavičiuses for many months, and I was like a son to them. The parting was very difficult for me, and the manner in which we parted did not make it easier. Life had taught me another lesson: I learned that unacceptable behavior toward others can cause grave damage that cannot always be mended.

———

After Jonas and Antanina left, my mother began dealing with our food, tentatively at first. However, her self-confidence quickly returned. Managing a household and preparing delicacies were right in her wheelhouse. Among our relatives and friends, she was known as an excellent cook. She had a lot of experience, and in the good old days, her kitchen had fed nine mouths: our six family members; my grandmother, my mother's mother; Mrs. Seitz, our Omama; and the maid, as well as other visitors and guests on holidays. The helper worked, and the products were supplied in abundance. The home's small chicken coop in the backyard provided fresh eggs and chicken, and three cows gave milk. Vegetables grew in the garden, and the trees bowed with the weight of their fruit.

The milk quenched our thirst like water, and the excess did not go to waste: it was collected in clay pitchers that were stored in the cool basement, and the fat that was separated from it was used to make butter, the fresh scent of which was like perfume. The sour milk was sealed in cloth bags sewn in the shape of a triangle, which were squeezed between wooden boards to remove the liquid. When the process was complete, flat bags of white cheese that could be sliced remained, rich and amazingly tasty—but also rich in cholesterol, a fact that was not yet known.

Unlike households in the city, where supplies were to a large extent purchased in measured quantities—in our home the flour, sugar, and groats were brought in large quantities and stored in cans. My mother used to mock the housewives who bought bread and challah for the Sabbath—could you imagine eating a challah that was bought? In our house, the loaves of bread and challah were baked in a huge oven, like in bakeries. And at the end of the summer, we prepared for the winter. Large wooden barrels were stored in the basement in which selected cucumbers and cabbage were pickled and sealed with wooden covers, pressed with a heavy stone, closing them tight. On the shelves were jars of preserved fruits and jam made from the surplus fruit, and on top of large wooden pallets stacked on top of one another were apples and pears of the finest quality, saved as part of the winter stock. From time to time, they were sorted to remove any fruit that may have rotted. In addition, potatoes for the winter were stored in sacks and placed one on top of the other.

At the end of winter, we again got ready for summer. The ice miners would bring large chunks of ice in their carts, which were thrown into a huge pit dug specifically for that purpose. The pit was closed and sealed with a roof. The ice was covered with straw, and just like that the pit became one huge underground block of ice, which held fast even in the heat of the summer and only partially melted. In the ice pit, as in our refrigerators of today, foods were stored to keep them cold and preserve them.

Managing the house demanded knowledge and skill. My mother mastered it all, with a helper—and when necessary two—at her side. The farm had a permanent staff, who lived year-round in a sort of boarding house on the premises. That was our house before the disaster came upon us.

That was how things once were. Our life's stable order was damaged with the arrival of the Russians and collapsed like a house of cards within a few days of the arrival of the Germans. Now, only my mother and I remained. Having sufficient food was not a problem. The big challenge was to cope with the memories. Every morning, my mother would go down to the mill yard where the farmers brought their grain to be ground on their way to the market to sell their produce, followed by a visit to the taverns to wet their whistle. Before the wagons left the yard, my mother, as well as some neighbors, would buy fresh food for our sustenance. And once again, the fire burned in our home. And my mother, seeing the fine, fresh food, could not stand the temptation and bought everything she could, far beyond our needs.

One day, when she was preparing lunch, much more than we needed—and you were not to throw away food—mother recommended I invite Jonas for a meal. She wanted to repair her relationship with the Paulavičiuses. I was so happy. I kissed her and ran to the mill to invite him. Jonas looked at me with smiling eyes and asked whether it was an invitation from my mother or one that I instigated. I swore that it was in fact my mother who had issued the invitation. Jonas hesitated. It seemed that he was concerned to be sitting opposite my mother after all that had passed between them. Then he suggested that his helper, Jurgėla, join us, and he asked that I get my mother's permission. I answered confidently that Jurgėla would be wanted and there was enough food prepared for all of us. And so the four of us ate together.

Jurgėla was a good-hearted, wise, and talented manager who served as Jonas's right hand. Jonas was meant to be the commander and instructor—Jurgėla was the man behind the scenes. Now, while sitting around the dining room table, he was guiding the conversation. He praised my mother for her culinary talent—she liked that—and he evaded possible conversational land mines. He must have known about the rift between her and Jonas.

Nothing brings people together like good food. From that day on, either Jonas or Jurgėla, or both of them, would occasionally join us, and we no longer regularly ate alone. My mother improved her cooking and made sure to enhance the aesthetic side of setting the table, as much as conditions allowed. When Antanina came by, she also joined the diners at the table. My mother had not lost her desire to demonstrate to her guests her superiority in food preparation and serving. And so my mother became the helper and cook of simple people, as she had once described them in her anger, and she even enjoyed it.

Her mood improved remarkably, and it was obvious that her preoccupation with the food, its preparation and serving, was therapeutic for her. She also enjoyed the company of people. She talked and joked, drawing on our family's stories and humor that I remembered from so long ago. But when she finished in the kitchen and the rest of the house, when evening came and we were left alone, she was overcome with melancholy. These evenings in the dark, with the shutters with iron bars in the big empty and dark house, were hard and awful. And the days were troubled.

One day, a tall, handsome officer knocked on the door of our house and introduced himself to my mother as Captain Dimitri Kuznetsov. My mother asked what he wanted, and he replied that he was looking for a room to live in. At that time, officers were allowed to live outside the barracks, and they sought out the larger houses in search of a room. Most of them were turned away, even if it was politically problematic to refuse. Most of the families lived in overcrowded conditions, so why would they want to be more crowded for the sake of a Russian officer and invite him into their home for free, without charging rent? This was not the case with us. Our house was almost empty, and my mother's nightly fears drove her mad. The officer's arrival—we called him "Dima"—came just at the right time, as if my mother's wish had been granted.

My mother accepted immediately and without any hesitation. The room near the main entrance was given, therefore, to Captain Dima Kuznetsov—and the presence of an armed man in the house gave my mother some sense of security during those frightful nights. But Dima did not come alone: he had a wife and baby, a fact that he hid at first in case my mother were to refuse a family. However, by the time we learned this, we had already come to like Dima very much, and my mother could not refuse. She welcomed the company because living with others and the bustle of a family around her was a cure for her loneliness.

At the service of Dima and his beautiful wife, Ninochka, was an orderly (*denshczik* in Russian)—a soldier who was determined to escape the life of the barracks and camp work. Sasha, whom we called Sashka, was like a house cat, who very quickly and willingly became my mother's right-hand man. She would order him to go here and there, bring wood, light the fire, turn on the stove, and do many other tasks. In short, instead of the joyful Fenka, Mother's helper before the war, my mother now had Sashka, who did whatever she asked of him.

With time, a friendship flourished between my mother and Ninotchka. My mother taught her how to cook, and I periodically tasted her food to monitor her culinary progress. Ninotchka's laughter filled the house; everyone loved her, and she loved and generously kissed everyone—I got a hug as well, unsure of whether it was motherly or not. She divided her time between the house and the barracks, where she had spent her youth. When war broke out, she volunteered for the army and plowed the battlefields with the other soldiers from somewhere in Russia all the way to our godforsaken suburb. Her marriage to her commanding officer had released her from military service, but her heart remained with the soldiers.

It was a June day in 1945. I had come home from whatever I was busy with that day and saw that my mother was not home. Through the open door to the room that served as Jonas's office, I saw him sitting leisurely at his desk. In front of him sat a woman, and they were in the midst of a lively conversation. When he saw me, he smiled and called me in. "Look, don't you recognize this young lady?" he asked. I looked. In front of me sat a thin woman, dressed in simple clothes, her face tired, her skin a yellowish-tan, and her shoes worn. Resting at her feet was a small, scratched-up suitcase—evidence of her long journey.

Yes, she looked familiar to me. I had not seen her in a long time, but when she got up to greet me with teary eyes, it removed all doubt: this was my sister Vera. We stood hugging each other for a long time, crying and silent. Five horrible years had passed since we parted. I was a ten-year-old boy when Vera and her husband, Asher Waldstein, had left for Vilnius.

They got married in 1940, the first year of Soviet control over Lithuania. Their wedding was celebrated in our home with a full house. Every room in our house was at the disposal of the guests, the tables were exploding with delicacies of all kinds, and the poor of the city ate to their hearts' content.

Asher was a communist in his views. When Lithuania became a Soviet Republic, he willingly put his talents to use in the service of the "land of socialism." He became an electrical engineer after completing his studies in Bordeaux, France. His classmate, Aaron Neumark, one of those saved by the Paulavičiuses, always used the word *genius* when he mentioned Asher Waldstein. And, indeed, his talents were exceptional. Asher and his older brother, David, were born in Simnas, a town in the Alytus district. As children, they lost their father, and their mother, a grocer, struggled to support them. They excelled at school, skipped a grade, made a living by giving private lessons, and finished high school early. With the help of their uncle Zalman Waldstein, who was a man of means, they continued their higher education. David, the older brother, became a distinguished chemist. After his graduation, he returned from France to Lithuania, where he met and married Vera, and they came to live in our house.

Vera and Asher continued living with us for a while. Asher, being typically withdrawn, locked himself in his room from morning to night to work on his inventions. With unbelievable concentration and detachment from the rest of the world around him, he sketched lines, wrote formulas, and drew spirals—a secret language to the foreign eye. Weeks later, when he was done, he sent his discoveries to a research institute near Moscow. In the spring of 1941, Vera and Asher moved to Vilnius, where Vera was to continue her third year of studies at the Economics Department of the University of Vilnius, and Asher worked at the Lithuanian State Radio in Vilnius.

By this point Europe was already burning, but they put their faith in the strong Soviet Union, which promised them a rosy future. Then came the answer from the institute, earlier than expected: Asher was invited to Moscow.

The earthquake that rocked Russia at dawn on June 22, 1941—the German invasion of the Soviet Union—interrupted all of Vera and Asher's dreams. The news broadcasting from the radio stations all day that told of the hastened flight of the leaders of government, the evacuation of the institutions, and the burning of documents left no room for doubt: the Soviet lines had been breached; everything had collapsed. The next day at dawn, Vera and Asher left their home and everything they had. They headed east with only a small bundle of possessions so that their load would not be too heavy. On the over-crowded, bombed roads, among masses of refugees, by foot and occasionally by car, clinging to freight cars, on crowded trains, and by any other mode of transportation they came across, they made their way eastward, without knowing where they were headed, where they would stop, or where they would rest or eat. Who could count the towns, suburbs, and villages they passed? The poor peasant huts, the people they met in meager clothing, and the prominent poverty they saw on their journey caused the first crack in Asher's ideological views.

A major stop along their way was the city of Velikiye Luki. While there, Vera worked in a public soup kitchen that fed refugees in order to support Asher and herself. While they were in Velikiye Luki, they found out after a lot of inquiries that the institute to which he had been invited was about to be evacuated. Asher's plans had reverted to being merely a dream.

Vera was still able to establish contact with the Gourevitch family in Moscow. The woman of the family, Berta—as we called her, Bertochka—was my mother's childhood friend, and after many years apart, their friendship was renewed when Lithuania became a Soviet Republic. In their despair, Vera reached out to the only address she had in the Soviet Union: Bertochka's home. It turned out that Bertochka and her family were about to evacuate to their relatives in Kuybyshev (now Samara). She gave Vera their future address. Who would have thought that even Moscow was no longer safe? With Bertochka's answer, Vera's last hope of finding shelter in a raging sea of refugees was snuffed out.

The Germans took over Velikiye Luki, and once again Vera and Asher were on the road. After months of misery, hunger, and deprivation, with hundreds of kilometers behind them, they reached the city of Gorky (now Nizhny Novgorod) and from there Kuybyshev. They located the Gourevitch family of three: Bertochka; her husband, Vladimir; and their daughter, Rita. The Gourevitches were also refugees who had found a narrow, crowded shelter with family. That was where Vera and Asher found support and a corner to lay their heads.

The days were cold, and the Russian winter was especially brutal for the homeless. Vera and Asher had no home and had arrived with no winter clothes or shoes to wear. But even times as cruel as these, when man is wolf to man, there were those who did not lose their humanity: that was what the Gourevitches were like. They gave Vera and Asher shelter. They shared their bread and gave them clothes from the little they had brought with them when they left Moscow.

Then, Vera and Asher decided to escape. This time not from the Germans, but from the winter. They again set off on their way, southward, to Central Asia. Hungry and emotionally and physically exhausted, they traveled thousands of kilometers to Tashkent, and from there to their final stop: the city of Osh in Kyrgyzstan. Here, they decided they could go no further.

They found a miserable place to live, their food was meager, their dignity was lost, and their humiliation was complete. They were bitter. For months they had wandered through Russia. On their way from Vilnius to Osh, they had covered over six thousand kilometers. All that Russia could show for itself they saw: heroism and cowardice, greatness and humility, loyalty and treachery, honesty and exploitation, volunteering and evasion, but above all, the endurance of millions of people who proudly bore their suffering.

Vera and Asher went through fire and water together, but when they arrived in Osh, the warm city of refuge where they were hoping to survive despite the poverty and difficulty, their time to part had come. They did not know, then, that this would be their final farewell. Asher was drafted into the Lithuanian Division of the Red Army, apparently in early 1942, and went to the fields of slaughter. He fell on the battlefield and was buried on the side of the road or in a deserted field; no one really knows where. His friends would have placed a stone on his grave and written his name on it, but it must have been removed and the field plowed.

In the beginning of August 1944, immediately upon my liberation, Magdė, a woman who had previously worked in my father's mill, arrived at the Paulavičius' with a letter in hand. Letters, at that time, were written on coarse paper, with the writing crowded into every corner of the paper, using every possible inch. Since there were no envelopes, the letter was folded into a triangle before it was sent. The letters wandered across Mother Russia—in mailbags, on trains, for weeks and months at a time. Folded into those letters were all the news and hope from the sender. Oftentimes, when wives and mothers read these letters, hands trembling at this sign that their loved one was still alive, the thought that he had already passed since its sending did not cross their minds. The soldiers who fell were like the stars: even when extinguished, their light continued to shine.

A letter addressed to us arrived at the beginning of August 1944. Vera had written it even before the Soviets' capture of Kaunas, assuming that by the time the letter would make its way on the trains, Kaunas would fall into the hands of the Soviets. The addressee was the head of the post office in Panemunė. To the best of her memory, this is what she wrote:

> Dear Sir,
> I am a daughter of the Fein family that lived in Panemunė before the war at 112 Vaidoto Street. I have a big request: please give this letter to anyone in my family who may have survived. If there is no one—please write me a few words, if you know what may have happened to them. I would consider this a good deed on your part.

Then a few words were written to anyone in the family who might read it. Vera wrote about being in Kyrgyzstan and sent us her exact address. She wrote that Asher had been drafted and was fighting in the Lithuanian Division. Apparently, when Vera wrote the letter, she did not yet know that Asher had fallen. She, too, had continued receiving letters from an extinguished star.

However, one day she received an official letter from the Department of Defense. She understood the bitter news even before she opened the envelope. The letter was filled with beautiful and lofty words: "a hero's death," "the Soviet Motherland," "Eternal Glory" for the "Liberty and Independence of our Homeland," and also a deep sorrow was expressed for her loss.

"A hero's death"! He fell with a weapon in his hands and not in the execution pits, which was at least some comfort, although very little. On behalf of socialism? Doubtful. After all that he had seen, his faith had been broken, and his higher power—communism—had disappointed him. On behalf of the homeland? In the place where he was born, all the Jews of the city of Simnas in Lithuania were murdered, among them his mother, with merciless cruelty by their Lithuanian neighbors who joined hands with the German occupier. Was this a homeland? A man's homeland is a place where he is loved. Lithuania was not such a place. If so, for what did Asher Waldstein die, after his faith was undermined? If I say that he fell for the eradication of Nazism, that would be the truth.

Two hundred years ago lived a man called Count Ferdinand von Waldstein. For many generations, his name was known to hundreds of thousands of people, not because he had been a count, but because of a sonata written by Beethoven in honor of his patron: the Waldstein Sonata. Had the title of the work been Sonata no. 21 in C Major, Op. 53, no one would know, two hundred years later, that such a count had ever existed. But the name of the count was included in the name of the piece, and so it continues to be memorable, as long as one musician remains on earth. While listening to the Waldstein Sonata, I think of my own Waldstein. A Russian proverb says that "what is written in ink, will not be uprooted, even with an ax!" The little I know of Asher Waldstein I have written here so that the sands of time will not uproot his memory.

Vera struggled for survival in a foreign and strange place. She worked in a factory for cotton processing, and she was barely making it; malaria had exhausted her strength, and the quinine drug had dyed her skin. After the Russians returned to Lithuania, she looked for ways to return to what had once been her father's house. Equipped with the appropriate permits, she set out again, destitute, wandering on crowded trains. She returned by the same way she had escaped with Asher from Vilnius to Osh. Now she was coming home alone, and all she had with her was a small, ragged suitcase. And so I found her one day in June 1945, and Vera joined Jonas in managing the mill. In those days, when flour was akin to gold, our house prospered financially.

One night in July or August 1945, we heard a light knock on the shutter of one of the windows: it was my sister Yehudit returning home. She had traversed a long and painful way since we had parted. In July 1944, she was transported in cramped freight cars to the Stutthof concentration camp, where she underwent torture that thousands of other women did not withstand, where so many others took their last breaths. She defied the odds, becoming one of the few survivors of that inferno.

As the front approached, hundreds of women were transferred from one place to another in endless marches. The bodies of the ones who dropped dead from exhaustion formed a trail on the side of the road. On a death march like this, Yehudit arrived at Chynowie, near Lauenburg (Lębork). On March 10, 1945, Russian soldiers found her—dirty, lice-ridden, and sick with typhus—crawling among the bodies, grasping at the fading thread of life. A military doctor treated her with devotion. She owed him her life.

Under his instructions and supervision, she underwent disinfecting procedures. Her hair, which had been the symbol of her beauty, was shorn and her head was shaved. She was hospitalized in one of the houses whose tenants fled from the Russians. Guards had been assigned to protect her and others who were hospitalized with her, from looters to rapists. For weeks, she was treated with medication and with sufficient, nourishing food. And so, in a slow process, medicine, devotion, and youth beat the Angel of Death.

When Yehudit got stronger and was back on her feet, she was required to pay her debt to the military: the survivors were put to work at various jobs, and Yehudit, who spoke Russian, was assigned to the post office in Toruń. Her officer promised that she would be discharged as soon as there was any sign of life from a surviving family member.

Indeed, one day, an officer from our hometown came into the post office where she worked. He recognized Yehudit. He was on his way to Kaunas—a precious letter had been given to him, and he had located us in Panemunė. Our letter to her was the exact sign of life she needed to get discharged. One night in July or August 1945, in military garb and with a head covering that hid her baldness, Yehudit returned home.

Who can describe the drumming of the heart, the tears of joy, and the sorrow of the survivors for the loss of their loved ones, when they fell into each other's arms upon their return? Who can understand what my heart felt when I saw Yehudit, my lifesaver, returning home? Hidden cords connected us. We had survived the dreadful years together with hands and hearts intertwined. Destiny intended for us to cross many more paths together.

We returned home, but we did not forget, nor will we ever forget, those who did not survive: our pure-hearted father, Menachem (Mendel), whose soul was stolen at the Dachau concentration camp; our handsome and talented brother, Zvi (Hirsch'ke), who was murdered at the Fourth Fort—a few kilometers from my father's house; my brother-in-law, who was intended for greatness; the branch of the family tree that was annihilated; and the neighbors, friends, and acquaintances who shaped the human landscape of our lives. They were all gone as though they had never existed. The four of us, four members of the same family, had survived the Nazi wave. Few families shared such a miracle.

26

THE JOY OF YOUTH

THE LOCAL SCHOOL IN PANEMUNĖ WELCOMED ME, AND I WAS accepted with sympathy by both students and teachers. There were a few boys in the class who were neighborhood children, so I had already spent time with them before I even came to that school. I was a curiosity to them and aroused their interest: I was the only Jewish boy in the whole region; I lived as an adopted son to a Lithuanian family; I spoke their language as well as they did; and, I knew the customs of the place and practiced them. I ate nonkosher foods and was called Juozukas—an authentic Lithuanian name. My original name—Yochanan—which was sometimes mentioned for purposes of formal registration, was the only marker of my Jewishness.

The story of my rescue became public knowledge. The mill and Jonas's management of it were seen as a good deal for the Paulavičius family. No one investigated the legal status of the family property. To those around us, the mill and the Fein family were bound together. They thought that as an adult, I would one day become the owner of a mill and a mansion.

Starting in the new school, I decided I would excel in my studies and be the best student in the class. I made sure to get my homework done, I wrote clearly and legibly, I underlined the headings of the chapters, and I read and reread what was being taught. In short—I was "a good boy." However, since I wasn't inclined to work diligently on subjects I didn't like—and what I really loved did not take place within the walls of the school—very quickly my studies dropped from their pedestal, and I became just an ordinary student.

My heart was with the military brigade, and especially with the military entertainment band, whose reputation preceded them at all the army camps in the area. The commander of the brigade, Colonel Shtulberg, paid special attention to cultural activities among the soldiers. When he discovered among them a prominent actor, a theater man from Leningrad (Saint Petersburg), he recruited him and gave him extensive authority to locate talent and establish a high-level entertainment troupe. Few knew the actor's real name, but he was known to all as "Chiuchiupal," the name of the character he created and developed—or perhaps it was his real name? I will never know. Chiuchiupal identified outstanding talent among the soldiers. Anyone who could do anything useful in the field of entertainment and drama was invited and willingly went to audition.

Joining Chiuchiupal's troupe released the soldiers from many tasks and made life easier for them. Dozens tried out, but only a select few were accepted. Although it was up to Chiuchiupal to create the entertainment troupe, he actually did more than that: he established a dramatic troupe alongside it. The entertainment was for the soldiers, but the drama was for his soul.

Chiuchiupal located a musician, who was then required to set up a choir. From among the hundreds of soldiers he auditioned, he established a choir of eighty singers, among them several excellent soloists. A female soldier with a deep alto voice was found, and her singing captured hearts. The choir was accompanied by mandolin players and a professional button accordionist (Russian Garmoshka). Anyone who could dance, danced; anyone who could sing, sang; and anyone who could play a musical instrument, played! All this extensive cultural activity was driven by one person: Chiuchiupal. He was the initiator, director, and scriptwriter for the shows, and his wonderful performances provided some relief for the soldiers' souls.

I was exposed to this wonderful world of artistic endeavor when Captain Dima Kuznetsov brought me to the shows under the guise of a boy-member and violinist. Dima himself was an amateur dancer and Chiuchiupal's commanding officer. There was mutual friendship and appreciation between them (though Chiuchiupal was a simple soldier and did not hold any rank). The entire troupe was under

Captain Dima's command, and all requests and demands were directed at him. I spent many hours with Chiuchiupal, and he took me under his wing.

My curiosity regarding everything involved in the artistic work and management of the band and drama troupe was insatiable. With Chiuchiupal's consent, I attended most rehearsals and performances. I followed the troupe everywhere, helped with various technical arrangements, and was well-liked by everyone. In time, I began telling Chiuchiupal's jokes, imitating his speech and movements. That was how the idea was born to dress me up and make me up like him.

It came to a climax when I went out on stage in front of hundreds of soldiers dressed as the character of Chiuchiupal. The character he had created and played was a combination of a circus clown, a Chaplin beggar, and the face from a Greek tragedy: he had long, pointed toe shoes that rolled up in front in the shape of a snail, patched trousers that were not the right size, and a jacket with all its buttons missing, closed with a safety pin about twenty centimeters long. His face was painted white and decorated with a tear coming from his eye, and he wore a red wig combed forward like a small arrow above his brow. To avoid collisions and falls in his oversized shoes, the character walked with a jerky jump. Chiuchiupal's entrance was preceded by a burst of wild laughter—played behind the scenes—signaling to the soldiers that Chiuchiupal would now appear! That was exactly how I made my own entrance. It was decided that I would not speak, but I would continue with the wild laughter of Chiuchiupal, whom I mimicked perfectly. The moderator tried to throw me off the stage with pleasant words and then threats, but to no avail. I bounced around and giggled on stage, and the soldiers in the audience laughed along with me.

Then Chiuchiupal himself came out on stage. He wore an ironed soldier's uniform as if ready for formation, his hair combed and his face serious. When I saw him, I stood speechless, like the sorcerer's apprentice to his master. The audience was in shock. How could it be, they thought, that the same man appeared simultaneously on stage as a clown and a soldier? A bustle and laughter broke out in the hall. With a vigorous hand gesture, Chiuchiupal pointed backstage and ordered me to leave: "Get out, impostor!" I left the stage frightened, limping, and whimpering. According to the plan, I was to remove the wig quickly, remove the makeup from my face, and return to the stage. In the time it took, Chiuchiupal engaged the audience in a joke.

"In London," he said, "there was a competition of Charlie Chaplin imitators." Here, he described the conditions of the competition, while glancing backstage to make sure I had managed to do what was expected of me. When he saw that I was ready, he finished and spoke about Charlie Chaplin participating anonymously in the competition, and how he won . . . third place! The soldiers laughed, and he continued, "We are also running a competition of Chiuchiupal imitators. I participated and was very successful: I won a prize . . . second place!" Then he motioned for me to come out on stage and with a fatherly hug he announced, "Before you now stands the first-place winner!" There were those among the soldiers who knew me because of my constant presence in the camp, but for most of them I was an unfamiliar boy. He continued, "Allow me to present to the first-place winner a prize: the title 'son of the regiment' [*syn polka* in Russian]!"

The soldiers greeted me with loud cheers and continuous applause. It was my first appearance on stage, but not the last. From that evening on, I wandered around the camp just as if at home. Everyone knew me and greeted me, and Colonel Shtulberg invited me to his office, shook my hand, and predicted a great stage future. But as we know, our world is full of false prophets.

Around that same time, in the year 1945, having reunited in our family home after those horrific years—my mother, my sisters, and me—we once again felt the warmth of a home. The emptiness and silence that had prevailed in the house after my mother's return gave way to a human hum. Aside from the family of Captain Kuznetsov, another officer had moved into our house, and Sashka, his orderly, spent more time there than in the barracks.

The wonderful cultural evenings that took place in our home are etched in my memory to this day. Our officer tenants would invite their friends on the weekends, and over time they became our guests as well. Some of them were Jews and spoke Yiddish, although poorly. When they heard that there was a Jewish house in the suburb, they searched for it and found ways to get there. My sisters—beautiful young women—were a major attraction.

Dima made sure that the assembled group would not be exclusively officers. He always brought with him three "simple" soldiers: Chiuchiupal; Vovka, the button accordion player; and one other— I've since forgotten his name—an excellent tenor. These three simple soldiers, the only soldiers without rank who were allowed to forgo a military-style buzz cut (could artists go without locks of hair?), were the ones who created these unforgettable cultural evenings.

Here we enjoyed Zoshchenko's reminiscences and monologues from Shakespeare's plays, all performed wonderfully by Chiuchiupal. Here, we heard Lensky's aria from *Eugene Onegin*, which the character sang before leaving for a duel in which he would be killed: "Whither, oh whither are ye banished, my golden days when spring was dear?" (A. S. Pushkin).

And more art songs from the Russian classics. If there is anything Russian in my soul, it was absorbed in that remote suburb, in the brigade, among the soldiers, in Chiuchiupal's troupe on those unforgettable nights that took place in our home.

My life continued to be a celebration of youth in school as well, mostly because of the friendships that had developed between me and some of the boys: the brothers Eugenijus and Romas Birmanas, Eduardas Šveikauskas, and last but not least—Mikas Vaitkevičius. I met Romas first, my classmate, and we immediately discovered our shared love for chess. After school, we would go to his house on Klevų Street, and before his parents returned from work, we would dive into our chess games. His family maintained a cultured home, as evidenced by the many books arranged on library shelves and a piano with scores of sheet music on it.

Romas claimed confidently that if I played chess against his brother, I wouldn't stand a chance. Indeed, his brother, Eugenius, was a fine player and later won third place in the Lithuanian Youth Championship. They inherited their love of chess from their father, who was a chess master and participated in the country's championships. I remembered that when I was in hiding at the Paulavičius's, Kęstutis brought me a weekly publication with a chess section. Once I followed the game of two masters, which was published in the weekly: one of them was Birmantas. This same Birmantas was Romas and Eugenius's father.

His real name was Birmanas, and with the Lithuanian ending "-as" removed, you would be left with Birman, which was not Lithuanian. Worse: it sounded Jewish. In order not to be suspected by the Nazis, their father changed their surname to Birmantas. This change—the addition of the letter *t*, legitimized the name in the eyes of the evildoers, but after the return of the Russians, the family returned to its original name.

And so, we became a trio of chess players in Eugenius's group. Later, we also added two boys to our group. One was a classmate of mine, Eduardas, and the second was an older boy, an architecture student named Paškauskas who was a neighbor of Eugenius's and who lived in the same building. We held competitions, and as soon as one ended, we would start another. It wasn't always possible to entertain such a large group at the Birmanas's, so often we played on the bench in the yard or in the stairwell. We were drunk on chess.

I remember very well the brothers' father, the chess master Birmanas. He treated me with sympathy. My being Jewish and a survivor moved him. My violin playing also aroused his curiosity, and I played for him several times. He was a composer. He devoted many hours to playing the piano. He played introspectively and with intention, as if there were no living soul around him. The hours I spent at the Birmanas's were hours of pleasure and relaxation, and I remember them with longing.

Mikas was my best friend. He was thin, short, reserved, introverted, and polite. Just as chess linked me to the Birmanases, music linked me to Mikas. When I met him, he was about fourteen years old and played the piano well. He had mastered the instrument and was a virtuoso at improvisation. He absorbed any theme or tune that he heard and could immediately add harmony and suitable accompaniment. I don't remember if there were other children in our school who stood out in their musical abilities, but Mikas and I became the regular musicians for every celebration or event at school and in the whole suburb.

And there were celebrations. The beginning and end of the school year, national and governmental holidays—all were celebrated in the only hall in the suburb: the local community center. It was a wooden house with a stage, wings, and even an opening in the floor, at the front of the stage, for a prompter.

A group of boys and girls, including Mikas and myself, made up a sort of cultural committee for the school. At the end of the greetings and the speeches at various gatherings, we had to present an artistic program. The young people in the area did not have many leisure opportunities at that time. The holiday celebrations in the hall were an opportunity for dancing and entertainment after the official portion of the evenings had ended. My playing, my experience in the military troupe, Chiuchiupal's lessons, the clown clothes, and the makeup box he had made available to me—all of these made me the life of the party in performances in the community center. And thus from one act to another, the audience saw a boy comedian in Chiuchiupal's costume reciting monologues about life in school, though the jokes and routines I borrowed from Chiuchiupal were not always age appropriate.

These were happy and joyful times. I drank them in, perhaps in compensation for my lost years.

Mikas and I spent a lot of time together outside of school. We worked hard to build a repertoire for the violin and accordion—Mikas had mastered that instrument as well—for any celebration that would arise. Over time, we became known as a pair of young and popular musicians. Mikas was a regular visitor to our home, loved by my mother and sisters, as I was in his home as well. The accordion and violin never left our hands. I introduced Mikas to the military regiment and its troupe, and we even participated in an interunit military competition for drama and art as "brigade boys."

As for my dramatic career, that came to an end faster than expected and in an undignified and even dangerous manner.

Kęstutis recommended that we travel to Kaunas to watch a performance of a well-known Lithuanian comedian-actor: Pupų Dėdė, meaning "Uncle Beans." The normal understanding of the word *travel* did not pertain to the manner in which we got from one place to another. Public transportation was not yet functioning and walking eight kilometers did not appeal to us. The accepted method was to wait for a military truck on the curve of the road, and when it would slow down—grab on and hang from behind, and, with some effort, scramble inside. Usually, the driver was not aware of what was going on, and the trip would end successfully by jumping out of the truck at the right moment. After such a trip, we usually ended up with some stains on our clothes, but we paid them no heed.

Pupų Dėdė was a beloved entertainer in Lithuania, and his loose tongue often garnered the anger of the authorities. In 1939, an incident occurred that was spoken of quite a bit. That year, the Soviet Union conquered Eastern Poland, including Vilnius, Lithuania's historic capital. Until then, the city was ruled by Poles. When the Soviet Union turned Vilnius over to Lithuania, and in return established military bases on its soil, Lithuanians were overjoyed. Pupų Dėdė then presented a rhyme: "*Vilnius musu Lietuva rusų!*" "Vilnius is ours, but we are theirs (Lithuania belongs to the Russians)!" It was said that he was put on trial for this statement.

Now, with the fighting over, Pupų Dėdė returned to the stage. He shared the stage with guest performers, but he was the main attraction. His jokes encouraged laughter from the audience, but his strength was in the rhymes he wrote on current affairs. These lyrics were paired with well-known melodies and were accompanied by a large bayan (button accordion). During one of his performances, he expressed satisfaction with the times because he and his household were running a tiny business and they were loaded with money—a reference to those growing rich from the black market.

I was fascinated with his performance, watched it again a week later, and memorized his jokes, especially his lyrics about the black-market business. Armed with all of this, I looked forward to an opportunity to perform, which arrived in the summer of 1945 at the end of the school-year party. At the community center hall, full of students and parents, teachers and youth, who came primarily to dance at the end of the ceremony, I performed as part of the artistic program by the school's students. Accompanied by Mikas on the accordion, dressed in Chiuchiupal's clown clothes, I sang the lyrics I had written about school life, but I also included Pupų Dėdė's rhymes and told some of his jokes, which in my opinion were appropriate for the event. After I sang the words of the stanza about the black market, the audience rewarded me with a huge round of applause.

After the official portion of the event, while everyone was still getting up and talking, I went out to grab a breath of fresh air, and everyone who happened across my path congratulated me on my successful performance. All that time, an officer in uniform was following me, and when I stood outside the entrance to the hall, he approached me, tapped me on the shoulder, and expressed his appreciation for my talent. I heard a foreign accent in his Lithuanian. He asked if I spoke Russian. I affirmed that I did and we switched to Russian. In spite of his friendliness, I was not comfortable with the discussion, and I wanted to return to the hall. However, he held my arm and asked that I answer the riddle he was about to ask. Half seriously, half jokingly, he asked if I knew who had built the Belomor Canal. At that time, I did not know about the existence of such a canal, let alone who its builders were, so I replied that I did not. At this point the man became serious, his face frozen. Pointing with a threatening finger he said, "Since I have your best interest at heart, I will answer the riddle for you: the Belomor Canal was built by those who tell jokes and write rhymes!"

Although I did not understand the meaning of his riddle nor its solution, I felt warned and threatened. "Ask your parents," he added. "They will surely understand the riddle and be able to explain it to you." He turned and left. When I returned home upset, I asked my mother about the Belomor Canal and those who built it, but she had no answer for me. Vera didn't know what it was about either. That evening, feeling contemplative, I entered Captain Kuznetsov's room and questioned him about the Belomor Canal.

I did not know then what I know today: The Belomor Canal was dug 227 kilometers long, 5 meters deep, and it connected the

White Sea to Lake Onega. It was opened to maritime travel in 1933. The builders of the canal were made up of thousands of prisoners who were exiled to camps and forced to work in hard labor. The stories of their lives and deaths are drowned in the waters of this cursed canal.

Dima knew about it in principle. However, when I asked who built it, he became alert and questioned me about why I was asking such questions. I answered in total innocence that I didn't have any special interest in it, and I only asked because I had been presented with this riddle. Since I did not know the answer, I was given one, but it was an answer that I could not understand. After Dima questioned me about how this unknown officer came to have words with me, and after he made the connection between the riddle and my performance on stage, he told me to translate the words of the song I sang and the jokes I told. He also asked about the color of the cap the man with the riddle was wearing. I replied that the cap was green, which apparently meant that he was an officer of the NKVD (Russian Secret Service)—later known as the KGB.

Captain Dima was alarmed. The bitter joke was that the canal builders were those who made anti-Soviet remarks, and it was known by word of mouth all over the Soviet Union. Dima understood well the riddle and its meaning. He also understood that I had been warned. I was surprised at his strong reaction to the matter, which in my eyes seemed so inconsequential—it was just a joke. Dima dragged me to my mother and told her what happened. He expressed his disappointment at my enticing the audience with anti-Soviet digs and said that I, of all people, was the last person who should behave in such a manner.

I tried to defend myself by saying that the rhymes and jokes were mostly copied from a famous entertainer who had performed publicly, but my excuses were not accepted: "If someone were to incite dissent against Soviet rule—could he take back his words and claim innocence using the excuse that he repeated someone else's words?" asked Dima. Now Dima revealed himself as a political person. Perhaps it wasn't coincidental that he was in charge of Chiuchiupal's troupe. He taught me a political lesson: "When the country is struggling—everyone has to step forward on behalf of its victory, even in jokes and satire."

My mother was very frightened, and her screams bordered on hysteria; she did not spare words. Since she knew Dima's influence on me, she went on about all of my deficiencies, hoping that she could get me to straighten out. My mother longed for the strict order of the old days, as she described it, which was no longer in vogue. It was not to Dima's liking either, but out of respect for my mother he did not say it aloud.

At this point, Dima tried to calm the situation. According to him, the man who claimed to have my best interest at heart was in fact giving me a warning but did not intend any harm. My mother and Dima asked me to give up comedy until the danger passed. My mother took it a step further and more or less demanded that I give up performing altogether and devote myself to my studies. She didn't like my chess playing either. She would see me sitting for hours at the chessboard analyzing positions or studying "openings," and she could not understand how a person could "play alone." While she did not see chess as a horrible pastime, she worried that I pursued it at the expense of my studies. However, my performing, she said, made me the laughingstock of the town.

Dima did not agree with my mother's criticism that I spent too much time on too many hobbies, and very politely he said so. He focused on one matter only. "You absolutely should not," he said, "make jokes at the expense of the authorities, to whom you owe your freedom, and moreover, that encourages those who are hostile to the government." Also, "The authorities are not forgiving to their critics." And more quietly, he said, "You must not allow yourself to have a black mark against you in the eyes of the authorities. You are too young to be involved in political satire, but old enough to understand this." I was thus forced to promise not to engage in further comedy.

As if my lesson from Dima regarding what I may and may not do related to politics was not enough, I got another jolt, which embarrassed me. Months after these incidents, placards were pasted all over town that a "popular performer—Pupų Dėdė," was going to appear at Panemunė's community hall.

In a packed hall, the comedian climbed on stage and was received with a roaring round of applause even before he opened his mouth. He executed his act as successfully as always, but after the first few segments—the peak of his performance—he received only lukewarm applause and laughter. They had already heard these segments in the same hall from the same stage from a local, amateurish boy. Things reached a peak when Pupų Dėdė posed a question to the audience, for which he would pause for several seconds before answering, and which usually caused a wave of laughter. But this time, before he even had a chance to finish his question, he heard a youth in the audience answering. The punchline was lost, and Pupų Dėdė had no choice but to agree that the audience was right in their answer.

I snuck out of the hall, embarrassed and accompanied by amused stares, but not especially angry ones. Most likely, the reason for the half-hearted response to those segments would have been explained to Pupų Dėdė. There were those who also explained to me the significance of what is known as copyright infringement. I felt like a kid who was caught with his hand in the cookie jar, and it turned me off to performing comedy. That was how my short-lived career as a comedian came to an end. However, I did return to the stage at a different time and place.

One day, an older boy from a neighboring town made me an offer, which I had no reason to refuse. He said he was a good drummer. He had heard about Mikas and me and suggested that we form a band that would play dance music for money. He said he knew of venues and could find us places to perform. "We will be a trio," he said, "and in places that have a piano, we can also include Eduardas, who plays well." Mikas considered what he said seriously, and he, Eduardas, and I all agreed. We happily went about our preparations. We got plenty of sheet music and prepared a large repertoire of dance tunes.

Our first performance was in a sunflower oil factory. The management of the company decided to throw a party for the employees for some event, and after the speeches and greetings, the hall was emptied of chairs and benches, and the three of us—Mikas, the drummer, and I—got on stage. There was no piano there for Eduardas. At first, the audience did not have any confidence in us. However, when we started playing and we did our job well, we earned tremendous praise. At the end of the evening, we were brought into one of the offices to receive our pay, as had been previously agreed. That was when the manager with whom we had made the agreement told us that he had no money to pay us and that payment would be made in *natūra*—in other words, in sunflower oil. The drummer grumbled, but to no avail—there was no money. We had no choice but to accept a generous amount of oil that made our mothers happy.

After our first experience, we continued performing, mainly at high schools. Dance parties were a very popular mode of entertainment, and the class student committees of different schools competed with one another for the best party. Those who attended the parties—students and friends—paid an entrance fee. The money was used to cover expenses, but most of it went to us, the musicians. We were a very popular band, and the fact that we were youngsters was especially appropriate for the mood of a school party. In other places or in post–high school venues, the dancing went on until the light of day, which demanded physical endurance from both the performers and the participants. At midnight, they would call for a break, during which we were expected to play musical renditions or popular songs for a singalong.

Later on, when all the members of the band were studying at the Green Mountain Technical School, we became the school's permanent musicians. We were paid well, for the time. After playing all night until daybreak, each of us walked away with between two hundred and three hundred rubles, which was comparable to a worker's monthly wage. My friends turned over the money to their families, or at least most of it. But I was able to keep all of the money for myself. Vera, who was supporting us at that time, did not need my money. Her job at the mill provided her with more than enough to take care of the family.

I was, therefore, a "rich" kid, and I could allow myself luxuries that other boys could not. I bought twelve books on chess openings from the chess trainer, Baršauskas, written by the previous world champion from Holland, Max Euwe. The books were in Dutch, but I understood most of it because written Dutch was similar to German.

Yochanan's sisters: Yehudit (*right*) and
Vera (Devorah), 1946.

I replaced my old bicycle with a new one, I went to the movies fre-
quently, and I enjoyed all kinds of other activities that my money
enabled me to do.

Life was good at that time. I felt independent and free. I made my
own schedule, and nobody at home told me what to do. I was mature
enough not to neglect my studies, and in spite of all my activities,
I did what was necessary to keep my grades reasonable. On occasion, I thought about what I would do next. In another six months,
I would be finishing school in Panemunė, and I had to decide what
my next step would be. However, the decision was made for me. In
hindsight, I find that the most critical events in my life occurred due
to circumstances beyond my control; as though the hidden hand of
destiny was charting my path.

27

MOSCOW

FROM WHAT I REMEMBER, THE TRAIN WE GOT ON CAME FROM Kaliningrad and continued via Minsk to Moscow. The trip took two days. We passed towns and wide-open spaces—Mother Russia is vast. The destruction left by the war was visible everywhere. The train stopped at many stations, and everything looked strange and neglected. About nine months had passed since the end of the war, but to an onlooker, watching from the window of the train, there were no signs of restoration. The railroad cars were packed with travelers, and more people kept getting on at various stations. They dragged their bags, packages, and torn suitcases—which were tied together with ropes—while looking for a less crowded car. Many of them wore uniforms without any insignia. They had just been discharged from military service and were returning to their homes and their dear ones. The disabled ones, who had to use crutches, stood out. They had earned a great deal of respect, preference, and assistance in getting onto the train. Life's struggles were etched in the dark, colorless clothes of the people, and in their blank faces, there was no smile or joy of life.

There was a different atmosphere in our cabin. In front of us sat an officer in a neatly ironed uniform. The two small golden star medals hanging on his chest meant he was a "Hero of the Soviet Union" who had been twice awarded a medal for acts of outstanding bravery.

He was a young man, happy with his lot and quite talkative. Next to him sat a beautiful young woman. They conversed among themselves, including us in their conversation. It was obvious that the hero was flirting with the young woman, and she did not reject his advances. We ate our food and shared some with our neighbors, and the officer brought us hot water, which was free at each of the stations.

Hours passed with brooding thoughts. From a young age, I had never liked the sound of train wheels running on the tracks—the bone-chilling horn, and the cloud of steam that clouded my eyes. After two days' travel, we arrived at the Moscow Belorussky railway station. Among the throngs of people, near the sleeper car stood a gaunt, frail, and gentle woman. Her goodness shone on her face, a woolen scarf was wrapped around her neck, and her eyes scanned and searched for us as we looked for her: this was Bertochka.

We liked her immediately. In the chilled air of the Moscow night, she cloaked us in warmth and love; she kissed us as though we were her own children, returned to her after years of separation.

—⁓—

It was not the joy of tourism that brought me to Moscow.

It was the beginning of 1946. I felt a very bothersome, burning sensation in my right eye, as though small grains of sand had gotten into it, and no attempt at rinsing it helped. Since this discomfort persisted, I went at my mother's urging to an eye doctor. His office was a little way from our house, in the same building my friends, the Birmanases, lived in on Klevų Street.

I awaited my turn. On the wall in front of me was a large poster with a heading: "Beware of Trachoma." Several pictures depicted the eye in various stages of the sickness, the last of which showed a blind man whose eyelids were twisted and distorted. It also stated on this poster that this disease was very contagious, treatment was prolonged, and in the absence of proper treatment, it could result in blindness. My name was called. The doctor, a kind old man, flipped my right eyelid and, with an instrument, examined the eye for a long time. After washing his hands well over and over again and sitting down opposite me, he said with restraint and frankness that I was suffering from a serious disease and that the treatment was long and required tenacity, perseverance, and patience. When I asked him how long it would take for my recovery, he replied that it would be a very long time. I was stunned. "Why?" I asked. "I don't have the disease described on that poster in the waiting room, do I?" But the doctor told me, sadly, that I in fact did have that disease—a neglected trachoma.

The members of our household did not understand the full significance of my illness; they reassured me, promising that everything would end well, and I was inclined to believe them. We entrusted my care to a well-known ophthalmologist in Kaunas—Kutorgienė, who was considered an excellent doctor.

The next day, I went to see her. She was an impressive, good-hearted, and pleasant woman. Her soft-spoken manner calmed me. I described my sensations to her, and I told her about my visit to the doctor in Panemunė and his harsh diagnosis. I expressed my certainty that he had to have erred.

She said that she knew that doctor and expressed her appreciation of him. For some reason, I was unhappy with that.

She checked my eye and examined my eyelid with a magnifying glass. The expression on her face gave away her thoughts. The old doctor was not wrong. She silently went to wash her hands, washing them over and over again. Dr. Kutorgienė confirmed that I was suffering from trachoma, that the treatment was a "long process," that it was a "stubborn illness" that required "unlimited patience," and that "neglect could result in blindness"—in short, I had a long road ahead of me, which would have a very significant impact on my quality of life.

The household was up in arms. My mother did not know what to do with herself in her sorrow. That same night, Captain Dima went to the camp and came back with the regiment's doctor. We knew him well from his previous visits to our home. We listened to what he had to say and asked his advice, the advice of a friend. The man, serious and reasonable in his words, admitted that his knowledge was very general and limited; he would not contradict the diagnosis of ophthalmologists. Still, he found it hard to believe that even a decade after completing his studies, no new drugs had been developed for trachoma and that it remained as incurable as it did back then.

He suggested that I travel to Moscow as soon as possible. There and only there would I receive the most innovative medical treatments and find the best specialists who could find a cure for my illness.

We were impressed with what he had to say. That same night, we decided that I would travel to Moscow accompanied by my sister Yehudit.

Two of my mother's childhood friends lived in Moscow. One of them, closest to her heart, was Bertochka Gurevich. You've already been told of the magnanimous nature of the Gurevich family. During the famine and the winter shortage of 1941, when they were destitute refugees, they shared their bread with Asher and Vera. Now, we were about to turn to them again and ask them to host me—while sick with a contagious disease—and Yehudit in their home. Had we known at that time in what conditions they were living, I doubt we would have dared ask.

The next morning, my mother and I went to the post office in Kaunas, and after much effort on the part of the operator, we managed to reach Bertochka. My mother told her through her heartbreaking tears that her son, who survived the ghetto, was now in danger of going blind and the medicine for his disease could only be found with the great doctors in Moscow.

Bertochka could have responded in many different ways to our request: that there was no point in coming until they checked out what Moscow had to offer in the area of ophthalmology; that their living space was only one room of a five-room apartment, which they shared with strangers; that my disease was contagious and in such close quarters the risk of contamination was that much worse; or that she would have to talk to her husband and her daughter, who lived with her in poverty. There were other reasons that were better left unspoken over the phone about why a visit from us would not be welcome: in the eyes of the authorities, we were considered "foreigners," and one of the people in her apartment was a representative of "Big Brother."

However, amid the silent sobbing that accompanied the conversation, Bertochka's voice echoed: she would not refuse her childhood friend, and she could not be indifferent to my tragedy. As if apologizing, she added that she would host us as best she could in the uncomfortable conditions of her apartment. We would have to make do with the little that they had. For our arrival, she declared, the walls of her room would expand as if they had been made of rubber. That was Bertochka's promise.

One would expect that traveling from place to place within the borders of the country would merely involve buying a train ticket, but in the post-war Soviet Union, we quickly realized that this was not so.

We had no documents. The bureaucratic wheels turned very slowly. To speed up the process of meeting with someone who could arrange matters with the authorities, we had to pay an appropriate "commission." Even purchasing train tickets was a complicated matter. The trains were crowded with discharged soldiers making their way to the center of the country. Captain Dima Kuznetsov came to our assistance. He arranged a meeting for us with Colonel Shtulberg, who had a soft spot for me. He, after hearing our story and tribulations, took a sheet of paper and wrote in clear, concise writing—to the best of my recollection—this approximate message:

> To all Soviet authorities!
>
> Comrade Yochanan Fein, son of Menachem, who was adopted as a son of our regiment, has come down with a harsh disease of the eyes, and must immediately travel to Moscow for treatment. I am requesting all Soviet authorities to assist him in this and to respond to all requests regarding his illness.
>
> His sister, Comrade Yehudit Fein, will accompany him.
>
> Signed: Colonel Shtulberg
> Commander of the Guard Regiment [details of the regiment were noted]

Alongside his impressive signature, he placed his round, all-powerful seal.

This letter would work wonders along the way. With the Colonel's help, we acquired two tickets—and not in a crowded car, but a sleeper car.

After arriving in Moscow, we made our way to Taganskaya Street, where the Gurevich family was living. Bertochka opened the door, and we went in. In front of us was a long corridor with four doors, which led to the apartment's rooms. Each door belonged to a different tenant. In the first room on the left lived a couple without children, who were close to retirement age. The second room was that of the Gurevich family. Opposite their door, to the right, in a very small room, lived a single woman whom I saw very few times in the months that I stayed there. The door at the end of the corridor led to the Odintsov couple's two rooms.

Ivan Odintsov was a major in the NKVD (initials representing the "People's Commissariat for Internal Affairs"—later known as the KGB—the Secret Service) and served in the Taganka—a notorious prison located at the end of the street. I usually saw him in the morning when he returned from his night shift at the prison, where he interrogated unfortunate prisoners. The things he did and the sights he saw destroyed his soul and shortened his life. I don't know how he got into this line of work that strangled his conscience like a noose. He found relief for his pain in a bottle of vodka, as though the bitter liquid had the power to wash away mental torments. I saw him when he came back in the mornings, pale and exhausted from fatigue, the smell of alcohol on his breath, the neck of the bottle peeking out of his trouser pocket. He would drop into bed with his clothes on. People were wary of him, though they knew that he had no intention of hurting anyone. His wife, Yelena Petrovna, many years younger than he, spent her years beside him, without children or friends, languishing in the walls of her apartment and looking after her husband, whose health was deteriorating.

Years later, I was told—then, I did not know—that NKVD officers and their families had lived in all the apartments in that section of the complex. In the late 1930s, during the great purges, the men were all arrested and never returned to their loved ones. Their wives and children were left, cut off, confined to themselves, carrying their suffering without knowing its cause. Their friends, neighbors, and acquaintances avoided them at all costs, worried that they could

suffer the same fate. The best the victims' families could expect was
a discreet nod if they ran into someone they knew on the street. They
waited alone in their homes and wished for better days. Few were
lucky enough to be granted this in their old age.

Bertochka received us, two strangers, into this environment of
oppression, fear, and suspicion. She had promised my mother that
the walls of her apartment would expand, as if they were made of
rubber, for our arrival. Yet, the walls were made of concrete, and
refused to budge. They encompassed a sum total of sixteen square
meters. We crowded in with our belongings. The father, Vladimir,
whom we called Volodya, received us warmly and their daughter,
Rita, regarded us with curiosity.

We told them our stories, and we listened to theirs—stories that
deserved to be told but would never be written down.

Bertochka was practical. She said that it was time to go to sleep
because tomorrow would be a very busy day. She had inquired about
ophthalmologists and sadly informed us that "the eye god," Professor Filatov, did not live in Moscow, but in Odessa. Still, she had managed to make an appointment in the Ophthalmology Department at
a well-respected hospital. Yehudit and I also received an invitation
from another one of my mother's friends, Marie Sobol, to join her
for dinner the next evening after my appointment.

The Gurevich's room was arranged for sleeping; there was the parents' bed, a couch which Rita slept on, a piano, a table with chairs, a
wardrobe, and some other furniture—their room was very crowded.
Now two more folding beds had to be set out, and the floor of the
room was covered with beds and linen. They took turns getting ready
for bed. One at a time, they would each undress behind a divider,
getting under the covers as the next person went to change.

We got up early. Rita, dressed in her school uniform, two carefully made braids, and a satchel on her back, left for school. She was a
young girl from a family that was rich with love. Later on, she would
become a math teacher. Volodya, the father—with his photography
equipment on his back—went to work. He had once been a wealthy
owner of a photography studio, and the apartment on Taganskaya

Street was entirely theirs. Now they had been left with one room to share. Still, you never heard any complaints from them; those were kept to themselves.

We got to the hospital at the appointed time. We needed Shtulberg's letter here as well to avoid many bureaucratic obstacles, which were imposed on anyone who was not a resident of Moscow and had not yet registered for a Moscow address.

It was finally my turn. I was used to the examinations, and this one was no different than the ones before. The doctor spoke. Her words were an exact repetition of what the old doctor from our secluded town on the banks of the Nemunas had said, as though there were a conspiracy against me and all the doctors were insisting on saying the same thing. There was only one difference between them: This doctor's voice was cold as ice and sharp as a knife.

There was no good news from her. At this point, I could have successfully, described the properties of this sickness myself: "persistent," "stubborn," "prolonged," "tends to break out again," "lengthy treatment," "medical supervision," and other well-known issues. I especially did not like the lecture on the need to separate my clothes and towels from those of the rest of the household. It was as though she were saying, "You are a lost cause anyway; just don't infect anyone else."

The Sobols had asked us to come early. We were miserable when we came to see them that late afternoon. They were eager to hear of our stories from Lithuania, and they promised we would eat well since they managed to "get" good food. In the Soviet Union, it was more often said that food was *gotten* rather than *bought*—although it was, of course, purchased—because the shortages were so great that one had to go to great lengths to acquire it. They received us warmly, as though we were old acquaintances who had been separated by the war for a little while.

The four-member family lived in one relatively large room of the apartment. The room was divided by a closet, and we crowded around the table in the smaller section. The Sobols's oldest son had perished during the war. Their second son, who was older than me, was an artist and worked as a designer in the Yiddish theater. The youngest son (who I believe was approximately my age) was a student.

They did not stop asking questions, but we cut things short and told only the main points about what had happened to us. And so we came to the story of my illness and its tribulations. We had hoped to find a doctor who could work magic in Moscow, we said, but in the hospital, it became clear to us that magic had its place in the circus and the imagination.

Suddenly, the Sobols's faces lit up. "There is a doctor who works miracles in Moscow!" they said. We thought they were fooling us, but they grew more and more excited. What had they heard about this doctor? That he succeeded where others failed, that he returned light to blind eyes, that he had been invited to consult at the renowned Kremlin clinic, and other such superlatives.

There must have been a great deal of exaggeration in their words to cheer me up, but even if the praise was only partially true, it was enough to improve my mood. "Who is this man? How do we get to see him?" They said their artist son's girlfriend, their future daughter-in-law, was an ophthalmologist, and her father was that same doctor whose name preceded him.

The mother got up decisively, as if to say, "Enough talk." She went to the phone and dialed. After a few seconds there was an answer. She spoke to Dr. David Moiseyevich Zwilling and kept it brief. She spoke of a Jewish boy who had survived the Nazi occupation in Lithuania and now had come down with trachoma. "The doctors are pessimistic." From her answers, we understood what his questions were. "He came from Kaunas looking for a savior in Moscow. He is the son of one of my childhood friends and is a guest in our home right now."

Dr. Zwilling had questions, and I was called to the phone. "Has your sight been affected?" I answered in the negative. "Has there been any change to the condition of your eyelid?" Again, I answered no. "Is your eye red?" Yes, in fact my eye was red, I confirmed.

He agreed to accept me, and he would immediately check his schedule. "No, no," said our friend loudly, "don't check your schedule—see him now!"

He calmed her, saying, "One more day will not make things better or worse, and tonight we are going to the theater." They *got* tickets to the Bolshoi ballet.

But she whispered persistently, "The boy is in distress." She looked at her watch and calculated that more than two hours remained before the start of the performance. She continued: "David Moiseyevich, please see him now, encourage him, give him back the hope he has lost!"

In the end, Dr. Zwilling could not resist her pleas. We hurriedly went out to meet our savior-to-be. We promised our hosts that we would return to eat with them so that all of their effort in procuring the meal would not be in vain.

We got to Pushkin Square, and from there we walked a few minutes to Dr. Zwilling's apartment. Everyone—the doctor, his wife, and their daughter—stared at us as though we came from another planet, survivors of the ghettos and camps. We felt Jewish solidarity and tremendous amity. "We want to know everything; we want to hear everything," the doctor said, but the evening was short and the time at his disposal was utilized for the intended purpose.

Dr. Zwilling had a very refined face that radiated wisdom and authority. His gaze was deep and penetrating. I had to tell him what I felt in detail, the progression of the disease, how and when I was diagnosed with it. It came time for the examination. First, he examined my healthy eye and then the infected one. With great skill, he flipped the eyelid, pinned my eyelashes to my forehead with one hand and held the two magnifying glasses in the other hand. He looked through them for a long time. I was used to examinations, but this one seemed to me more important than its predecessors. The man in front of me was like the supreme court of appeals, and after the ruling was passed, there would no longer be anyone to appeal to. The washing of hands and wiping of the instruments with cotton balls soaked in a liquid reminded me again that my illness was one of the more infectious diseases.

"First of all," said Dr. Zwilling, "I want you to get the word *blindness* out of your dictionary. Who drilled that nonsense into your head?" he asked as if in wonder. Briefly and very concisely, he went on to say that the other doctors' words were certainly misunderstood by us or that they had exaggerated the dangers to convince me that neglect and lack of treatment would cause me to go blind. His words pleased me. "Trachoma," he said, "causes blindness only in extreme cases due to lack of treatment and neglect for many years." My situation was far from being similar to these cases, especially since I was about to receive some of the best treatment possible. He measured his words carefully. "Your disease is not in its early stages," he said. "It was diagnosed late, but, young man, I will heal you! This process will not take days or weeks, but months, and I will heal you!"

I wanted to keep listening to him. I wanted him to confirm that the words, "I will heal you" would become binding, like a contract that could not be breached. And to be absolutely sure of his optimistic diagnosis, I blurted out impertinently—regretting it immensely after—"It's incurable!"

Everyone was shocked at my outburst. Yehudit looked at me, stunned, and spread her hands in question. "Why would you say such a thing?"

There was an awkward silence. Dr. Zwilling looked at me angrily, pointed to the door, and ordered, "Get out of here!"

I did not move. I waited for someone to save me from the embarrassing situation I was in. Yehudit tried to approach him, but he refused to listen. His wife and daughter had tiny smiles on their faces, and I noticed that the doctor winked at Yehudit. This was a show! Angrily, he turned to my sister and asked, "What is the name of the village you came from?"

"Panemunė," she answered.

Now he sneered at me, "Did you finish medical school in Panemunė?" Everyone laughed.

My sense of humor came back as well. "No, in Kaunas," I answered.

"Tell me, Dr. Fein, why do you think that your disease is incurable?"

"I read it in journals," I answered.

"You read it in journals," he repeated what I had said, emphatically. "That's where you got all the nonsense about going blind?" Now he got serious, and he spoke to me in a manner that everyone could hear. "A requirement for the healing process," he said, pointing in a threatening manner, "is your faith that you will be healed. Your faith is what will give you the strength to fight and cope, and despite the suffering that is still to come, to persevere!" Dr. Zwilling ended the meeting, apologizing for his haste because they were late for the Bolshoi. He ordered me to come to his house the next day for another conversation and to determine treatment. Yehudit asked how much was due to him, but he refused and asked us not to embarrass him. On his way out, he stroked my head and said, "Poor Jewish boy."

Cheerful and happy-hearted, we returned to our hosts, called Bertochka, and told her the good news. She was beside herself with happiness. The next day, we registered ourselves with a Moscow address. I cannot recall if we were required to do so at a police station or in some other office. I also do not remember whether the registration was stamped in our passport or whether we were given a separate certificate, but I do remember that we succeeded with the registration procedures with relative ease: Shtulberg's letter worked like magic on everyone.

That evening, Yehudit and I went to Dr. Zwilling, and we did not go empty-handed: Bertochka gave us some of the food we had brought with us from Panemunė, a smoked country sausage and a round bowl of butter, to give to the doctor. He refused even this modest gift. This was no pretense—the resoluteness of his refusal was a testimony to his principles. I was asked to write my personal details clearly, my address and telephone, and he would arrange all the exhausting administrative matters with the hospital administration, using shortcuts accessible only to him.

Dr. Zwilling questioned us about our living conditions in Moscow. When he heard that we were five people crowded into one room, he was not surprised. He knew how people lived there, and he instructed me on how I was to behave. "Your hosts," he said, "are wonderful people." However, my illness, rightfully defined as very contagious, certainly intruded on their peace of mind. Not only was I to keep my things separate, especially my towels, but I was to do so demonstrably. Finally, we decided that at a certain hour I would arrive at the clinic on Gorky Street, where, at a spot near the entrance, I would wait for the nurse's arrival, and she would pave my way through the crowd that was pushing at the doctors' doors. All this would happen two days later: I was granted one day off before beginning the torture.

Bertochka was surprised that we brought the food back with us. We told her of Dr. Zwilling's adamant refusal to accept it. "Do people like this still exist?" she asked. After some thought she turned to me. "Yeika [that was how my name, Yochanan, was spoken in Russian], who do you think cooks the meals at the Zwilling's home?"

What did this strange question mean? I was surprised and answered, "Probably his wife."

"True," she said and went on. "So why are you bringing supplies to the doctor and not to the cook?" We laughed.

The next morning, I went to the Zwilling's house. His wife was surprised to see me. I handed her the package. "I beg you to accept it—they won't let me back home with the package," I said. She was embarrassed and refused halfheartedly. I left the package and ran out.

That same night, we saw a play, in fact, two plays. The artist, the Zwilling's intended son-in-law, got us two tickets to the Yiddish theater. The name of the play was *Freilachs*, which translates as *Joyous Occasions*. The performance, and the surroundings, made our heads spin. The hall was filled to capacity. There were military personnel in uniform in the audience. There were constant whispers heard throughout the performance, helpful explanations for those who did not speak Yiddish.

During intermission, the audience wandered around the entrance hall. Russian with a smattering of Yiddish was heard all around. I had never seen a play in the language of my home, the language in which I spoke my first words, the language they spoke to me in my crib. I felt good being a part of this audience. It took me only one evening among my Jewish brothers to revive the feelings that the years and circumstances of my life had dulled.

It was a great privilege to see the pearl of this Jewish culture before it was liquidated. The great actor Michoels, the head of the theater, was murdered in a staged car accident in 1948. With his death came the end of Yiddish theater in the Soviet Union. The theater's patron, Zhemchuzhina Molotov (originally named Pearl Karp), who was the wife of the foreign minister Molotov and a minister herself, was removed from her ministerial capacity and was arrested and tortured in the interrogation cellars. Jews were being forced out of the institutions of government, senior executive units, and the press, and Yiddish language education disappeared as though it had never existed.

In August 1952, the greatest Jewish writers, who were not dissidents, were executed; under Stalin, their having written in Yiddish was reason enough to murder them. In January 1953, a group of prominent Jewish doctors was arrested, accused of conspiring to murder the country's leaders by poisoning them. The death of Stalin in March 1953 saved them from execution. These were dark years in the history of Soviet Jewry. After Stalin's death, the darkness began to fade, but the hardships did not completely pass. But I digress— that Moscow evening of 1946, I was excited, happy, and emotional.

I remained awake a long time in my bed reviewing over and over the voices and scenes of the wonderful *Freilachs* play. However, later that night, another performance awaited us that was not *freilach* (a joyous occasion)—a small drama, for which no one had to *get* tickets.

It was after midnight when the sound of boots was heard in the stairwell, followed by a loud and persistent ringing at the door. The house was awoken—whose turn was it? The tenant of the room closest to the entrance opened up to the police. Voices: "There are foreigners visiting here—where are they?" Poor Bertochka—I can only imagine what thoughts must have been running through her head— and the relief the other tenants of the apartment must have felt. There were steps in the hallway outside our room and a knock at the door: "Open up, police!" We opened the door. Three policemen entered the crowded room into the spaces between the beds and brought with them fear and the cold of the night. Our clothes were strewn all over the room. The women were in their nightgowns. We felt our privacy being trampled; our honor was being crushed by gruff boots; we felt helpless. "Which of you are visitors from abroad?" asked the senior officer of the group.

In the most assured manner she could muster, Bertochka answered with the last of her emotional strength, "What visitors from abroad? Our guests are citizens of the Soviet Union!"

"Papers, please," ordered the policeman.

"Yehudit, give the police comrades your passports," said Bertochka. With our shaking hands, we rummaged through our belongings, which were strewn all over the room, looking for our documents. We turned these over to the police.

"You are registered?" asked the superior.

"You can see for yourself," answered Yehudit.

"What is the purpose of your visit?" he continued.

Bertochka regained her composure. "Yehudit, give the Colonel's letter to the comrades." We took out the letter—and what an impression it made, the imposing signature of the Guard Brigade Commander and the round, all-enabling stamp. The Colonel had written it perfectly, as if he had foreseen the arrival of the police: "a son of our regiment," "a harsh disease of the eyes," "he must immediately travel to Moscow for treatment," "I am requesting all Soviet authorities to assist him," etc.

The policemen were surprised and unsure how to treat us. The informant, apparently the building's janitor, knew nothing about us, and for his safety had found it necessary to report us to show his loyalty. After a long moment that felt like an eternity, one of the policemen spoke with ostentatious grace, "Everything's fine. Sorry for the interruption. Good night!"

———

In the morning, I went to the hospital. A nurse brought me into a room full of medical equipment, where Dr. Zwilling was waiting for me, together with another doctor. The other doctor was older and bespectacled, with a tuft of hair tied up in a small bun with pins that stayed put—a real Russian *babushka* ("grandmother"). "This is the boy I told you about," Dr. Zwilling said.

The examinations started. The two of them tested my eye alternately. They came to an agreement regarding which treatment they would proceed with. Both doctors spent a substantial amount of time on me. I felt as if I were more than just "another patient" of the dozens waiting in the clinic. They treated me like a parent treats an only child. Dr. Zwilling's treatment was painful. First, he put drops in my eye (numbing drops, presumably), and after a few minutes he spread a coarse powder on the eyelid, which felt as though it were made of finely ground glass. He started rubbing my eyelid with the powder. I had to wait a long hour until I could open my eye to the light of the sun. After a long time, I went home with a painful, bleeding eyelid.

That morning, Bertochka and Yehudit spoke at length. Yehudit wanted to go home to Lithuania soon. We knew I was to stay in Moscow for several months. She knew I had a home here—crowded but warm. My illness would be treated by a prominent physician, devoted and supportive. Now that these important matters had been taken care of, there was no longer any reason for her to remain by my side. She asked me if it would be okay for her to leave, and I said that it was. After the police's nighttime visit, when it became clear to all that we were not a danger to the security of the state, the neighbor, Yelena Petrovna, the wife of the officer, who lived in the relative luxury of two rooms, offered me a place to stay, for pay, of course, in her section of the apartment. There was no better solution.

Yehudit traveled home. She left me with most of the money intended for our expenses in Moscow, so even here I was a "wealthy" boy.

Several days later I underwent an operation. I arrived at "Moscow's large regional clinic." The huge yard and the hallways were packed with people. I felt like a tiny ant in this huge maze. I was sorry for those who had to wait there so long for salvation from a doctor, whereas I knew nothing of waiting in line and dealing with bureaucracy. Dr. Zwilling himself came out to greet me and placed his arm around my shoulder. Just like that we walked down the endless corridors to the operating room, while the crowd made way for us in awe. In order to justify this, from time to time, he would blurt out loud: "*Synok, moi synok*"—"My little son, my son."

That was how my healing process began in Moscow. It lasted for six months. I was operated on four times during that period, and I visited the clinic multiple times. I quickly became familiar with the treatment routine: numbing drops, rubbing the eyelid, surgery, and so on and so forth. Occasionally, I was also treated with injections. Experts assumed years later that I was injected with antibiotics, which at that time in the Soviet Union could not be obtained by ordinary mortals—only senior officials could expect to receive it in times of distress. There is no other explanation for Dr. Zwilling's success in healing my illness within a few months while other doctors predicted years of struggle without any promise of success.

When Dr. Zwilling informed me that my illness had been overcome, I was beside myself with happiness. I told Bertochka, and her tears were testimony to how emotional she was. We hugged like mother and son, and the Gurevich household celebrated with me.

It was time to leave Moscow, a city that I had come to love—the places where I had spent six months, to those who loved me and from those whom I loved.

Taganskaya Street, where I lived, was famous for two contrasting symbols: the infamous Taganka Prison and the Tagansky Theater. The theatre was not so well thought of at first, but later rose to prominence due to its management by the famous director, Yuri Lyubimov, and its actor Vladimir Vysotsky, the greatest protest singer in Russia. There was a riddle that was whispered: What is the difference between the Tagansky Theater and the Taganka Prison? The answer: one travels on his own to the theater and one is transported to the prison!

However, from the Gurevich home to the theater there was no need to travel: I could get to the hall in only a few minutes' walk. To me it seemed like a holy shrine. For the first time in my life, I was introduced to theater art. It was quite different from the entertainment I had learned to know before at the military regiment.

I visited this theater consistently and persistently, and when I finished the whole cycle of performances, I went to see them all again.

Sometimes, I frequented the theater twice a week. When one of the actors said his lines incorrectly in the play *Kashirskaya Starina,* my loud reaction aroused the attention of those sitting next to me. The ushers already recognized me. One of them once brought me backstage, introducing me as a hardworking critic.

To get tickets for the Bolshoi, one had to wait for many hours in line. Sometimes, when I lost patience or when they hung a Sold Out sign, I bought a ticket from scalpers. Here, I saw *Prince Igor, Swan Lake,* and *Eugene Onegin.* And so I discovered the source of the melodies that had been running through my ears for years.

While I stayed in Moscow, the chess capital of the world, I did not ignore my beloved game. At the time, there was a Moscow-Prague intercity competition, and each evening, I sat for hours in the famous Pillar Hall and followed the progress of the matches. When there was no competition, I spent days in the chess club at Gorky Park. Equipped with sandwiches and food I bought at the stalls, I played for hours until I was senseless. Now I had to part from all of these wonders. I did not know then that I would not return.

Sometimes you meet beautiful people who are good and pleasant, open-hearted and easy to talk to, passing friends. That was what it was like with Misha, whom I met at the automat, which to me was a technical wonder. In exchange for payment in coins stuffed into a slot, a selected sandwich was transported on a moving compartment in a transparent sleeve. Beside me stood a young, handsome man in a uniform without insignia—discharged from the military—rummaging in his pocket for coins. He was not near the sandwiches, but at a small tap that poured one hundred grams of vodka for a fee. I watched him, wanting to see the "marvels of technology" automatically pouring a drink. But when he could not find the money, he smiled sadly at me and spread his arms as if to say, "No matter, another time."

That was Misha. He took the crutches that he had leaned on the side of the machine and returned to one of the tables. I, on the other hand was a "rich" kid. I immediately bought one hundred grams of the sharp liquid and a sandwich, which I served to the handsome young man. Although somewhat embarrassed, he did not refuse.

"Thank you, my friend, but what about you?" I brought another sandwich and sat opposite him. "Where is your drink?" he asked. I explained that I was not accustomed to drinking. "I don't usually drink either," he said, "But this time I need to drown my sorrows." I did not ask why, but he continued to tell me that yesterday he parted forever from someone he loved very much, someone he had dreamed of while he was in the trenches. I felt so sad. "I couldn't meet her demands," he said.

And then I dared ask, "What demands did she have?"

"Actually, she only had one demand," he said bitterly. "She demanded that I stand on two feet and not on one! I left my second foot in the fields of Vitebsk, and I will not go back there to find it." I got chills.

Misha was a literature teacher. After a long period of inactivity, he was about to begin working at the start of the next school year at one of the high schools in the city.

Leading up to my return home, I said goodbye to him. I was a boy then. Even now, after fifty-seven years, I still think about that chance meeting and the inexplicable and short-lived relationship with the stranger, Misha. Perhaps it is because of the life story I had heard from him: a story about love. I have convinced myself that Misha ended up living a happy life.

I parted from Marie Sobel's family, thanks to whom I got to be in the care of Dr. Zwilling. I parted from Dr. Zwilling. I do not know what his status in Moscow's medical community was. Was he unique in his gifts, as described by those who loved him, or perhaps only an excellent doctor, one of many? For me, he was a savior who managed to heal me within months, while others predicted a years-long struggle. I don't think he saw my healing as something extraordinary, and it is doubtful whether my case merited special note to him.

I will not forget the humanity of his attitude toward me nor his ethical behavior. Throughout the entire course of my treatment, he vehemently refused to accept any payment from us—even the most symbolic—for his work. In answer to Bertochka's question, "Do people like this still exist?" I reply, "Absolutely, there are still good people."

I parted from the wonderful Gurevich family, and most of all, from the person who was like a second mother to me: Bertochka. Never Berta—always Bertochka. They suffered with me for six months straight, and I hope I was a good guest, that I behaved well, and that I was kind to them. Bertochka took care of me, guided me, cooked for me and fed me, laundered and ironed my clothes, and boiled my towels separately. She did all this in such horrible conditions, the crowded living space shared with others, yet they closed their ears to any compensation we offered. They were extraordinary in their good-heartedness—that was what the Gurevich family was like. "Do people like this still exist?" Not many, but there are still some.

On the return trip, I boarded the train and settled into a sleeper car, this time alone, without Yehudit. Looking out the window, I parted from Bertochka and Volodya. The engine blew a hair-raising whistle, and slowly the train left. I kept looking back at them, as long as I could still see them. They cried, and so did I. There are no happy partings.

I did not know then that I would never see them again.

28

A BRIEF RETURN HOME

IN JULY 1946, AT THE END OF THE SCHOOL YEAR, I RETURNED home. After living in the big city, Panemunė seemed like a small, dismal place. But soon enough I got back to my old self.

Both of my sisters got married while I was away. I already knew Vera's husband, Fima (Ephraim) Shagal: he was one of those who had frequented our home. Fima had served in Colonel Shtulberg's military brigade. He was discharged from the military a while after the end of the war, and once he married Vera, he never returned to his childhood home.

Yehudit's husband, Yeshayahu Zhelezniak (later he changed his name to Barzilai), was confined to the ghetto. In spite of his limp— a result of having had polio as a child—he jumped off the train on the way to the death camps and thus was the only one of his family to survive.

My two friends, Mikas and Eduardas, decided to continue their studies in the technical school in Kaunas. The school was located in the Green Mountain district, and I very much wanted to study with them. I remembered how hard it was at the beginning of my schooling in Kaunas, and I wanted to have at least two friends in my class to make me feel more comfortable there.

As a result of my illness and my long absence, I had not finished my studies at the school in Panemunė, and I had not acquired a diploma, which meant that continuing my studies at any institution was impossible. I was very concerned. After the war, I was forever playing catch-up with my studies. I was aware that learning a lot of material in short periods of time and using shortcuts was inferior to a continuous education. I knew that I fell short in my knowledge compared to other students my age and was determined to make my studies a priority.

I arranged my affairs at school as best I could. The principal, Mr. Grybauskas, was very kind to me and assisted me as much as possible. Some of the subjects had dates set for alternate exams, and for other subjects—if there was no one else taking the tests—I could take an examination individually, he said. I wrote down the dates of the exams and began studying with persistence and perseverance. I had quite a few meltdowns. I had all of a month and a half, and in such a short time it was hard to read all the material I had missed, and it was even harder to remember what I had read. Once again, I went back to the method of shortcuts and diagrams Gražina had taught me, which was, in truth, more sham than knowledge.

At the same time, I went to register at the technical school in the Green Mountain district. I had a letter from the principal of the school in Panemunė, explaining that due to my illness I was not able to take my exams with everyone else at the end of the school year. However, I was registered to take the exams on the alternate dates, and the principal expressed his assumption "based on knowing the student" that I would pass. At first, the school's acceptance was conditional; however, when I presented my long-awaited diploma, they accepted me fully.

As the start of the school year at Green Mountain, I moved in with Yehudit and Yeshayahu. My path to school was shortened and I was spared a lot of time and physical effort. They had a one-room apartment with a very large kitchen that was not connected to it. To get to the kitchen, one had to cross the stairwell. The kitchen became my room. It had a separate entrance, and I could manage my life undisturbed and do whatever I wanted. Here, I immersed myself in my studies until late at night. The large, bright table made it easier for me to do technical drawings, a subject I loved very much and in which I excelled.

My studies at the technical school were a step up for me. There was a huge difference between the perfunctory studies up till that point and the serious and demanding atmosphere of the studies that prevailed here. No more going to school just because "everyone goes." School now involved a great deal of serious work. I became obsessive in my studies, and all the rest of my activities were set aside. Games and idleness were no longer at the top of my daily schedule, and chess was reduced to a few minor games at the club, which were not supported by studying opening moves and participating in competitions, as they had been in the past.

On the weekends, I would return home to Panemunė and get together with my friends, and those were my only leisure hours. My violin was neglected as well. My dream to go back to studying and playing music under the tutelage of instructors was not possible. In fact, I did not make any progress—my playing might have even worsened. On occasion, I played for my enjoyment, just focusing on what I liked and knew by heart. There were no new additions to my repertoire.

Our small band, with Mikas and the drummer, got back together, but we did not play with the same intensity as before. On occasion, I played until the light of day at dance parties in order to keep my status as a "rich" boy. However, my status as a weddings-and-parties musician was no longer to my liking, and not too long after, I left it for good. Music apparently did not burn in my bones as a goal like no other, which in fact is a condition to working in this art. This was evidenced by Mikas. After a while, he abandoned his engineering studies and returned to his music. He later became a well-known composer in Lithuania, authoring dozens of melodies, some of which became popular songs known by all.

In 1946 and halfway through 1947, there was a turning point in my life. The activities that just yesterday were at the top of my world, were now set aside in favor of my studies and education. From a happy-go-lucky lad, I had become a mature, even somewhat reclusive boy. My classmates, boys my age and even younger, invested much of their energy in entertainment. They courted girls and were constantly trying to figure out where they would go dancing on the weekends, while I—if I found myself in a group of dancers—sat alone and contemplative, and any girl who dared to pull me to the dance floor would probably require orthopedic care afterward.

The 1946–1947 school year could have been my best as a student, but it wasn't to be. In May 1947, a family meeting took place: something bad had happened.

A few months before, my brother-in-law, Yeshayahu, switched jobs and became a bookkeeper for a new company, with better compensation than the last. It quickly became clear to him that the books were being mishandled and that his predecessors had left irregularities and a great delay in registering transactions. His efforts to bring things to order did not bear fruit, and the people around him did not make any effort to rectify the situation. Yeshayahu suspected that things were being done in the company that should not be done, and that the gaps between what was registered in the books and what was actually in the warehouses indicated theft and embezzlement.

In the meantime, Yeshayahu's friend, S. Bloch, a man with connections, came to Yeshayahu with a shocking story. He learned of an informant's letter to the police stating that Yeshayahu was responsible for the missing merchandise from the warehouse. Yeshayahu was accused of theft and embezzlement. The informant's name was also provided. He was one of the company's employees, who for some time had shown Yeshayahu open hostility. Bloch also said that he had the power to delay the handling of this letter for a number of days, by which time Yeshayahu was to disappear.

The chances of standing up in a Soviet court, proving your innocence, and being judged accordingly were slim. At that time, thefts were at their peak, and the punishments imposed on all those prosecuted were extremely heavy. Ten years was the norm. A bitter joke was told at the time: A new prisoner is asked by his cellmates why he is serving twenty years. The prisoner swears that he was sentenced for nothing, but his cellmates shoot back, "Liar, for nothing you only get ten years!"

There were very few ways of getting out of Lithuania at that time. The least dangerous way was by purchasing forged travel documents, which served Polish citizens who got caught in Soviet-controlled areas during the war and were now permitted to return to Poland within the repatriation agreement between Poland and the Soviet Union. Another way was to sneak across the Lithuanian-Polish border, which was not well guarded since it was a friendly border between two countries within the Soviet camp. There was also an escape movement via trains and cargo ships, which arrived in Western ports and cities. However, this path was available only to a select few.

Within such a short timeframe, the only way to escape was by stealing across the border. Initial inquiries indicated that it would require a physically agonizing trek on foot; Yeshayahu's limp and Yehudit's pregnancy placed some doubt as to whether they would be able to manage it.

Everyone was staring at me. Would I be willing to join them and encourage them by my presence, as well as by carrying most of their baggage—as little as it may be—on my back? I was already a mature young man, seventeen years old, capable of endurance. It was clear that our family was once again being torn apart, and it was equally clear where I was most needed. At this next crossroads that destiny sent our way, I stood beside Yehudit and Yeshayahu.

━━━

Frantic searches were initiated to establish contact with groups of smugglers who specialized in moving people from Lithuania to Poland. It was not easy because these groups acted in strict secrecy, using precise compartmentalization methods, and were careful not to be infiltrated by undercover agents.

The smugglers' organization operated in four groups: one group dealt with locating candidates for escape; a second group brought them to meeting points at the border; a third armed group transferred the escapees to Polish soil; and a fourth Polish group took them out of the border area.

In our distress, we turned to Jonas. He knew that of all those who had hidden with him during the war, not many were left in Lithuania—I may have been the last. He did not know how the others had escaped. Jonas had given Mania money to buy Polish citizenship and travel documents, but he did not know the identity of the people who helped smuggle her out. It occurred to him to refer us to Prapuolenis, the man who had brought Shima'leh Schames to him, the first of those saved.

It turned out that Jonas's intuition was correct. Prapuolenis in fact dealt in illegal matters, as he had always done under other occupations in the past. He knew us and spoke openly: he had connections to smugglers. The cost of our escape, along with bringing us to a city distant from the border within Poland, would be ten thousand rubles. The money would go through him. He would keep a small sum for brokering the deal, and the rest he would pass on.

He explained that the smugglers come to specific places without knowing the entire route. Everything worked according to a strict time frame. We asked how we would know that we were not simply being cheated and how would Prapuolenis know that once we turned over the money, minus his cut, that the anonymous smugglers would stick to their deal. How would he know that the smugglers would not rob or kill us on the way, with no one knowing what had happened to us?

For all the troubling questions, his response was but a single word: "Faith!" He provided a simple explanation: up until then, no one had been robbed or killed by the smugglers. An act of betrayal would become widely known, the news would spread like wildfire, and that would end the smuggling enterprise that was a gold mine for the smugglers.

We weighed the possibilities, but we did not have many options. Vera gave us the money for our escape from savings she still had from the flour business, and that same day we paid the money to Prapuolenis. After a nerve-racking week, we were given the exact logistical details of our escape.

The distance from Kaunas to the Polish border, about eighty-five kilometers, was divided into three segments. We would travel the first fifteen kilometers in a horse-drawn carriage where the one holding the reins had to be reliable and resourceful. At the end of this segment, we would have to wait for a contact person, who would tell us where the second meeting point would be. The journey to this second point we would need to make alone. There we would be picked up by a third person who would bring us in his carriage to the destination.

We were worried. Many parts of this plan seemed vague, and any hitch along the way could jeopardize the entire journey. Naively, we had assumed that from beginning to end, our transportation would be handled. It never occurred to us that we would have to make our own way to a yet unknown location. But these were the rules, and we could do nothing to change them.

In those days, the role that military trucks played in public transportation was still considerable: people would wait at pickup stops, and a soldier-driver would stop for them, collect the fare, and then bring them to their destination. Riding to the border to cross it on an army truck was, in our eyes, like voluntarily placing our heads in the lion's mouth. We decided to look for a private driver and not risk standing at the regular stops.

Our date for leaving was finally set: May 17, 1947.

That was how all my plans were ruined. My studies, which had seemed so regular and established, were once again cut short. Throughout the month of May, until my escape, I continued to attend school, but my heart just wasn't in it anymore. My thoughts were already on the road. My homework wasn't done properly, and my instructors felt it. I had to leave without saying goodbye to anyone, without shaking my friends' hands or looking them in the eyes. What would they think? What would they find out? Perhaps they would understand that I had no other choice, that I could not reveal my secret. I parted with my saviors, the Paulavičiuses, to whom I could say goodbye and embrace. They knew my secret.

I was headed on a voyage full of unknowns. Our family's home—even after our lives were flooded and it took its victims—remained a fortress, and now I had to leave it forever. The sunny spring days of May 1947 were terrifying for me. What would happen next—would we be caught or perhaps worse? Would we be able to continue our trek westward or would they give us a "free trip" eastward to Siberia?

May 16 was our last night at home. I didn't get a moment of sleep. Thoughts and reflections ran through my head—what would the next day bring? My feelings were intertwined with the words of the poet:

Что день грядущий мне готовит?	What will the coming dawn reveal?
Его мой взор напрасно ловит,	In vain my anxious eyes appeal;
В глубокой мгле таится он.	In mist profound all yet is hid.
Нет нужды; прав судьбы закон.	So be it! Just the laws which bid
Паду ли я стрелой пронзенный,	The fatal bullet penetrate,
Иль мимо пролетит она,	Or innocently past me fly.
Все благо: бдения и сна	Good governs all! The hour draws nigh
Приходит час определенный;	Of life or death predestinate.

A. Pushkin, *Eugene Onegin*, Chapter 6, 21
Translator: Lieutenant Colonel Henry Spalding, 1881

PART

III

29

GOODBYE, LITHUANIA

ON THE MORNING OF MAY 17, A FARMER ENTERED OUR HOME through the back door. After scrutinizing us with a glance, he informed us that he was going to Kaunas where he was told to pick up a few items. These were the code words. When we confirmed that we in fact needed a delivery, he asked if there were three items for him to pick up, and this we confirmed as well. Apparently, this was the man, along with his anonymous group, who held our fate in his hands.

We knew we had approximately twenty kilometers to travel with him (to a location I no longer remember), where we would be told where to go next on our own. We had recruited an acquaintance ahead of time, Dr. Shemkovitz, who owned a pickup truck, and who promised to join us at the meeting place. At the appointed hour, he would drive us to our next location.

Our possessions were already packed. My mother wanted us to take everything, and she tried to justify why each item was necessary. But we had to consider the size and weight of the packages. From life's experience, we knew of instances where not being able to part with belongings brought on tragedy. What we had packed would suffice for the next two weeks.

Vera came home from the mill to say her goodbyes. She returned to work as if nothing had happened, her facial expression giving nothing away. Parting from Mother was very difficult, she cried bitterly and expressed her pain: "God only knows if we will ever see each other again." She ordered us to watch over each other and always to stay together. We calmed her. We told her that if she didn't control herself, her expression would give away to any casual visitor that something had happened here.

And so we headed out. We had to leave Panemunė on foot as though it were a regular morning walk, head toward the Aleksotas section of Kaunas, and wait there for the wagon driver who would pick us up. It was my last look back at my father's house, and my last steps on Vaidoto Street: where I played as a kid, where they led my brother to his death, and where Yehudit was marched under guard to the trains. We passed the Jewish cemetery, then the pit where I was hidden and the Paulavičius house. I took one last look back before everything disappeared from our view.

The wagon driver was waiting for us. I sat in the front passenger seat, while Yehudit and Yeshayahu sat in the back. We rode in silence. After a two-hour ride, we arrived at an inn. The pickup truck was waiting for us on the side of the road. We sat on one of the benches, and we were surprised to see another group of five people waiting. They sat on one of the other benches. Among them was our friend, Sarah Urin. We knew she wanted to flee Lithuania, and she also knew that Yeshayahu was to escape. Yeshayahu had even stayed in her house for a few nights to avoid arrest. Without ever having discussed it, using different agents who worked independently of each other, we were brought to the same place to escape.

This was a hitch. With so much compartmentalization and conspiracy, no one knew what each other was doing. The two agents gathered their groups on the same day, in the same place, at the same hour. As I was later told, the optimal number of people for crossing the border was a group of three, and certainly not more than five. Small groups of this size could be brought in a wagon with their possessions. Our group of eight people was too large and could possibly draw attention to us.

In the second group, in addition to Sarah Urin, were two young men whose names I do not remember and the Gertner couple. Like Yehudit, Mrs. Gertner had set out on her way despite her pregnancy. After a long wait, a man arrived. He identified us easily but was shocked by the size of the group. The pickup truck on the side of the rode aroused his suspicions, but when he realized that it was ours, he explained to the driver where he was to take us, and then disappeared.

We drove for about an hour and stopped at the side of a small market square that was winding down for the night, near a few village inns in the town of Kalvarija. It was about fifteen kilometers from the border. So that our large group would not arouse suspicion, we split up into two small groups: we sat with our friend Sarah on one bench, and the other four sat some distance away from us. One of the carts in the market was already waiting.

The driver also expressed his displeasure with the size of the group and was trying to figure out how he would take us. Finally, he decided that four people would be on his cart, and the others would walk, two-by-two following the cart. Occasionally the two groups would change places. All our belongings were put in the wagon. We were instructed to say, if asked, that we were going to a wedding in a certain village near the border.

The trip was about three hours long and went at the pace of those who were walking. Yehudit and Mrs. Gertner speculated over what was less dangerous to their pregnancies—bouncing around in the cart on the dirt path or walking. I chose to walk and did not change places with any of the passengers.

As we got closer to the border, tensions grew, and the driver kept staring at us nervously. We stopped in a small grove at the edge of a village. The road then crossed a wide-open field and wound toward another village, the last on our way, only a few kilometers from the border. The presence of our group in this area during the evening hours could have aroused suspicion, especially since we were not residents of the area. We still had the excuse of traveling to a wedding in the nearby village, but beyond that, if we were to come across a military truck or a foot guard, we would be in big trouble. The border guards knew the local farmers, and our clothes could easily give away that we were not villagers. But so far, our luck was with us, and we had not encountered any people in uniform.

Following the driver's instructions, four of us got in the wagon—
our party of three with our friend, Sarah, while the others were told
to wait in the grove. The wagon continued on its way. After crossing
the field, the path began skirting the edge of the forest. At this point,
the driver became tense. He scanned his surroundings. When he was
convinced that there were no people and no vehicles approaching, he
whipped the poor horse, and with a sudden sharp turn, he steered
the wagon into the forest.

After we had gone deeper into the forest and were immersed in
darkness, we stopped. We got off the wagon and were ordered to
wait in the bushes. The driver then drove back to pick up our four
waiting companions. After a nerve-racking wait, we heard the cart
approaching and thundering into the forest. All eight escapees were
together again.

The farmer tethered his horse to one of the trees, fed him, and
continued leading us on foot into the forest. For about the next half
hour, carrying our belongings in the dark, we encountered broken
branches and prickly bushes, kept falling and getting back up, and
strained our eyes so as not to lose each other. We walked until we
reached a group of shrubs. We paused there. We were surrounded
by tall trees, one of which stood out in size. Here, the driver ordered
us to lie down, keep quiet, and wait a few hours until the arrival of
those who would help us cross the border. The driver then disappeared into the darkness.

Tired and sweaty, we dropped to the ground. Through the treetops, the moon occasionally peeked out at us. We whispered, es-
timating that many dangers were already behind us. We put our
belongings under our heads and laid down. We felt confident that
no one would look for us in the thick of the forest. We fell into a
deep sleep.

I felt a forceful jolt. I opened my eyes in alarm. In front of me
stood an armed man who ordered me to wake my friends. I got up
and did as he instructed. We shivered with cold. In front of us stood
three armed men. One spoke firmly, but in a whisper. We were told
what was ahead of us and how we should behave. We would walk

until we reached the edge of the forest, where we would have to cross through an open area about half a kilometer wide. That was the border. Across that plot of land, he explained, there were alarm wires that must not be tripped. In order to hide them, a layer of sandy soil was poured over the alarm wires, and on a clear night like this, they could be identified relatively easily. We had to try our best not to drag our feet, but to step from above so that even if we stepped on one, we would be less likely to set it off. I thought of my brother-in-law, Yeshayahu. His limp was severe, and when he was tense it worsened even more.

I loaded as much as I could on my back. We started walking. Traveling through the forest at night was arduous. After a while, we finally made it to the border. We stopped and were allowed to rest but only standing up, so we would be ready to take off at a moment's notice. The smugglers waited, looked around and scanned the area. When a cloud obscured the moonlight, the signal was given.

We walked single file. We were forced to walk very fast, almost to the point of running. Our eyes searched for the hidden alarm wires, and we concentrated on lifting our feet. So with great tension and strain, especially for my brother-in-law and the two pregnant women, we reached a row of trees behind which stood a few single buildings.

We hid behind a farmhouse and leaned against the barn wall, thoroughly exhausted and breathless. That was when the head of the group asked us to pay him. He claimed that because of the size of our group, his men had taken upon themselves a double risk, and for this they had to be compensated. We tried to argue and explained that the size of the group wasn't our fault, but a demand supported by weapons always prevails over arguments supported by logic.

A farmer came out of the hut, insisting that we end the argument. A terrifying howling of dogs pierced the night air. The ensuing cacophony came to our rescue. With no introduction, the farmer ordered us to run after him to the threshing floor. Then he turned to the armed group and demanded, or perhaps begged them, to let us leave. It was a commotion that could attract guards from the border. Frightened by the noise, the smugglers turned around and disappeared into the darkness of the night.

After a while, everything calmed down. In the light of an oil lantern, we were led to the threshing floor, where we fell weary and slept until the morning light. That was how we passed our first night in Poland.

———

Our group was perhaps the last to successfully steal across the Lithuanian-Polish border. The group that tried after us tripped the alarm, and their people got turned around. They were returned to Lithuanian land where they were caught by Soviet border guards. After this failure, security at the border was increased, and the group of smugglers stopped their activity.

The KGB invested a lot of energy into tracking down the network, and after two years, in 1949, the investigators followed and arrested Prapuolenis. According to him, as published in a newspaper interview on April 6, 2002, "*Kauno diena*"—"A Day in Kaunas," the prosecution was unable to prove his guilt. That was how his relatively easy penalty could be explained: he was given ten years in prison, which he served in the infamous Norilsk camps. He was freed in 1955 after Stalin's death (1953).

———

About two years after our escape, in the spring of 1949, my mother and my sister Vera, with her baby in her arms, were exiled to Siberia.[1] They were taken under arrest about six thousand kilometers away to a remote location near the city of Irkutsk, west of Lake Baikal, about four hundred kilometers from the Mongolian border, where they were integrated among exiles from previous generations.

Fima, Vera's husband, against whom no deportation order was issued, accompanied his family as a free citizen and became a voluntary exile. A bundle of objects, hastily packed on the night of the arrest, was all they were allowed to carry with them. The story of their tribulations is part of the agony of millions of people who were uprooted from their homes and resettled in the seemingly never-ending vastness of eastern Russia.

On occasion, they would write requests for pardons to the authorities, but all their requests were ignored. Finally, one such request, in 1955, following Stalin's death (1953), was accepted, and they were permitted to return to Lithuania. They did not return to our home. In a modest apartment in Kaunas, they had to start their lives over again.

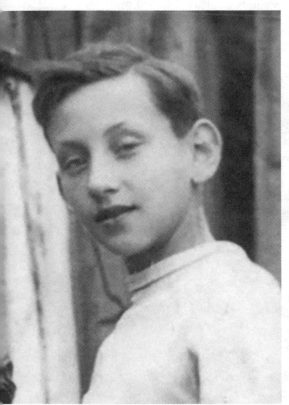

Left, Yochanan after the war, 1945; *right*, Yochanan in Poland, 1949.

30

∽

STRANGERS IN POLAND

WE STAYED IN THE FARMER'S HOUSE NEAR THE BORDER FOR about ten days. We were not allowed to walk outside, so that we would not be seen by others. The men had to remain on the threshing floor and the women in a cabin. We counted the days.

According to the plan, the farmer was to take us to Suwalki, about thirty-five kilometers from the border. Traveling close to the border was dangerous for those who did not speak the language and did not carry proper documentation. The Polish guards did not cover the entire border, but they did patrol the border area and knew the locals. Transporting strangers in broad daylight was therefore impossible. Traveling at night required an explanation, and an explanation could only be given two days a week: market days. On those days, the peasants went to sell their agricultural produce.

The trip to Suwalki required approximately three and a half hours, and to get to the market early, farmers would leave around three o'clock in the morning at the latest. The patrols were accustomed to seeing a lot of wagons on the road on market days, so they were not as alert. The farmer took the first group—everyone who had joined us except for Sarah, who stayed with us. When the farmer returned in the evening and spoke of their success, we were happy and encouraged.

Before our trip, we were presented with a bill for the hospitality. Prices for food and lodging on the hay of the threshing floor were calculated according to the rates of a decent hotel. Our money was made up of two universal currencies, which in those difficult times would maintain their value. These currencies were known in Yiddish as *Harteh un Veicheh*, in other words, "hard and soft." The hard money was gold coins from the Russian Tsars' era, and the soft money was US dollars.

We also needed Polish money to continue our journey. That was when we realized that the farmer, in addition to being a shrewd "hotelier," was also a money changer. In exchange for our "room and board," we had to part with a considerable amount of the money we had brought with us. We were afraid that if we needed other intermediaries at such rates, we would run out of our meager amount very quickly.

It came time to leave. The large cart, harnessed to two horses, was loaded with milk, homemade butter wrapped in pieces of cloth, cheese, eggs, and other agricultural products, which when sold would be far less profitable than his smuggling business. We all wrapped ourselves in coarse woolen coats. The men also wore country hats, and the women wrapped woolen scarves around their heads. Bundled in these clothes, we went out into the chill of the night. In these dark hours, we looked like real villagers, and only a check of our documents could reveal that we were not.

I sat by the farmer, and the others sat behind us. We hadn't been able to sleep that night, but very quickly the motion of the cart on the road rocked the travelers in the back to slumber. This was a good thing: their sleep saved them from unnecessary anxiety. After a few kilometers, the horses stopped, reared on their hind legs, and made frightened snorts; they sensed danger, felt the presence of other people. Even the horses knew that meeting up with unknown, armed people on an isolated path at night meant danger. The farmer prayed for help from his God and crossed himself.

Within the bushes was a small point of fire: a lit cigarette. My heart was pounding. Two armed Polish soldiers came toward us. Standing by the side of the road, one started interrogating us: "Who is driving?"

"Malinowski," replied the farmer.

"Where to?" he continued to investigate.

"To the market—*Na targi*," he replied.

With a wave of his hand, the soldier signaled us to continue and called out to us, "May God bless you!" The farmer answered with a blessing and whipped the rebellious horses. The role of the guards was to capture escapees like us, but the routine of the market days lulled their alertness. How good it was that my fellow travelers were asleep.

Very early in the morning, we arrived at the Suwalki market square, which was full of people and bustling with activity. We straightened ourselves out and removed the farmer clothes. What next?

The farmer pointed to the corner of the street where a few canvas-covered trucks stood surrounded by a group of travelers. These trucks were for intercity transportation. We stood in line, paid the price of the ride, climbed a small ladder, and sat on one of the four wooden benches available for the passengers: two along the length of the sides of the truck and two back-to-back in the middle. After about two hours, we arrived in Białystok and stood on the street of an unfamiliar city with no documentation and no ability to speak the language.

Yehudit's Polish was less than basic—we were like mutes with no address to turn to and no friends to guide us. Our crumpled clothes, the pallor of our tired faces, and the bundles in our hands were all witnesses saying, "They are strangers; they are not from here."

We wandered down the street and looked for a Yiddish-speaking Jew. After a while, we met two Jews who spoke Yiddish. We told them that we had arrived from the Soviet Union a little while ago, and we were looking for a Jewish institution through which we could get some assistance. The two knew that there was indeed a Jewish organization that handled refugees and various types of homeless people, and they gave us the address. We dragged ourselves there with the last of our strength.

Our new home was a refuge for refugees, repatriates, and displaced persons who needed temporary shelter and assistance through their wanderings. The war had ended two years ago, and survivors of the camps and returnees from the Soviet Union were still wandering across the country in search of their future. Here, we were greeted by the person in charge of the place, who heard from us a summary of our story. To our credit, we gave him as few details as possible. He promised that the next day his superiors would visit here, people with authority and the ability to help and guide us with options for our future. What he could do for us now was give us a place to stay, an initial shelter until our status was clarified. We did not have much choice, so we accepted his offer.

They took us into a hall that had approximately twenty beds, but only a few were taken. We chose for ourselves beds in the corner of the hall, dropped our things, sat down on the beds, and were silent for several minutes until we calmed our nerves and released some of the tension. As we regained our composure, we realized we were hungry. It had been hours since we had had anything to eat or drink. Yeshayahu and I went out to a nearby market square to buy food, and the women went to find a place to get washed up. In a store right next to our lodgings, I bought a chess set, and after several hours of rest and idleness, we got ready for a good night's sleep. It was agreed that the next day, when the supervisors came who could help us, we would ask them to get us documentation of some kind—something in writing and stamped, similar to the all-enabling letter from Colonel Shtulberg, to provide us with a shred of legality.

The next morning, a three-person entourage visited our lodgings: a superior, whose behavior attested to his position, and his two assistants. They were reserved and grave. Their conversation with us in Yiddish was like an interrogation of an unfavorable and was hostile in nature. We did not understand the reason, but we realized that we should be very careful in providing information. However, as it turned out, the man knew everything about us. From what he said, it was clear that our four companions, who had arrived in Białystok about a week before us, told anyone who was willing to listen—out of basic unfamiliarity with local politics—about the heroic deeds of eight people who had succeeded in deceiving the border guards of two states. They said that our whole group was Zionist and that our goal was to reach the up-and-coming Jewish state: Israel. This did not make a favorable impression on the heads of the organization.

After our conversation, we came to the conclusion that we would not be given any assistance, and that we were really not wanted there. Although we were not driven out, it was clear to us that we had to leave, but we did not realize how urgent this was.

At that time, a rigid communist regime had not yet been introduced in Poland, and the Communist Party, which was dominant in the government, had joined forces with several other parties. Relatively extensive grassroots Jewish political activity was still permitted. Out of the ruins of Jewish culture in Poland arose Zionist parties. The War of Independence in Israel in 1948 was perceived by the government as an anti-imperialist struggle, and the regime somewhat sympathized with the left-wing Zionist parties. It was a short-lived sympathy that would gradually dissipate and vanish by the end of 1949.

The Zionist parties, which operated politically and ideologically in Poland at that time among the surviving remnants of Polish Jewry, promoted the idea of *aliyah*—Jewish immigration to Israel (then still Mandatory Palestine). This put them at odds with the Jewish branch of the Polish People's Party—the Polish Communist Party, which at that time formed part of the ruling coalition, but would soon take total control of the government. The party's Jewish members were called by the derogatory name *Yevsekim* (short for Yevrcyskaya Sektsia—the Jewish Section). They were the most committed opponents of Zionism within the party, fiercer than the mainstream party. In their ideological struggle they brought to bear all the administrative and material means available to them as members of the government.

A short while after the three visitors left, we were taught this political lesson by a Zionist activist from the HaShomer HaTzair[1] movement, who had heard about our arrival at the lodgings and rushed over to warn us of danger. We learned from him that we were in lodgings controlled by the local Jewish communists, which accounted for the coldness and loathing demonstrated toward us during their visit. We were not only Zionists in their eyes, political opponents who were not worthy of their support, but worse: a criminal group that had come to Poland illegally. According to the activist's assessment and inside information, the heads of the organization would have to inform the government authorities of our presence, either out of ideological motives or the need to show loyalty, since the affair could reach the authorities through other sources. What were we to do? We had to run for our lives immediately so there would be no one to report and no one to arrest.

Most of our belongings were still packed. We replaced those things that we had taken out for immediate use, snuck out of the lodgings, and followed the man, who led us to the train station. We kept our distance from each other so as not to stick out as a group, but we made sure to stay within eye contact. A quick pace was required for us to catch the train to Warsaw, which was about to leave the station. All of this happened unbelievably fast, in just minutes.

We gathered in the square near the ticket office. The man hurried to purchase four tickets for us and quickly left the place. We offered to reimburse him, but he refused. And again we ran into a problem: in the speed and tension of our departure, we forgot to ask the good man for an address in Warsaw where we could turn for help. Now we would once again have to wander the streets of a strange city to find a place to sleep, and in light of our bitter experience in Białystok, we already knew that this was no simple matter.

The trip was difficult. We were crammed into a packed railway car, at the entrance of which there was no orderly queue but a violent and powerful crowd. In addition, we had a language barrier: we couldn't complain or argue with anyone who pushed us or stepped on our feet. It was as though we were mute. It was also important that we be crammed into the same car so that we would not lose each other. Much of the way, we stood next to other passengers, and only later on, when people got off and before others got on, we managed to get a seat. We kept our eyes down and pretended to be asleep so that no one would want to make conversation with us and ask unwanted questions.

The first person we met in Warsaw was a street photographer, who insisted on photographing us four strange people (Sarah was still with us). When we refused, he moved on. Too bad—it could have been a sad reminder of our suffering. After walking back and forth in an attempt to locate a Yiddish speaker, a wagon stopped near us, and the driver offered his services. Yehudit had a basic understanding of Polish. She had worked for a few months in the post office of the Polish town of Turun, so she became our chief spokeswoman. In a language that was more Russian than Polish, she asked the driver if he knew the address of any Jewish or Zionist organization. The poor driver found himself dragged into Jewish politics, but even still, he very badly wanted to drive us and earn a few *złotys* (Poland's official currency before the Euro). "Yes, I know a Jewish place where people pray—is that what you mean?" We confirmed that this was indeed what we needed: a prayer.

And so we rode in a wagon in the ruined streets of Warsaw, viewing scenes that we had never seen, ruin and destruction everywhere, a terrible reminder of the Warsaw Uprising that engulfed the city from August to September 1944. We finally arrived at a partially destroyed building that had a Hebrew and Yiddish sign above the door. A Jewish bearded man wearing a yarmulke greeted us.

We had one request for him: Did he know the HaShomer HaTzair movement's address? We explained that we had been active in the movement in our youth in Kaunas, before the Russians arrived, and one of their activists had extracted us from a great deal of trouble in Białystok. In fact, the man did know an address for the movement, "Thirty-Eight Poznańska Street," he said.

We then asked if we could leave our things with him while we looked for the address to be free of the burden and avoid suspicion. The man agreed with some reservations; he did not want to be responsible for our belongings. It was decided that I would stay back to keep an eye on our things while Yehudit, Yeshayahu, and Sarah would go on without me.

I was brought to a small hall furnished with five wooden bunk beds with straw mattresses on them. In the empty part of the hall there were benches and stands, enough for a minyan[2] to pray. The hall's appearance was neglected and shabby; the rotted wooden floor had not been washed for quite some time. A small room next to the hall served as an office for the man in charge, who welcomed us warmly. I gathered our belongings onto one of the bunks and sat beside them in a gloomy mood. The hours seemed to drag on forever.

After a long while, Yeshayahu returned with two young men at his side, who came to get me and our things. My misery passed instantaneously. Yeshayahu told me that everything was working itself out and that the HaShomer HaTzair people, headed by Haika Grossman, the movement's driving force, who was a fighter and member of the underground, had welcomed them in a friendly manner. (Years later, she would become a member of the Israeli parliament, the Knesset.) Alongside the two locals, who spoke Polish, I felt confident. We stayed for a few days at the municipal kibbutz of HaShomer HaTzair in Warsaw, where we found food and a safe roof over our heads.

The next obstacle we had to overcome was getting from Warsaw to Łódź. Haika Grossman explained that she would do her best to take care of everything but that we could not stay in Warsaw. We had no documentation and didn't speak the local language, and they had no place for us to stay. She told us that the main offices and leadership of the movement were in Łódź, as well as the Mother Party newspaper, the Jewish Workers Party, and a concentration of activists, all of which were located within a considerable Jewish cluster where we could easily intermingle. We made our way to Łódź accompanied by a local activist, who was well acquainted with day-to-day life in Poland and in whom we felt some confidence.

Łódź was the last stop that Yehudit, Yeshayahu, and I made together. From here on, our paths to Israel diverged. Yehudit, Yeshayahu, and Sarah were housed in an activist's apartment on Wschodnia Street. Yehudit and Sarah were expected to manage the place and take care of the food and other needs of the tenants, a group of about ten people. My brother-in-law Yeshayahu, who was an expert at his profession, was employed as an accountant at the party newspaper: *Mosty* (*Bridges*). In exchange for their work, they were paid with a safe roof over their heads, or as safe as could be arranged under their circumstances. The HaShomer HaTzair movement provided protection for them and promised to do its best to look after their future.

I was taken to live in the movement's kibbutz in Łódź, on Kilińskiego Street. I was the only boy in a group of adults. I couldn't go out to work and earn my keep because I didn't have documentation or speak the language. I helped out as much as I could in the house. However, my idleness and wasted days put me in a terrible mood. I had to minimize my expeditions outside the lodgings, as my situation dictated, and I felt like a prisoner: a young man with no documents and no identity.

Poland was just a stopping station on our way to Israel (then Mandatory Palestine), and we knew that the sooner we left, the better it would be. In the three years after the war, tens of thousands of Jews had left Poland in every possible way, some with passports issued by the country, and others by very roundabout methods. Poland was a massive graveyard for its Jews and the Jews of Europe in general; its soil was soaked with Jewish blood. If the events of the past were not enough, the country was flooded with anti-Semitism and murder even now that the war was over. The events reached a peak at the beginning of July 1946, when a mob murdered forty-two Jews in the city of Kielce, and the local police stood by and even helped the murderers. Such atrocities hastened the departure of Jews from Poland more than any Zionist propaganda.

That was the situation and atmosphere in which we found ourselves as illegal residents. The question of how we could get out of Poland hovered in all its severity. Yehudit's pregnancy was progressing, and in that situation, stealing across borders seemed impossible. The only practical thing for us would be to obtain personal documents, which could be used to submit an official request for exit visas with a Polish passport. Indeed, our patrons succeeded in finding us documents from repatriates who had left Poland without their papers. My brother-in-law's name Yeshayahu was changed to Bernard Gar, my sister was no longer Yehudit, but Chaya Ginsh, and I became Chaim Krengel.

My certificate was problematic; it made me three years older, which did not match my outward youthful appearance. After a while, however, they found me a more appropriate certificate. I became Avraham Wolner, the son of Moshe, a native of Vilnius, and with this borrowed identity, the details of which I learned well, I spent three years in Poland.

A few months after we arrived in Poland, my uncle, my mother's brother, Isser Braude, a Norwegian citizen, joined us in Poland. He had managed to acquire Norwegian entry visas for us, which enabled us to put in applications for Polish passports. Norway would also be just a stopgap in our wanderings, but the need to escape Poland forced Yehudit and Yeshayahu to move on, further north.

Yehudit gave birth to her first-born son, Reuven, in Poland, in November 1947. His certificate listed him as illegitimate because no one knew that Bernard Gar was Chaya Ginsh's legal spouse. The legal became illegal and the illegal legal.

After a few months, the long-awaited Polish passports were issued, and Yehudit, Yeshayahu, and their son left Poland in February 1948. They stayed in Norway for about a year and a half. In July 1949, they immigrated to Israel. This ended their wanderings and tribulations; they finally reached a safe haven where they could build their future. I did not go with them. Despite my mother's request that we not split up, we parted ways.

31

AT THE CHILDREN'S HOME

I SPENT A FEW WEEKS AT THE KIBBUTZ IN ŁÓDŹ, WHERE MY days were filled with idleness and boredom. I read a book of Russian poetry, and I played chess with anyone who had time. But mostly, I was alone. There were those who discussed my situation and promised to find a way to ease my isolation.

While I was in Łódź, I met Peretz Kaganovsky, a young man about two years older than me. He was educated, witty, humorous, fluent in Russian, Polish, and Yiddish, and a counselor in the HaShomer HaTzair youth camp in Łódź. Peretz was the son of a famous Yiddish writer, and my acquaintanceship with him eased my loneliness significantly. It was the beginning of a wonderful friendship.

One day, a representative of the movement's main leadership came to see me. We spoke in Yiddish. He questioned me about my hobbies and what I liked to do. Finally, he suggested that I join the movement's children's home in Lower Silesia. The name of the place was Biały Kamień, near the city of Wałbrzych. "Among young people, including a group of your peers, you will feel great," he said. He added: "In a group of dozens of children you will not stick out as a foreigner, and not knowing the language will be less of an issue." I agreed to the suggestion without any hesitation. I told Yehudit of my decision. She understood and gave me her blessing. This was the beginning of my separation from Yehudit and Yeshayahu. A few days later, Chaim Mendel, the director of the children's home, came to Łódź on business, and I made the long trip from Łódź to Wałbrzych with him at my side.

The children's home was in a handsome two-story house, a kind of small palace built in the Bauhaus style with ten or twelve rooms. There were large courtyards around the house for formations and games. Next to them was a garden of fruit trees. There was another two-story building in the courtyard, with a storeroom on the ground floor and a small, enclosed hall, which apparently served as a stable for horses or a garage for the owner's car. The second floor was where the maintenance workers had once lived, but it was now occupied by the counselors. The front of the house was adorned with two proper terraces, one on each floor, and the entire complex was enclosed by an iron fence and tall vegetation. Apparently, a well-to-do man had left this property and fled for his life with the retreating Wehrmacht from the Allied forces that were fast on his heals.

After the war, the place served as a children's home for the HaShomer HaTzair movement and a stopgap on the long and illegal road to the Land of Israel, then known as Mandatory Palestine, where the British still ruled. At the beginning of 1947, after the previous group of the movement members had departed, a crowd of about fifty youth found their temporary home in this handsome complex. Few of them had survived with one of their parents; the rest were orphans. A small group of them returned from the Soviet Union. The others had survived the Nazi occupation in Poland, either through the help of a few good-hearted Poles or compassionate peasants, or by wandering from village to village, begging for money and food.

A unified group of about twenty-five children came from another Jewish children's home, which was established in the town of Otwock in 1945. It was an initiative of the local Jewish Committee, with most of its budget coming from the American Jewish Joint Distribution Committee (also known as the Joint or JDC). The Otwock home was run by Luba Bielicka-Blum (the widow of Abraham "Abrasza" Blum, one of the leaders of the Bund[1] in Poland and one of the leaders of the Warsaw Ghetto uprising), along with a team of excellent teachers and assistants. There, children went to a local school, they received tutoring at home when necessary, and enjoyed extracurricular activities. They sang in a choir, learned dance and music, received proper medical treatment, and were educated in the spirit of

the Yiddish culture. They instilled in them the ideals of good citizenship and loyalty to the new social order envisioned by the movement,
which was a regime of justice and brotherhood among the nations.

But all those noble ideals did not stand up to reality, as the children saw and experienced themselves. In early July 1946, an armed
military unit surrounded the house in Otwock, and snipers were
placed on its roof. These were the days following the pogrom in
Kielce, and the army was deployed to defend the Jewish children's
home. Two years after the war, the lives of Jewish children in Poland
still required protection. The pogrom was a traumatic event, in the
wake of which tens of thousands of Jews emigrated from Poland. It
was deeply etched into the hearts of the children. There were also
daily reminders of the hatred of the Jews: when the children marched
in and out of school, they were attacked with stones by groups of
Polish youth, and physical confrontations within the school were
routine.

Therefore, when emissaries of HaShomer HaTzair secretly arrived
at the children's home in Otwock to convince the children to immigrate to Mandatory Palestine, their work was easy. As a result of this
secret activity, a group of about twenty-five children were transferred
from Otwock to Biały Kamień.

The living conditions in their new home were far worse than in
their former residence. There were cramped quarters and poorer
food, and their studies were interrupted. Yet their spirits were high.
Even when the promises of rapid immigration fell through and the
dates for their departure were delayed time after time, they kept their
optimism, and their faith in their counselors was not undermined.

I was exposed to this house, to its special atmosphere, and to the
wonderful group of youth that lived within its boundaries when I arrived there in June 1947. For the first time since my early childhood, I
found myself in a group of Jewish youth. I was no longer a stranger,
different from the rest. I was one of them. I no longer had to hide my
origins, nor did I have to behave in a subdued manner so as not to
stand out. I could be open about who I was with my head held high.
I no longer had to go by my borrowed name, Juozukas, which was
given to me by my Lithuanian saviors. Now, I could go by my Jewish

name, Yochanan, as my parents had named me at birth. Even though according to the documents my name was Avraham Wolner, none of my new friends knew that—only the house manager was aware of it.

Everyday life was conducted according to a regular and well-planned routine, which included elements of scouting: formations and ceremonies around the flag that was raised to the top of the mast, regular exercises, uniform shirts, ties and various symbols, hiking in the surrounding areas, and sometimes sleeping in tents on the shores of the lake—these activities were all meant to create social cohesion and were not goals for their own sake. Most of the effort was invested in imparting the idea of immigration to Israel and kibbutz life at a level suited to the age of the group members. This was done by means of lectures, discussions, stories about the Land of Israel, and a description of the Haganah's and Palmach's[2] acts of bravery in the War of Independence that was taking place in Israel at the time.

The children learned songs of Israel and sang in Hebrew without knowing the language. The words were written in Latin letters and learned by heart. The evenings of Kabbalat Shabbat ("Welcoming the Sabbath") were really special. Everyone wore white shirts, dined around tables set for a festive meal, accompanied by a specially invited pianist, danced Israeli folk dances, and sang Yiddish, Hebrew, and even Polish songs. Those evenings, which I remember with longing, were not religious in nature, but they had an abundance of *Yiddishkeit*[3] and love for the Land of Israel.

Some followed this path out of recognition and ideological persuasion, as much as children could understand these things. Others came to be with their friends. The orphans had found within this circle of friends a replacement for the families they lost in the Holocaust, and this new community framework was like an extended family to them. I am encouraged by the fact that to this very day, more than six decades later, those friendships continue. During the many years that have passed since then, we've matured, worked hard, met many new people both in school and at work, raised families, and became grandparents. Yet more than half a century later, the connections that we made by chance in the children's homes in Poland are still a key part of our social circle.

I lived with this group for five months. Sometimes I wonder how it's possible that such a short period of time could cause the profound mental and emotional changes I experienced. Some of this group would later become my friends. One charming girl would later become my faithful wife, and her two brothers became my brothers-in-law. The three of them had their own difficult story. They were orphaned, wandering for two years through villages alone. They slept in fields and in hiding places they found themselves, even throughout winter. Their survival is a testimony to the power of the soul, the drive to live in the face of death.

During my short stay in the children's home, I acquired a conversational level of Polish. Later, as my language skills improved, my speech would become fluent, and my accent would no longer telegraph the fact that I was a foreigner. Yet even then, language was not an obstacle. The management of the house sympathized with me, and I believe my friends did as well. They bought me a nice chess set, and, more importantly, a precious violin, handmade by an artist, was purchased for me. I was given the freedom to pursue my hobbies.

My studies, as well as the studies of my friends, had been interrupted. Only a few of the members of the group attended high school in the nearby city. The younger members attended the Hebrew *Tarbut* (cultural) school, which was not a particularly rigorous institution; the others were homeschooled, with our counselors as their teachers. Naturally, the counselors taught material with which they felt most comfortable, not following any accepted curriculum. The children's home was a transit station on the way to *Eretz Yisrael* ("the Land of Israel") and its temporary nature created this haphazard approach to our studies.

My time was my own, and I was free to pursue my hobbies. I found a Jewish chess club in the city, and when I did not find any appropriate opponents, I transferred to a citywide club where I stayed until the late hours of the evening. Freedom and lack of discipline characterized my days.

One day, I was called in for a conversation with the house manager, Chaim Mendel. Sitting by his side was Misha Lewin, a central figure in the movement whom I had already met at summer camp, where he had been one of the lecturers and directors. Chaim and Misha complimented me. They spoke highly of my hobbies and appreciated the fact that I had improved my Polish, which they saw as testimony to my impressive learning abilities. I was embarrassed. I did not know why these compliments were being voiced, but I had a feeling that they were going to ask something of me. And so they did.

I was offered a counseling position at the HaShomer HaTzair branch in a nearby city, Wałbrzych. My task would be to instill in the young people the ideals of the movement, mainly: immigration to Israel and the fulfillment of our principles in kibbutz life.

I was taken aback. To me, the offer made no sense, and I voiced my opinion aloud. "I myself adopted the movement's ideology only a few months ago, and my devotion to it was emotional and devoid of theoretical roots. How can I instill this path in others?" I had no experience working with young people, and my Polish language ability was still in its infancy. When I conversed with Polish-speaking youth, they would giggle and mimic my speech. Most importantly, all the children of the house were to leave for Israel within a few weeks, so what was the point of starting a new job that would end so close to its start?

My interviewers were not impressed with my objections, and they had an answer to each and every one. They said that my Polish was reasonable, and the need to speak Polish would soon lead me to a solid command of the language. As for lacking deep ideological roots, I would have to read and learn a lot, but it was not necessary to convince young people whose hearts should be acquired more with emotion rather than ideology. I could tell stories, take advantage of my hobbies of chess and music, sing and use my dramatic skills—all this would attract young people more than Zionism, Marxism, socialism, and other -isms. My interviewers conceded my point about the futility of starting what was about to end in a matter of weeks, but they had a solution for that as well: I must give up my trip with my friends, stay in Poland, and immigrate to Israel with the rest of the movement's activists.

I was speechless. Was it conceivable that I—the foreigner, who was living under an assumed identity and brought here to hide out from my persecutors by intermingling with masses of young people to get out of Poland with them as soon as possible—would be left behind and confined to a life of loneliness and danger? I did not inquire about how I would live and who would take care of my sustenance and my basic needs because it was obvious I would decline. My interviewers sensed this and asked me not to rush my reply, but to consider their proposal seriously before I responded. In the meantime, they thought, they would continue their persuasion efforts. I agreed to their suggestion and said that I would consult my friends and my sister who was living in the activists' apartment in Łódź.

The idea that I would consult with my friends was not to their liking. They were afraid that I would be influenced by them and would not accept their proposal, so they wrapped the matter in a cloak of secrecy and asked me not to tell my friends anything. I was offered a two-day visit to Łódź to talk to my sister and was then to go to the headquarters of the main leadership for another conversation about my affairs.

My sister was surprised by my sudden arrival. When I told her the reason, she was absolutely shocked. "Are these people responsible for their actions?" she asked. First, a formal matter: I was not yet eighteen, and she still had a say regarding my future. While she said that she did not intend to take advantage of her formal position and that I was the master of myself, she questioned whether my interviewers thought of the life of a boy of this age, alone, in a remote province at the edge of the country. How would I live? What would I eat? Who would take care of my most basic needs? Had I thought it through? "You must remember," she said, "that you live under an assumed identity, illegally, and that any slip could bring disaster upon you, and no one would know what had happened to you." Yehudit also reminded me of something I had forgotten: in a short while, we were supposed to receive our passports, and we would be able to leave

Poland in a normal manner, not by stealing across borders. Living outside the law would come to an end. We would live in Norway, and from there, when the time came, we would leave for Israel. Yehudit spoke calmly and rationally, asking me to consider things in depth and not to be tempted to embark on a most dangerous adventure.

Dejected and thoughtful, I went to the head office. The place was bustling with activity: a girl was typing; a duplicating machine was working at full speed; another girl was collating pages for a pamphlet; young people were coming and going; and members of the leadership—some of them familiar to me—were sitting at a table discussing their affairs. I was invited in.

The movement was short on counselors. New graduates who were thought to have potential as guides were identified and offered a position, which was then followed by a period of training and study alongside experienced counselors. Most of them were native-born and lived with their families; the movement was not responsible for their sustenance or their fate. But my situation was different.

I sat timidly in front of people much older than me, prewar veteran members of a movement, well-educated and high-ranking, and in my eyes—esteemed. Sitting with them affected my self-image. I felt that I would not be able to refuse these people. The first speaker was Avraham Pashstein, the emissary from Israel. Contrary to my expectations, he did not begin by trying to convince me. "You have complete freedom to refuse the movement's offer, and no one would see it as unacceptable. However," he added, "the movement did help you and your family in your first most critical days in Poland and continues to keep you under its protection. Yet this does not obligate you in any way." From what he said, however, I understood that I was in fact obligated, if not formally, then at least morally.

Another member described how satisfying educational work with youth was, especially for such a lofty goal: a fulfilling life on a kibbutz in the Land of Israel. "Living independently," he continued, "will build your character; the constant independent learning that will be required for this will broaden your horizons, and you will have a full life."

Now it was my turn. I spoke shyly. I was embarrassed in front of my interviewers. I stated that my illegal status was frightening and that I would soon receive a passport that would allow me to free myself from that problematic situation and leave Poland legally and safely. Much to my surprise, my last argument worked against me, contrary to what I expected. "You will have a passport?" I was asked.

"It in fact has been verified," I replied.

"So," said the man, "you will have a first-rate document duly issued by a competent authority, not just a note of a repatriate, but a passport bearing your picture." He explained further that a passport was issued for a specific period of time, which could then be renewed, or a visa could be obtained for a country other than Norway, and perhaps soon I would be able to proudly acquire a visa issued by the future State of Israel.

When I asked where and how I would live after I parted from my friends, it was clear that in principle, I would accept their offer, and the rest of the questions would be mostly logistical. Everyone welcomed me and shook my hand. Then, one member of the group went out with me to arrange matters in which the whole group did not need to be involved.

Lyova—better known as Lyovka—handled the money matters. He was able to tell me that the mother party of the HaShomer HaTzair movement, known as the Jewish Labor Party, was about to take over the building after the children left and make it into a guesthouse for members of the party and its wide circle of sympathizers. "You will continue to live in the house as before, or in the building next to it in the courtyard. The home will be converted to a guest hotel, and you will receive all its services. You will also be given proper pocket money, and you will live in luxury. You will lead a comfortable life, and you will be able to study, read, and train yourself for your 'noble work': bringing Jewish children into the ranks of the movement, bringing them closer to the noble ideals we all believe in."

Nowadays, such an agreement would have been taken care of by lawyers—back then an oral agreement and a handshake were enough. One could assume that a lawyer would probably have asked what would happen to me if the guesthouse were to close, but since the question was not asked, no answer was given.

—⁓—

In October 1947, my friends from the children's home left on their long road to Israel. They were enroute for half a year. They were stuck in France for several months—in Quantilly, a small village, and in the port city of Marseilles. In March 1948, they got off their ship during a stopover in Haifa. The children, accompanied by supposed "relatives" and "parents" for a "tour," did not return to their ship. That was how they fooled the British Mandate authorities.

32

MY STUDENTS—MY FRIENDS

OUR SMALL PALACE WAS EMPTIED OUT OF ALL ITS RESIDENTS. The dancing stopped, and singing was no longer heard. There was silence. The home was remodeled. Its rooms were cleaned, painted, and set up as guest rooms. The house opened its doors, and the first guests started to arrive. I was left to guide the teenagers at the HaShomer HaTzair youth clubhouse in the city of Wałbrzych along with Tamara Buchman, an experienced counselor my age.

I arrived at the clubhouse daily. I learned its routine, participated in all of the meetings together with the experienced counselors, and learned how to present programs to the youth. I checked the work schedule carefully and read all the printed material sent to the counselors by the leadership.

In the beginning, I was guided by the head of the clubhouse, Feivel Pudamski, who was a senior and experienced counselor. Later, standing in front of my fourteen- to fifteen-year-old students, I discarded some of the models from the experiences of the other counselors, creating rules of my own that suited me. I used my skills in singing, music, chess, and acting and tried to explain the movement's ideological ideals rather than lecture. If one of my meetings did not go well, it would sully my mood and prompt me to try and figure out what had gone wrong. Over time, I learned not to stop the singing and dancing of the students, even if according to the plan it was time for a discussion. I learned that it was better to end a discussion before the allotted time than to drag it out beyond their will and ability to listen. I did not let the clock guide me, but followed the expressions on their faces. Students went to school because they had to, but the clubhouse had to be alluring since they attended it by their own choice.

Tamara and I worked hard to make the clubhouse a pleasant place to be. Different people on duty took care to clean and wash the floors, and they hung pictures and decorations on the walls. A chess group was created for chess lovers, an editorial staff was chosen to publish a newspaper to be printed and displayed on the clubhouse wall, and a cultural committee prepared artistic programs that we performed for both parents and a general Jewish audience. The clubhouse was open most days of the week. When I was gone, it was opened by others on duty. We went on camping trips, spending many evenings around the campfire, sleeping in tents, and reaching the treetops with our singing.

I earned the students' trust. They were my young friends, and I was their adult friend. They shared their problems with me and sometimes told me about what was going on in their homes, things that could only be revealed to those they trusted. When they came to the clubhouse and found it locked, they would go to my room that was just across the street and turn it into a club. I made sure, of course, that my room was clean and tidy, as would befit a counselor.

Some of the parents were against what they perceived as excessive activity in the clubhouse. They claimed that it interfered with their children's studies, and they made it difficult for their children to attend the activities. We decided that we should talk to the parents. From time to time, we held parent meetings in which we described our activities as a complement to school, sang our songs, and presented an artistic program. The parents came to appreciate that their children were in good hands: Tamara was a well-educated college student and counselor. I played my music for them, and my title as runner-up chess champion of the town of Wałbrzych raised my status in their eyes.

We succeeded in creating a "HaShomer experience" that carried more weight than the ideologies. Those who were my students are now pushing the seventh decade of their lives, and to this day they remember with nostalgia their youthful life in the HaShomer clubhouse.

The HaShomer HaTzair movement taught universal behavioral norms; moral behavior and integrity were its hallmarks. We had our own rules, the "HaShomer commandments," which gave us a sense of superiority and separated us from our surroundings. These strict demands on the students were often decrees that were difficult to meet for long. They certainly contradicted our aim to become a mass movement: "HaShomer is a helpful and trustworthy brother," "HaShomer does not smoke," "HaShomer does not drink alcohol," "HaShomer does not go ballroom dancing," "HaShomer stays sexually abstinent before marriage"—these were just a few of the duties and prohibitions.

At one of the summer camps, a young lady from my youth group came to me angry and emotional: she had seen one of the leaders of the movement smoking in secret! I, too, was surprised by the discovery—and I was nineteen then. I spoke to the man—"Could it be?" I asked.

He looked at me questioningly—how could you be so innocent at your age?—and gave me two answers: To the young lady, he said, I had to explain that he was more than twice her age, and that in the war he had gone through hell in the trenches. In the company of his fellow soldiers, smoking had been a refuge for calming the nerves. From then on, it became a habit that he could not stop. He identified with the ideological ideals of the movement and did not want to give up his active membership because of this bad habit. If they were to demand that he stop smoking, it would be akin to demanding that an asthma patient stop coughing. I needed to present this as an exception that strengthens the rule. And as for me, I had to understand that certain prohibitions were good for the youth but could not possibly survive into adulthood. "Members of the kibbutzim in Israel smoke," he said, "and yet their ideological world does not collapse."

I had earned the trust of my students not because of my virtues as an educator, but because I believed in everything I said. I did not lie to them and did not preach what I did not believe. It was a period of youthful innocence and honesty.

The winter of 1948 was especially cold. I had a burner in my room, and it was lit for many hours to warm my frozen limbs. My friend Tamara's room was across the street on the floor above the clubhouse, and it was absolutely freezing. Later, she told me that she would warm up in the train car on her way to study at Wrocław University. We spent many hours in my room; we read, studied, and ate.

My bed stood along the length of one wall, and opposite it was a sofa. I inherited the furniture from those who were in my room before me. Late at night, Tamara would leave for her frigid room and would cover up with a pile of blankets so as not to freeze. Sleeping together in my warm, heated room was rejected out of hand: the students would not understand this, and even if they assumed that we did not break the morality rules, their parents would interpret this as reckless behavior, and our sacred monastic image would be irreparably damaged.

And if it was done in secret? The counselor who smoked also did so covertly. He forgot that there could be no secrets from the students. We would not be looked upon in the same manner if we were to stumble in our behavior. Integrity and honesty are transmitted at hidden frequencies, and young people sense this with their youthful innocence. The proper rules of conduct had to be adhered to even when the risk of being caught was negligible, like religious dogma that must be observed day and night.

Once, late at night, I was on my way home from the chess club and happened across a drunk, sprawled on the sidewalk, trying unsuccessfully to stand up. He had blood on his face, indicating that he had hit his head. "Help me," he begged. The option to simply keep going and not get into trouble with a drunkard did not occur to me. "HaShomer" was, after all, "a helpful and trustworthy brother," and therefore it was my duty to offer him help. With considerable effort,

I managed to get him to his feet. Now he grabbed my clothes, hugged my shoulders tightly, and asked me to lead him to his home, which he said was nearby. I agreed to that as well: I knew that if I let go, he would fall.

This was a big problem, and a lot of thoughts were running through my head. How would I explain to anyone who happened across me embracing a drunk that we were not a couple of friends returning together from the tavern? And if we ran into a policeman? The police used to stop drunks, pour cold water on them, and send them home shivering from the cold. But if they do not settle for the standard punishment and decided to file a report, they would demand that I testify. This would be a dangerous encounter for me with the people of the law, which I needed to avoid at all costs.

Worst of all, it would be just my luck if the parents of one of my students were on their way home from a night out and saw me embraced by a drunk. No explanation would satisfy them; they would have plenty to say about the young man who was supposed to be guiding their children to good and virtuous behavior. They would surely conclude that their children's counselor was not as "holy" as the image he portrayed to his students. "He is just like everyone else," they would say, "he speaks of lofty ideals, the proud symbol of the movement on his chest, but his words are empty. He does not practice what he preaches."

I used to keep a notepad in my front pocket where I wrote down my chess games. Now, I pulled it out a bit, so it would hide the HaShomer symbol. The drunk noticed this and said, "My friend, are you a scout counselor?" Half asking, half stating, he started crying bitterly as is typical of drunks. "This is what has become of me," he mumbled, "that a scout counselor is ashamed to be seen in my company." I, however, was relieved that I had succeeded in "saving" the dignity of the movement and only relaxed when we reached the door of his house.

However, my troubles were not over yet. The man did not let go of me and begged me to come inside with him. If not, they would kill him. By "they," he meant his wife and her sister. I had rejoiced all too soon at the end of the adventure that no one had seen me. Now I had to meet his family.

We went in. This was my first and only visit to a Polish family home. The apartment was neglected, things were strewn all over, and poverty screamed from the walls. My presence stopped the two women from pouring out their anger on the man, and his bloody face aroused their sympathy. They sat him down, rinsed his face, and took care of him, all while voicing their troubles. Like many in this town, the man was a coal miner and used to spend much of what little he earned at the tavern. "You see, mister, how we live?" his wife said, spreading her arms to the sides. "See, sir, how my child is growing up?" She pointed to a bed where their little son slept. "What will come of him when he grows up with such a father? He will not grow up to be a man like you," she concluded.

The drunken husband felt that the worst with the two women was already behind him and said to his wife, pointing at me, "He's decent; he saved me. He's a scout counselor. Show her; show her." He demanded that I uncover the movement's emblem that I had been hiding, and when I did not respond, he tried to get up and pull the notebook out of my pocket. The woman wanted to understand what he was talking about. Finally, I pushed the notebook back into my pocket, and the emblem of the HaShomer HaTzair, which had the words "strength and courage" written under it, peeked out for everyone to see. "You see, you see, I told you." The man was proud of me.

"What are you so proud of?" the woman scolded. "You might have thought it was you who brought him up. His father did not drink his money at the tavern, but invested everything in his upbringing."

She did not know that I spent half my young life apart from my father, and my upbringing came from the ghetto, the hideouts, from wandering, and from the dreamlike years of innocence and purity at HaShomer.

⸻

One day, a young boy came to the clubhouse dressed in a plaid shirt of bright colors. Its collar was coarse and raised upward. This

Twelve-year-old Nurit (Irka)
shortly after liberation, 1944.

mode of dress was against HaShomer's modest code, and it was thought that he was taunting it. He was at the receiving end of contemptuous stares, and when other boys copied him, it was decided by open vote to remove them from the ranks of the movement. No one defended them from among their friends. This episode was accompanied by a letter, at the end of which it stated that the movement would consider returning the children to its ranks when they arrived in Israel, if they followed the way of the kibbutz and not that of the "street."

Fifteen-year-old Nurit, in the children's home,
1947, where she met Yochanan,
her future husband.

All of them immigrated to Israel but followed neither the ways of
the kibbutz nor the ways of the street. They were all decent people
who would come to tell their children about those three wonderful
years in the HaShomer clubhouse, in that remote secluded place, that
had given them back their childhood and the joy of youth.

We got together once in a small forest in Israel—here the forests
are not like in Poland—and we reminisced by singing songs from
back in those days. I accompanied them on my accordion. I still get

together with a few of them to this day. When one of their children said, pointing to me, "He was the counselor of HaShomer HaTzair," I felt a slight tug at my heartstrings.

—⁓—

A year after I came to Wałbrzych to be a counselor, I became the head of the clubhouse, and I was invited to join the main leadership of the movement. I was the youngest of that group. My role was terminated after two years since the Polish authorities forbade Zionist activity at the end of 1949, and with that ends another chapter of this story.

33

THE COURT

MY LIFE IN THE GUESTHOUSE WAS COMFORTABLE AND PLEAS-
ant, but unfortunately it did not last long. The guesthouse did not
attract enough vacationers to make it economically sound. It closed
after just a few months, approaching the spring of 1948. It was unfortunate. While I lived there, I had my own room that was cleaned
every few days, my clothes were laundered and ironed by one of
the workers for very little money, and the food that was served was
excellent.

While living at the guesthouse, I set myself a rigid schedule and
tried to stick to it. My older friend, Misha Lewin (who later became
a professor of history at the University of Pennsylvania), taught me
how a single, independent person must live if he did not want to
waste his days: get up early, do twenty sets of exercises, and take a
cold shower—these were the key elements for a successful day. And
most importantly, learn, learn, and learn.

That's what I did. I read a great deal every morning, learned the
material that was needed for the activities in the clubhouse, and
planned every detail for the meetings with my students. In my free
evenings, I spent many hours at the chess club. I had no worries and
was not particularly concerned about my future. Everything here
was temporary, I thought. I'd immigrate to Israel, live in the kibbutz,
and help develop the fledgling nation of Israel.

But all of this comfort came to an end, as I mentioned, in
the spring of 1948. Tamara and I continued to live in the empty

house as guardians of the "palace." Now my life was difficult. My self-sufficiency took up a lot of my time, and my meals were meager and prepared in a rush. The budget for my expenditures increased. Every month, I was sent a package of canned food and various commodities from the central warehouse of the movement, but some of them required preparation before they could be put on the plate, and I had no idea how to cook.

The nights in a big, empty house were frightening. The chances that the movement would be able to assemble another group of youth to stay at the house were slim. It was therefore necessary to remove the remaining valuables from the house and return them to the authorities. I made it clear to the administrators of the property that being the guardians of the house didn't suit us, that Tamara and I were out of the house for most of the day, and that the palace was neglected and abandoned. I recommended that they place a guard on it because we were going to move to town soon. We were looking for an alternative place to live.

⁓

At that point, I already had a passport that would allow me to leave Poland. Before Yehudit's trip with her family to Norway, the question of my joining them was again raised. Yehudit did not pressure me; she just asked me to reconsider my path. "If you don't take advantage of this last opportunity," she said, "you will no longer be the master of your own destiny, and you will have to rely on the promises of others. Doesn't it scare you to be alone in a strange land with a borrowed identity? Does the goal for which you are endangering yourself warrant it?" In theory, I had not yet made up my mind about accompanying Yehudit to Norway, but in reality, I had made the decision much earlier, when I agreed not to leave with my friends and stay in Poland. Even then it was clear that my stay was not for a few months, but for a more significant period: as long as HaShomer HaTzair remained in Poland, so would I.

I was exposed to the HaShomer HaTzair movement by chance. I took my first steps in studying its ideological foundations, but I was mainly influenced by the special experience that this movement managed to impart on its youth. The desire to immigrate to Israel conquered all logic, and the love of the Land of Israel captivated our hearts through song and dance. By then, I was deeply invested in imparting this message to my students.

However, I took Yehudit's warnings about my dual identity to heart. I realized that the slightest misstep could have disastrous consequences. So I was determined to arrange my papers in the best way possible to appear perfectly legal. Based on my passport, and with the help of a lawyer friend, I was able to obtain a local identity card and also a certificate as a youth counselor in the Jewish Labor Party. These documents bore my picture and greatly strengthened the legality of my position—or so I thought. A person who lives under an assumed identity—no matter how good their documents are—is always subject to unexpected dangers.

One night, after I had locked the doors to the house, I lay down to sleep in my room on the bottom floor. Tamara slept in one of the rooms on the top floor. Suddenly, I was awoken by the sound of smashing glass. I sat up on my bed and listened. I heard the sound of a person stepping on broken glass. I left my room and yelled, "Who's there?" I heard the sound of someone running away. I went out to the hallway. As I stood opposite the hall that had once been a classroom, I saw two figures leaping over the railing of the porch, disappearing into the darkness of the night.

I turned on the light. The porch door was wide open, and its glass had been smashed to smithereens and strewn all over the hall floor. The second-floor light was turned on. I yelled to Tamara that everything was okay and no one was in the house besides me.

Our empty palace had attracted thieves. They had broken the glass in the door, turned the key that was in the door on the inside, and had come in. When they were interrupted, they fled. Tamara recommended we call the police immediately, but she gave up when I strongly opposed this. The last thing I wanted was to meet up with the police. The next morning, I checked for the results of the break-in in the light of day, and I found that nothing had been stolen. The members of the party who were responsible for the place recommended we replace the window, clean up the mess, and not involve the police in the matter.

As days passed, the incident was forgotten. Yet there was someone who did not forget: the police themselves. We received an official letter requiring the representatives of the house to report to the police station for the purpose of giving testimony in connection with the break-in, which had taken place on such-and-such date. I was stunned. How did the police know about the break-in? The mystery became clear when Tamara and I, accompanied by my lawyer friend, arrived at the police station. From the interrogator, we learned that the two thieves had been caught. During their interrogation, they had revealed the addresses of the houses they had broken into, one of which—of course—was ours, from which they had not stolen anything.

But that is not where the story ends. We were subpoenaed to testify against the two thieves in court. This was exactly what I had feared and had been so careful to avoid! My lousy luck landed me in court for the first time in my life, in Poland, of all places. Before my court appearance, I was instructed on the rules. I acted in accordance with the motto that my attorney drilled into me: "Keep it short, and do not volunteer answers to unasked questions."

And indeed, my testimony was simple and smooth. After I got back to my seat from the witness stand, I could not understand why I had been so nervous. I confirmed my personal data: Avraham Wolner, youth counselor. I stated that, on the night of the break-in, I was home. I saw the thieves escape, saw the broken glass on the floor, but nothing had been taken. It couldn't have been any simpler: formality for formality's sake.

After me, Tamara testified. She said she had also heard a noise, had gone down the hall on the lower floor, and had found me there. No, she did not see the thieves: they had run away before she arrived.

"What did you see that indicated a break-in?" asked the judge.

Here is where she blurted out a terrible sentence: "I saw the signs of the break-in as described by my friend Yochanan!"

The judge rummaged through his papers. At that moment, we knew we were in big trouble. "I don't seem to remember," said the judge, "that there was anyone in the file named Yochanan. Who is this Yochanan?"

I was speechless. The seconds passed, and no answer came out. The lawyer rose to his feet, and, with demonstrative composure, turned to "the honorable judge" and explained: "These young people are Zionist activists, and their intention is to move to Israel. In their movement, it is customary to give themselves Hebrew names before the trip, and their new names are used in everyday life. The Hebrew name chosen by comrade Wolner is Yochanan."

"Very nice," said the judge, and later on he expressed his appreciation for these "enthusiastic young people" and their identification with and devotion to the cause.

We left the courthouse. It took me some time to get over my shock. I felt as if I had stood on the edge of an abyss and had been saved by the resourcefulness of the lawyer. But as for the logic of the lawyer's reasoning, I had something to bring to his attention: Why, in his opinion, was the name of John (Yochanan) the Baptist more Hebraic than the name of our forefather Abraham (Avraham)?

34

SOLITUDE

AFTER A RELENTLESS SEARCH, I WAS ABLE TO FIND A ONE-room apartment with a separate entrance across from the Hebrew school and the HaShomer HaTzair clubhouse. I couldn't have expected any better. Nachman, the secretary of the Hebrew School, had been living in this apartment and was leaving to immigrate to Israel. The apartment was apparently an abandoned property; it was owned by the municipality at the time. I registered as an additional tenant, in agreement with the tenant who held it legally. As far as the municipality was concerned, there were now two tenants in the apartment.

After Nachman left, I inherited his belongings: a bed, a couch, a dilapidated table, three mismatched chairs, a chest of drawers, a sort of buffet cabinet, some dishes, and a large wooden crate to store coal. There was a coal burner for cooking and warming and a sink with running water.

Days passed, and rose-colored dreams turned into a gray reality. In my mind, I imagined a life of independence traversing a consistent and challenging agenda, doing whatever I felt like. I simply needed to make choices. These grand dreams were shattered in the face of a grim truth, which no one takes into consideration when they are handed things on a silver platter. Yet no one had handed me anything, and most of my time was spent trying to take care of myself. My food was meager, monotonous, and lacking in nutritional value. Hot meals at the restaurant consumed my money.

I was particularly upset that I was wasting my time on mundane daily needs, and that I was no longer setting aside time to learn, as I had done during those glamorous months, under the auspices of the guesthouse. Now my room was neglected; I was embarrassed by its shabby state when my students came to see me from time to time.

My life experiences had taught me how to survive in moments of peril, but in everyday trivialities, I failed. I lacked experience and practical skills, and resourcefulness escaped me. Perhaps my young age was not meant for such coping either; I still needed a warm home with an environment of human support, which I did not have. Outside of the clubhouse and meetings with the youth, I was simply alone.

Until Greta came along.

One rainy day, there was a hesitant knock at my door. In the doorway stood a forty-year-old woman, pale, fair-haired, simply dressed, with a weary smile on her face. Beside her stood her young son, about ten years old. This was Greta. She greeted me, apologized for the interruption, and asked if I could spare her a few moments of my time. She spoke basic Polish with a heavy German accent. I had met her previously in the stairwell, usually with her two children in tow, on her way to or from the school. We continued our conversation in German. I invited her to my room and apologized for the mess. "This is no job for a young man like you," she said. I invited her to sit down, but she refused; in front of such an "important" person, she chose to stand.

Greta was German. Like many of her people, she remained in the city that was previously known as Waldenburg and was now called Wałbrzych. Once the Germans had been rulers of this land. Now, they had become a hated minority, insular, living on the fringes of society. Her sickly husband worked in the coal mines. They were poor. My predecessor, she said, had employed her on occasion to clean, and she even laundered his clothes. Now she came to ask if perhaps I needed her services as well.

If anyone had a star looking out for them from above, protecting them every step of the way and helping them through their troubles, it was me. It was my good star that sent Greta to save me from my distress. I stood before her thinking for some time: according to my financial calculations, which I made occasionally, I did not have enough money left to pay for this service, which I needed so badly.

Greta read my mind and was concerned that I would turn her away. "I'll settle for little," she said. In order to convince me, she added that cleaning one room and washing one person's clothes was not so much work, and payment would be expected accordingly.

I asked if I could pay her with groceries. She did not understand what I meant. I went to the dresser and opened a drawer. The drawer held a two months' accumulation of mine and Tamara's canned goods and other groceries—quite impressive a quantity. She clasped her hands and blurted out, "Oh my God ['Mein Gott']—there's a whole grocery store here!" I explained to her that this was a bi-monthly portion. Some cans I would have to leave for myself and for my friend who ate with me, but the rest could serve as payment.

Greta could not hide her joy. We agreed that she would clean my room once a week and launder my clothes as needed. She could not stop thanking me.

After Greta's arrival, my life changed. She removed the principal burden that had hovered over me, which I could not manage without her. Now my room was spotless, and I enjoyed being there, lounging about like a housecat. I avoided leaving if I didn't have to. I loved the clean scent. Greta did her work thoroughly and with devotion. My shirts came back laundered and folded as they hadn't been in a long time.

Greta accompanied my stay until my last day in Poland, until the end of January 1950. At first, she would clean and do my laundry, but through her own initiative she became my "house mother," if my room could be called a house. In the morning, when she went to the market, she would also buy the little that I needed. Politely and in an inoffensive manner, she would bring things to my attention and guide me on daily matters, which, due to my lack of experience, had not caught my attention.

Sometimes she spoke of herself with such self-deprecation that I became embarrassed. I asked her to stop calling me "Mr. Wolner" and to call me by my first name, my Hebrew name. She had a hard time pronouncing "Yochanan," so she called me "Johan."

Gently, she remarked about the inadequacy of my *Kleidung* ("clothes"). In fact, all I had was three shirts, one of which—due to so much laundering and ironing—had come to the end of its usefulness. Greta said it was not nice for the students and the other members of the movement to see me wearing the same two shirts. She whispered, as if there were people around us, that I really needed to buy a pair of pants, otherwise she would not be able to wash the ones I had. I made a note and promised to buy two shirts and a pair of pants. She added a few pairs of socks to the list. She assured me this was not because of her frequent laundering, but because she worried about my appearance, and I believed her.

Since I did not have enough money for such a "long" shopping list, I decided that for the next month, I would not eat lunch at the workers' restaurant where I spent a good part of my money, and I also decided to stop my obsessive habit of buying books. I tended to buy more books than I could possibly read, books that "every home should have," but I had forgotten that my life and room were not exactly a home in the conventional sense and that my current life was temporary. I bought every chess book, and when Pushkin's and Lermontov's books came in—I bought those too, without thinking twice. I purchased books by the fathers of socialism. In a used bookstore, I found a biography of Napoleon in two volumes, an academic publication from 1931 by Kircheisen. I bought those for a lot of money.

I had to forgo all this, and not just for the sake of buying clothes. I felt more strongly that the groceries I was paying Greta for her services weren't enough, and the thought that she might leave her position worried me.

The purchases on Greta's short shopping list doubled my wardrobe. I was very proud of my ability to show restraint in managing my finances, and felt that giving up hot meals that month was a sign of my character. I refused to acknowledge that the asceticism in which I lived was forced upon me, and I saw it as a way of life that was adopted by choice. I lived by the saying, "It is not shameful to be poor," but I forgot about the rest of it: "It's no great honor either." My intellectual-political insight and my work with the youth for "the most just cause in the world" filled my heart with pride and satisfaction. The song from the HaShomer HaTzair tradition we sang around the bonfires was almost true for me: "On my body there is only a shirt, but my heart is aflame!"

Almost true—because unlike in the song, I now had four shirts, three intact and one in shreds.

——

Near the winter of 1948, several things happened that made life easier for me. As mentioned before, I won second place in the municipal chess championship, and for this I received a modest monetary prize, an unexpected surprise just at the right time. As a league player in the "coal miners" team, Górnik, I was also provided free coal throughout the winter months. Therefore, my room had unlimited heat.

Furthermore, before the school year, I found a part-time job: I taught music at the Tarbut Hebrew school. I do not recall whether it was through the initiative of the principal of the school, Mr. Tushman, or if the authorities had mandated that the school have a music teacher. The principal did not have a written document regarding what was required of a music teacher, but when I looked into what was being taught in other schools, I concluded that the students should be taught the notes in treble clef and to sing in two-part harmony. The principal asked that the repertoire of the students always include two songs, prepared to be performed at the spur of the moment, for occasions such as an inspector's visit or a performance for the parents.

This small job added a little to my budget, and I was now able to pay Greta not only with canned goods, but with money. She was beside herself with joy. At first, she refused out of politeness. I insisted she take the money, so she accepted it, though with embarrassment. She looked at me with tears in her eyes. "What will I do when you leave?" she asked.

"There is still time before that," I answered.

"Time flies," she replied. She gave me a kiss and ran.

We once spoke about the history between Germans and Jews; this topic had hovered over us for some time. I knew about Greta, from the little she had told me, but to her I was an enigma. Still, Greta was afraid to pry.

One day, when I was still immersed in my reading at my table, Greta had finished washing the floor, and I felt her looking at me. I raised my eyes from my book and looked at her in a moment of confusion. A sad beauty rested on her pale face that her poverty and difficulties had hidden from me until then. She asked if Nachman, my predecessor in the room, was my friend. I answered no. My acquaintance with him was superficial and accidental. She told me that Nachman was lonely and that his family was murdered in the war. He hated all Germans, she said, adding that she could understand it. Still, he treated her decently and paid generously for her work. "Do you have a family?" she asked.

"I have no one here," I replied.

There was silence. "How old are you?"

"Nineteen," I replied.

"I am German—do you hate all the Germans? Please be frank with me; I will understand."

"Do you feel hatred on my part toward you?" I asked.

"Oh, no, I feel incredible sympathy and kindness," she replied, but begged me to answer her question.

I replied, "I can't hate everyone, but I hate those Germans, the Nazis, and their leaders, who murdered my family and my people."

"Were there many?" she half questioned, half stated.

"Yes," I replied. "There were many, and I hate them." She understood and was saddened. "You're not 'all those Germans'; you are Greta," I said.

"Yes." She nodded in understanding. There was silence. "Many generations of Germans will have to endure the sins of their forefathers," she said thoughtfully. She told me that she had known better days than this, that she had not always been a housekeeper and cleaning lady. She used to be a clerk-typist, and her husband a shift manager in the mines. He was not drafted because of his age and position, and he had never carried a weapon, she added. Now she was willing to do any job as long as it was not degrading. Because she didn't know the "terrible" Polish language, she did not expect a respectable position. If I could possibly find her a job before I left, she would be grateful to me. I promised I would try. I decided to speak with Mr. Stulgiński, whom I had met by chance.

One day, I was asked to speak at a party meeting to talk about the activities of the clubhouse and to ask those assembled to send their children to join us. I was introduced as the head of the clubhouse, and to make a good impression, they noted that I was the runner-up city champion in chess. At the end of the meeting, a man approached, introduced himself as a chess fan, and asked me to play with him. I never refused to play chess. We came to my apartment and played a few games. After being easily defeated, he offered to introduce me to his brother-in-law, who, according to him, was an excellent chess player. I agreed, of course.

The next day, the man came to my apartment, and together we walked to a big, upscale shoe store. The owner of the store came out to welcome us. He already knew I was coming and greeted me warmly. That was Mr. Stulgiński, his brother-in-law. He noticed that my shoes were very worn and ordered the worker to measure me for a nice pair of new shoes. I politely declined his offer for another time. I knew that a handsome pair of shoes would empty my wallet, and I did not want to starve for another month. However, he noticed my hesitation and insisted that I pick a pair of the best shoes, and I could pay at a substantial discount of my choosing when I had the money. "You can feel good about this," he said. "I know that you are a 'party functionary' and that money is not pouring out of your pockets." I couldn't refuse such an offer. I felt as if I had just greatly increased my assets. I was invited to his house the next day for dinner and a chess game.

A beautiful home, nice dishes with an abundance of delectable food to please the palate, table manners that I had forgotten—that was what the Stulgiński home was like. He was a worthy opponent, and the evening passed in a homey, warm, and enjoyable atmosphere.

After that, we would meet periodically in a nice restaurant on the top floor of a huge commercial building, where we ate a well-rounded meal and played chess. The man was at home in the place, and the waiters waited on us hand and foot.

One evening, we came and ate, but we talked instead of playing chess. He wondered who I was, how I had gotten to Wałbrzych, how I lived. I told him a little of what I was allowed to reveal about myself, my modest and purposeful life, and my beliefs. I told him about one of the neighbors in the house, who for a small fee cleaned my room and did my washing and ironing.

I added that Greta was desperately looking for work. If he learned of something, he assured me, he would tell me. That was what everyone promised, I thought. But suddenly he remembered that here in the restaurant they had recently been looking for a waitress. He asked to speak to the manager, who joined our table. Yes, in fact, he needed a waitress, he said, for the evening hours.

The next day, Greta and I went to meet him. She impressed him by being nice, gentle, well-mannered, and quick. Greta said that she was willing to work shifts and that she would even prefer to work the evening shift. A week later, Greta started working there, and it was clear that she was pleased. She thanked me warmly and said that she had never met a young man who could understand others' difficulties so well. A young Jewish man, after what her people did to him, who would help a German woman and her family survive. She would never forget this.

My time in Poland was steeped in political and ideological struggles. The Communist Party's hold on the government increased until it took complete control in 1949. In the 1930s, even before the outbreak of the war, there was a Polish sentiment that it would be preferable to relocate its Jewish citizens outside its borders. This trend did not seem to change, even after the Holocaust in communist Poland. Exit passports were issued generously, the authorities turned a blind eye to the exodus of Jews by other means. Anti-Semitism in Polish society was still rampant and murderous in its expression, which further accelerated the process.

Along with this policy, and even in contradiction to it, the Jewish communists conducted a collective ideological war against Zionism, which was defined as contradictory to the principles of Marxism. Such a definition would eventually become a political-criminal accusation, but at that time, as long as Zionist activity was permitted in Poland, a confrontation took place on every stage between supporters of Zionism and its opponents.

One particular confrontation took place in the city of Wrocław, as I recall, in April 1949, between a central communist activist, Kwaterko, and an emissary of HaShomer HaTzair, Matityahu Mintz, who had arrived from Israel in early July 1948. Mintz was a young, twenty-six-year-old man, impressive looking, highly educated, and later a professor of history at Tel Aviv University. He was active in Wrocław and the counselor and educator of a large group of scouts in the HaShomer HaTzair, which was of great importance in deepening their ideological roots.

The ideological battle was waged for the hearts and minds of the Jewish youth, who, unlike their parents' generation, were still looking for an ideological direction for their lives. Many of them were torn between loyalty to the Soviet Union, whose army had liberated them from the clutches of the Nazis, and the national feeling that was awakened within them to realize a Jewish life in a country of their own.

The HaShomer HaTzair movement fulfilled many dreams for these troubled youth. It defined itself as Marxist, revolutionary, and Zionist, identified with the Soviet Union ideologically and politically, but disagreed with it about the solution to the Jewish dilemma, by advocating the building of a Jewish state.

In early April 1949, the Wrocław Jewish committee of the Communist Party was ordered to organize a youth meeting, as part of their ideological struggle against Zionism. The full hall was crowded with youth from all political streams, including the local HaShomer HaTzair and their Israeli counselor.

Comrade Kwaterko's lecture was sprinkled with quotations of Marxist doctrines, as was the custom of those days, and drew on Stalin's thesis in his 1913 article, "Marxism and the National Question." The hands of time had not eroded the power of this article, because the *great* Stalin's words were timeless in the eyes of the Communist Party. In this article, Stalin claimed that the characteristics that made a group of people into a nation were language, territory, and an integrated economic life. The Jews were given as an example of a group who did not meet these criteria, and therefore were not a nation, but a people that existed "on paper" alone and did not merit national rights.

Stalin rooted the Jewish dilemma in anti-Semitism, which was a by-product of capitalist regimes. By contrast, socialism advocated the brotherhood of nations, fought and outlawed anti-Semitism, thereby eliminating the ground on which anti-Semitism could grow. In the absence of anti-Semitism, there would be no Jewish dilemma. Hence, the Jews should not emigrate from one capitalist country to another, but join the Communist Parties in their countries of residence and join in the struggle for the implementation of socialism, which would also solve their problem. Regarding the question of anti-Semitism, which persisted even in socialist Poland, a standard answer was provided: that a battle was being waged against it, and Jews, instead of deserting, must take part in it.

To further strengthen his arguments, Comrade Kwaterko referred to an article by Ilya Ehrenburg. On September 21, 1948, Ilya Ehrenburg, a prominent Soviet Jewish writer and journalist, published in *Pravda* a harsh anti-Zionist article that was spoken about at length and became the focus of political discourse in Jewish public circles. The article, titled "Regarding One Letter," was later demonstrated to have been personally commissioned by Stalin. It was written in the form of a response to a supposed letter from a Zionist, Jewish student from Munich. Ehrenburg's answer articulated the position of the Soviet leadership on the Jewish question. It is reasonable to assume that the student in question never existed and was invented as a pretext for Ehrenburg's writing. The publication of the article, deemed necessary because of a growing Zionist sentiment among the Jewish public in the Soviet Union itself, was a part of an anti-Jewish campaign. Later, Ehrenburg wrote in his memoirs, "Fascism invaded our lives before it invaded our land." The article emphasized the thesis that Jews were united because of anti-Semitism, just as redheads would unite if they were persecuted.

The lecture ended. It was evident that the core of these new ideas was the old Stalinist thesis of 1913. The speaker had to be answered, but no one volunteered to do so. The HaShomer HaTzair students' eyes were directed at their Israeli instructor. Matityahu Mintz lived in Poland on a one-time "temporary" visa, which had to be extended from time to time. In this special situation, he had to consider carefully whether taking part in a public political debate in which he would attack the communist activist's arguments was prudent. However, when the speaker mentioned the famous article by Ilya Ehrenburg, it was impossible not to respond.

Mintz asked for the floor. In an impressive performance of rhetorical and scholarly ability, he contradicted Comrade Kwaterko's arguments, one after another. He made extensive use of the words of the Gromyko Declaration—a speech given by the representative of the Soviet Union, Andrei Gromyko, to the United Nations General Assembly on May 14, 1947, for the establishment of a Jewish state in Palestine. All the principles of Zionism were included in Gromyko's speech: the desires of the "great part of the Jewish people" were connected to the Land of Israel; the Jewish people experienced untold torture and suffering, with six million dead; the hundreds of thousands of Jews who survived in Europe had no homeland, so their desire to create their own state was very understandable. The Jewish people could not be denied the right to realize their aspirations. Mintz's ability to quote Gromyko from memory impressed the audience. He was interrupted from time to time by loud applause. Thus, a meeting aimed at condemning Zionism ended up promoting it.

And yet, the game was already rigged. At that time, comedians had a riddle: Who had the upper hand in the argument between a scholar and a bully? The answer: the strong hand of the bully. In the same manner, they could have asked: Who has the upper hand in the debate between a communist and a Zionist? The answer: the hand of a police officer in the department of foreign affairs.

Marko Tomasz, of the foreign-affairs police, was the man who had the authority to extend the visas or permits of foreigners who lived in Poland. This procedure was usually just a formality, and Mintz's visa was extended generously. The last extension was given in September 1948 for a period of eight months until May 31, 1949. But no longer: when he faced his old "acquaintance" Tomasz for further extension, Mintz was required to leave the country no later than mid-July.

⁓

This debate, which had been forgotten by its participants, nevertheless had a continuation.

A few decades later, an academic meeting was set up for Professor Mintz with a man named Shlomo Strauss. When Strauss entered the professor's office, he was unable to hide his embarrassment. The two had known each other from when Mintz was in the position of emissary in HaShomer HaTzair in Poland and Strauss was in his position within the foreign-affairs police. He had taken on a Polish name to hide his Jewishness: Marko Tomasz.

As I was told, the main speaker at the meeting in Wrocław, Comrade Kwaterko, also made it to Israel with many other Jewish communists, who struggled back then with Zionism and immigration to Israel. At the top of the list were persons who were of the highest ranking in the party: David Sfard, who was central in the party and cultural activities of the Jewish communists; Leopold Trepper, who was known by his underground name of Domb and established the Red Orchestra, a Soviet spy network that he headed; and most prominently Hersz Smolar, a Jewish communist who dedicated his life to the service of the party and devotion to the Jewish communist culture.

That was how many of those who loved Israel arrived there, as well as many whose feelings were split or were opposed. Yet Israel did not retaliate against them. Israel forgave and adopted all who arrived with open arms. The Soviet Union did not succeed in defeating Zionism but managed to defeat itself. When it collapsed, the nature of the Soviet solution to the Jewish dilemma was revealed to anyone who was not yet aware of it: a million Russian Jews immigrated to Israel within a decade, and that was the end of the debate between Zionism and "Marxism and the National Question."

How ironic and merciless history's verdict can be.

35

GOODBYE, POLAND

TOWARD THE END OF 1949, THE POLISH AUTHORITIES AN-
nounced that the Zionist parties must cease their activity and set
a deadline for the organizations to adhere to this order. The party
activists were promised exit visas, and no obstacles were expected.
The movement's leadership gave its activists an unequivocal order
that they should obey the law and not hold further gatherings or
group meetings that could be misconstrued as underground activities. They wanted to avoid giving the authorities any reason to take
administrative measures against the movement and its activists.

My passport, which had not been used for traveling to Norway,
was handed over to the person who had previously managed my
affairs, but by now it had expired. I was promised that an attempt
would be made to renew it, and if that weren't possible, a request for
a new passport would be submitted on my behalf. Another possibility was that the movement activists would leave Poland in organized
groups with group exit permits.

The formal procedures did not interest me, nor was I familiar with
them. Living with a borrowed identity mandated that I stay as far
away from the authorities as possible. I relied on the organizational
know-how of my friends, who dealt with matters of immigration
to Israel on behalf of movement activists. There was no doubt in
my mind that my leaving Poland would be legal and safe. No more
stealing across borders; I would be leaving through the main gate.

However, during one of my visits to Łódź, my friends hinted to me about some difficulties in the handling of my immigration issues. They said that they were trying to determine the cause of the problem. I started worrying. When I returned to Wałbrzych, the reason became clear. I had received a letter from the Ministry of Defense: Comrade Wolner, in other words, myself, had to appear for a medical exam before military recruitment into the Polish Army. There are no benefits without obligations: Avraham Wolner was a Polish citizen, and I, his impersonator, had to fulfill my obligation to the homeland, which wasn't really my homeland at all.

What great trouble I was in. What did I care about the Polish Army? I could not consider the possibility of enlisting. I knew that after two years' military service, my dream of immigrating to Israel would be out of reach, and I would lose my purpose in life. I would not have a home to return to, and the movement that took care of me and in which I was active would no longer be at my side. When I would return, I would not find a single soul to talk to about my secret identity, and my immigration to Israel would by then be impossible.

I consulted with my friends in Łódź. The possibility of stealing across the border was considered, but discarded. Crossing the border from Poland to East Germany, and from East Germany to the West, and from there onward—such a trek was fraught with obstacles and dangers, and arranging it for one person was nearly impossible.

A more likely option was to try to get out of the military service or to be rejected for medical reasons. I remembered my bout with trachoma. The idea of exploiting it seemed like a lifesaver. We found an ophthalmologist to examine my eye. He found signs of surgery in the eyelid. The scars and drops that had reddened my eyes would testify like a hundred witnesses that I was suffering from trachoma, which was a dangerous and contagious disease in which the patient would have to be separated as far as possible from the other soldiers. Once the idea was in play, the rest was relatively simple. The Łódźian doctor referred me to his colleague in Wałbrzych, and he provided me with appropriate drops, which I was to put into my "sick" eye before I presented to the medical committee. The doctor advised me to take the vial of drops with me in case I needed more color during the many hours of waiting.

Early in the morning, in my room, I experimented with the drops for the first time before I left for Wrocław, where I was supposed to present for examination. The drops worked beautifully, and my eye was impressively red. I got to the large military base, where thousands of people were wandering around the courtyards, some in uniform, most civilians, young people like myself who had been summoned for military service. Like a small ant, I tried to find my way in that maze. For the first time, I found myself among thousands of young Poles my age, loud, brutish, pushing and being pushed, working their way into the barracks or military offices to which they were summoned. I felt terribly out of place. I read the directional signs, presented the summons to the administrators, and finally reached the barracks, where hundreds of young people were crowding the corridor.

After a short while, an officer came out and demanded silence. When the clamor died down, he announced that there was no reason to push. Those whose names were called would be summoned in alphabetical order. One of the young men raised his hand. When he was given permission to speak, he suggested that the names be read from the beginning and from the end of the alphabet, alternately. His proposal was supported by many, but the officer sternly, firmly announced that no one would teach the army how to conduct its affairs. I realized that due to the Ws place at the end of the alphabet, I would have to spend many hours there, and therefore I had to take care of the redness in my eye.

At the end of a long, exhausting day, they called my name. I entered the hall where doctors were sitting behind individual tables examining recruits. I was referred to one of them. After confirmation of my personal details, the doctor looked at me and asked, "What happened to your eye?"

"I have trachoma," I answered.

The doctor got very serious. "Are you sure about that?" he asked.

"Unfortunately, yes," I responded.

"What are you doing about it?" he asked.

"I am under ongoing care by a doctor," I answered. As long as they did not ask, I did not volunteer the doctor's name, as we had discussed. He continued by asking about my general health, but I had no complaints. He measured my height, checked my mouth and throat, listened to my lungs, and immersed himself in writing. He then recommended to defer my recruitment for a year, dependent on further confirmation of a military ophthalmologist. I was happy, but worried as well. I was very tense about my upcoming exam.

I was ordered to accompany the sergeant, who was carrying my papers, and was led to a room at the other end of the corridor. On the way, I looked into a small mirror I carried with me and relaxed slightly. About two hours before, I had dropped too much of the medication into my eye, and my eye had gotten too red. Now the red had faded a little, and the eye looked reasonably pink but not excessively so. I turned to the ophthalmologist and noticed the uniform peeking out from under his white robe.

The doctor read my paperwork, examined my eye, flipped the eyelid, and looked at the eye through a magnifying glass. Afterward, he washed his hands repeatedly, which reminded me of days long past. It had then been a sad sign of my illness; now it was a happy sign of the deferment of my recruitment. I was provided with a certificate indicating that my recruitment would be postponed for a year. "The Polish Navy will be waiting a year for you," the doctor said.

"Navy?" I asked in amazement.

"Yes, you are a nice tall man, and this is what our navy needs," he explained.

I wondered, "Does the Polish military know that I don't know how to swim at all?"

―――

The HaShomer HaTzair clubhouse closed its doors, the tumult of the youth stopped, and my path in Poland had come to an end. There were still a number of months before my estimated departure from

Poland at the beginning of February 1950. These were months of letting loose. Nothing was pressing; nothing brought my mood down.

—⁓—

During this period, I spent a lot of time playing my violin. I spent long hours playing day after day, with insatiable fervor, until I was worn out, and I felt an immense satisfaction that I hadn't felt in many years.

I returned to the violin not because I reflected on the matter and found the conviction to play again, but because of an accidental acquaintance with the conductor of the local orchestra. At that time, the chess club was on the same floor as a small concert hall where the orchestra rehearsed. Symphonic music was a closed book for me, since record players were hard to come by. Moreover, the circumstances surrounding my life has not allowed me the opportunity to enjoy such pastimes.

On rehearsal nights, I would leave the chess club and go into the rehearsal hall to listen to the orchestra, especially the conductor playing the piano. After the rest of the musicians would leave, he would stay behind and continue playing, engrossed, endlessly in love with music flowing into the night. The sight mesmerized me.

When the conductor noticed me and investigated, he learned that I had played the violin some years before. "Why don't you start playing again?" he asked.

"It's too late," I answered. That was when he expressed his view: there is no too late in music; you do not have to be Bronisław Huberman.[1] With transcendent passion, he described the satisfaction of making music for everyone at their own level.

That night, I could not get any sleep. My dream of musical greatness had reawakened.

My musical path had had many ups and downs. The wanderings, the lack of a supportive environment, and the temporariness that characterized each stop along the way interrupted my flow of study. These were the main reasons, but not the only ones, for why I had stopped playing.

Yochanan in Poland, 1948.

In retrospect, my approach to playing was fundamentally wrong. I had not wanted to be one of many nameless musicians, simply following a path and finding contentedness in anonymity. I had aspired to be more than that; I had dreamed of playing like one of the greats, achieving perfection in my playing. But it was beyond my skill. I dreamed of peaks I couldn't conquer.

Years later, when once again I returned to playing the violin, my bitter disappointment would be as great as my uncompromising aspirations, as is the case with many who want all or nothing. I would only come to understand this many years later. Yet that night, I returned to my lofty dreams.

The next day, I went to see the violinist Ziskind, a respected teacher in the city, who came recommended by the conductor. So I once again returned to studying the violin, although, my return would be short-lived.

In addition to my old and beloved pieces, which I spent much time playing and fine-tuning, a few more pieces were added to my repertoire: two sonatas for the violin and piano by Tartini and Handel; "Love's Sorrow" by Fritz Kreisler; and the first two movements of Bach's Partita no. 2 to be played as a solo.

That was how I continued playing until my last day in Poland, when my violin was taken from me.

———

I didn't know many people in Wałbrzych, so there were not too many goodbyes. Members of the chess club expressed their sincere sorrow over my leaving and swamped me with well-wishes. They shook my hand warmly as I was accepted among them. The deputy mayor, who was a chess enthusiast, found out I was leaving. He wanted to say goodbye to me in person and invited me to his office.

During my visit, I was joined by a local Zionist administrator, Mr. Farber, who, for the occasion, wore a decorated military uniform with several medals. He was a reserve officer in the Polish Army.

I was so emotional. I was not used to dealing with people in official positions and always avoided them. During our conversation, which was unlimited in time, the deputy mayor inquired how I came to his city. That was how he learned that I came from Vilnius, was sent here to guide youth, and had lived in Wałbrzych for three years all alone with no family. I always had a ready-made biographical story that matched my documentation, and I had to be careful not to make a mistake.

It was such a shame that he did not know about my situation, the deputy mayor said. He could have helped me quite a bit. He didn't know that I had kept my distance, as much as possible, from any authorities, especially ones of his level, so that they would not learn more about me. The deputy mayor expressed his regret that a young man with such high values from the top chess group in Wałbrzych was leaving the city. I received a gift from him—a statue of the coat of arms of the city. He wished me well, and we separated with a warm handshake.

I left the key to my room with Greta. I suggested that she take anything she might want and advised she do so while I was still living there so that no one could claim she was stealing.

Greta came to say goodbye to me along with her son. She cried, and I teared up as well. She kissed me and hugged me at length. We finally parted, and I left on my way.

I sent my baggage ahead, mainly books from the customs office in Wrocław. The amount a person could carry with him in traveling was limited. I boarded the train in Warsaw with a small bundle in my arms and my violin. We were a cheerful group of HaShomer HaTzair members, and the hardships of the road did not diminish our joy. I played my violin, and everyone joined in singing until we reached the Czech border. My violin was confiscated at the border station: I was forbidden to take a musical instrument from Poland. I was overtaken with sadness. Once again, I had lost my violin.

A rickety Israeli ship named *Independence* transported me from Venice to the port of Haifa on February 9, 1950. I will not describe what I felt; I do not have the literary talent for that. I imagined the entire Land of Israel as gold. As I disembarked, I found a concrete platform, but what significance did the ground carry—gold or concrete—to those who did not step on it, but floated in the air with their heads in the clouds?

I was singing as I reached the registration officials. They must have thought, "A *meshuggeneh!*"[2] I declared that my proper name was Yochanan Fein and not Avraham Wolner. I was Wolner for the Poles; here I was Fein. I asked that they register me accordingly, but they, of course, could only register me as stated in the documents: Avraham Wolner. They doused me with a double dose of DDT[3] powder—perhaps in part to get rid of me sooner. Now my clothes looked like shrouds, and my hair appeared aged.

In a rickety bus, common in those days, I made my way to the Upper Galilee, to Kibbutz Amir, which was my first home in Israel.

A local little boy who happened across my path pointed at me and asked his friends, "Is that a boy or a girl?" It was the first sign that I had to part with my full locks of hair so that I could blend in with the locals and no longer be different and alien. Years later, I would do this wholeheartedly.

I had arrived in Israel, my wanderings finally over. With this my story ends. I don't remember if my first residence was a shack that was replaced with a tent or whether the tent came first and was replaced by a shack. A tent or a shack, no matter—it was home.

———

My story is a testimony. Millions of people did not survive that horrific era. Millions of stories were buried in mass graves. The mind cannot possibly grasp the significance of these numbers. The survivor's story grabs the heart and wails about man's inhumanity to man. Think of all those who did not survive, of those who were murdered and whose names have been erased and wiped from memory, those who make up that astounding number of deaths that our minds cannot grasp.

I was determined to document and describe those nine years of my life. The start of my story begins on June 22, 1941, with a deluge that inundated my childhood, and then continues through a series of ebbs and flows, finally ending with my feet securely on the shore in Israel.

I am not a brave swimmer, nor very resourceful. I made it to shore with the help of wonderful people, who in that cruel era did not lose their humanity and swam toward me against the currents of evil. They were few, very few. Those who did not meet them did not make it to shore, and they were many, so many: an entire people.

36

ME AND MY PAST

MY FRIENDS WILL ATTEST TO THE FACT THAT I AM NOT SAD person. Destiny was kind to me, and I am naturally optimistic—happy with my lot. Yet sometimes, here and there, the sadness returns.

The terror of my childhood accompanies me, not like a constant burden on my shoulders that stifles the pleasures of life, but as memories, deeply engraved in my heart. From time to time, at the various crossroads in my life, they come out of hiding to the forefront—the pictures and faces, as if it were only yesterday, as if six decades had not passed.

The most intense image is that of Ghetta'leh. She was born on August 15, 1941, in the inferno of the ghetto, from which her chilling name was derived. Our oldest son was born on August 18, 1960, and he carries my father's name—Menachem, or Hemi, as he is known to all. The proximity of his and Ghetta'leh's birthdays is frightening. Many thoughts creep in.

Our daughter was born on November 16, 1962. She carries Nurit's mother's name, Lia. When our children were two and a half years old, we hugged them tight and spoiled them. When Ghetta'leh was two and a half, I closed a backpack on her and smuggled her beyond the barbed wire fence in an attempt to save her life. Having become a parent, I now understand deeply the tragedy that befell Berta, Ghetta'leh's mother, what she felt, how traumatized she was, how she agreed to the rescue attempt, and how she withstood it. My heart breaks.

When our children were three years old, they had hardly begun to live—exactly at that age, there in the basement, Ghetta'leh's life ended. In my mind's eye, I see the flames. Before me the bodies and embers are ascending. These visions could drive one to madness.

During the decades that have passed, from time to time, my thoughts have uncontrollably returned to the ghetto alleys. I have discovered that the experiences that brought relief for my soul as a child still accompany me to this day in the autumn of my life.

In the ghetto, I was exposed to the game of chess. I remember the boy, Leibke Solski, who accompanied me in the first steps; the Berliner chess master, Kopelman, who embraced me lovingly; the boys Welpert, Griliches, Rubenstein, and Oscar, who were my rivals, none of whom survived; perhaps no one but me remembers their names, as though they had never existed. Because of the game of chess, they remain in my memories, and because of them, the game made my life more pleasant. To this day, like a ritual, I go to the chess club and sit opposite my opponents—my friends.

I am sure that many music lovers played musical instruments in their childhood, discontinuing as they got older, but keeping their love for the world of sounds. But I played the violin within the hell of the ghetto, and to this day, the strings of this instrument shake my heart with a special vibration. Very late, to my embarrassment, I admitted that piano, cello, flute, and vocals were beautiful as well, but the kingdom of my heart reverberated in the violin. For me, the pieces that were played there are filled with the sadness, the emotion, and the memories of that time. In front of my eyes stands the anonymous boy who played the Chaconne out of Bach's Second Partita for solo violin. He did not survive. The Chaconne remains engraved in my heart; as a prayer, it is whispered in my home in many different interpretations.

Sometimes, when I listen to the Second Partita, I stop the car on the side of the road and wipe the tears from my eyes. Then I continue on my way.

I did not always have the opportunity to make choices. The carpentry that hurt my fingers was thrust upon me. A person had to be "productive" in the ghetto; we thought that would give us a better chance of survival. But when I stood in front of Nazi officers and took my carpentry tools out of my pack as proof of my productivity, it did not help. They ordered me onto the bus going to the Ninth Fort; a fortress that for many would be their last stop.

Many years have passed, and the carpentry that was forced upon on me in the ghetto has become a hobby that has accompanied me all my life. The furniture in my home is my handiwork, and many have said that my work surpasses that of a hobbyist.

All of these are remnants I carry with me from the ghetto.

But I also carry with me something much deeper than these symbols of the past. I have two mottoes of my life, which were born in the ghetto and that over time have become the doctrines by which I live and think.

Until the end of my days, I will remember my wonderful father's words: *"Men darf zein a Mensch!"* ("Man must be a good person!") and beyond its literal translation—a person must maintain his humanity. As I often repeat these words, I discover more layers in their meaning.

Being a mensch is a seemingly simple pursuit, yet so many have failed to live up to it, and so many still do.

To volunteer to help when a person is in trouble, to feed the hungry, to find work for the unemployed, to give to charity anonymously, all of these are wonderful attributes, and being blessed with them means being a mensch. But there are times and circumstances in which man is required to pay a high price for this degree of humanity, and it is at such times that my father's words were said.

When my father distributed potatoes from our field to the hungry, he knew that hunger would greet our home sooner. His sensitivity to others' suffering was more important.

When Jonas and Antanina saved the lives of others, they were well aware that the price they might have to pay was their lives, but they continued and gathered sixteen fugitives into their home.

Many will say that my father sinned against his family. Many will ask how the lives of those being saved were preferred over the lives of the saviors. The answers to these questions are found far beyond the reaches of reason and logic. The logic of those holding the title of mensch is hidden in their hearts. Some call the logic of the heart conscience, some call it morality, some call it humanity. My father called it—"*Men darf zein a Mensch!*"

With these simple words, my father summarized all the volumes of ethical teaching.

There is one more motto that I have formulated for myself and have vowed to maintain: "Not to resemble *them*," which I don't mean literally, but in essence.

In my childhood, I experienced horrors that cannot be described; I witnessed unimaginable evil. These experiences formed my perspective. I wondered—How do people become so evil—so monstrous? I was searching for answers—and I found that words preceded actions.

It didn't start in Auschwitz—that was the end. It started with words dripping with hate and venom that fell on attentive ears and fertile ground. The race theory was composed, and with it, the racial discrimination codes were drafted in Nuremberg. Poisoned words can kill. Hate-dripping words herald the drawing of knives. With those poisoned words, they ordered the burning of books before these same words commanded the burning of people.

Racism is the father of evil. Racism is not something you are born with; it is perpetuated. With persistence and stubbornness for many years, the venom of racism was injected into minds and arteries, and with it, the addition of money, strength, dominance, status, and power. This is how the tens of thousands of descendants of Schiller, Beethoven, and Goethe became evil and monsters.

"Not to resemble them" in evil or cruelty, not to display even a morsel of racism—this is the second motto by which I live, think, and practice.

—⁓—

As previously mentioned, I married Nurit, whom I met in 1947 in the children's home in Poland when she was just fifteen years old.

Our son, Hemi (Menachem), is married to Anat née Dinari (Zilberman).

Anat and Hemi gave us four grandchildren. Our oldest grand-daughter, Sapir (Sapphire), will soon be twelve years old. Sapir has a little sister, Osher, and two brothers, Noam and Stav, all of whom are five and a half: a joyful set of triplets.

Our daughter, Lia, is married to Yigal Dziesietnik.

Lia and Yigal gave us two more grandchildren. Yuval will soon be four years old, and his little brother, Alon—ten months.

That is the whole tribe, my loved ones and those who love me. I intend to live alongside them and within them for many more years to come.

Life is indeed beautiful.

February 2004[1]

EPILOGUE

ABOUT MY BOOK'S HEROES

ABOUT SIXTY YEARS HAVE PASSED SINCE THE EVENTS DE-
scribed in this book. What happened to the heroes of my story? I
have only minimal biographical information about a few of these
people, as was told to me over the years.

All those who had been in our hideout left Lithuania in different
ways, obviously illegally. The Soviet Union's borders were sealed to
emigration to the West.

The Schames family went as far as Peru. I don't know any other
details about them.

Chaim and Tanya Ipp traveled to South Africa, where Dr. Chaim
Ipp perished in a car accident. Dr. Tanya Ipp immigrated to Israel
and lived in Jerusalem for a time. Due to her loneliness and advanced
age, she immigrated to Canada and now lives in Toronto near her
son. When I visited Canada, she hosted my wife and me in her home
very warmly.[1]

311

Aaron Neumark, Jonas's contact person, immigrated to Israel. After his divorce from Manya, he lived with his second wife, Bronya, in Givatayim. After her passing, he moved to a nursing home. I maintained contact with him until he passed away in 1988. He was eighty-four years old.

—⁓—

Manya Neumark-Gershenman immigrated to Israel and married Moshe Gershenman. They lived in Givatayim. After his passing, she moved to a nursing home. She helped me with her testimony in describing several events in my book. I am in constant touch with Manya.

—⁓—

Miriam Krakinowski and her husband, Moshe, immigrated to the United States and live in New York. I am still in touch with them.[2]

—⁓—

David Rubin, who was with me in the hideout, immigrated to Israel and married Shoshana. They lived in Bnei Brak. I stayed in touch with him until he passed away in 1996 at the age of seventy-three.

—⁓—

Riva Katavushnik immigrated to Israel, lived in Rishon LeZion, and died in 1998 at the age of eighty-seven.

—⁓—

Dr. Abrasha (Avraham) Kronzon, the little girl Ghetta'leh's father, was captured in the Action of February 1942 and was transferred to the Riga Ghetto. When the ghetto was liquidated, he was transported to camps on German soil, where he was eventually liberated by the Red Army and was later able to abscond to the West. He immigrated to Israel, raised a family, and lived in Holon. Dr. Kronzon, who was my doctor when I was a child, became my children's doctor as well. He passed away in 1977 at the age of seventy-four.

The Gurevich family.

In 1950, Vladimir Gurevich, the father, became paralyzed and suffered in his bed for seventeen years. He passed away in 1967 at the age of seventy-one.

Berta and Rita took care of him with such devotion until the end under impossible living conditions. They struggled with the bureaucracy to get a small apartment of their own. With the intervention of people in high places, at the top of which was Soviet Premier Nikita S. Khrushchev, they were given a two-room apartment for which they waited thirteen years.

Three months after they moved into their new apartment, in 1963, Bertochka passed away of a heart attack. She was sixty-six years old when she died.

Rita continued bearing the burden by herself. She sustained the family by teaching math and giving private lessons. The rest of her time was devoted to taking care of her father. She sacrificed her youth and her best years until his final moments.

My connection to Rita was reestablished during Mikhail Gorbachev's time. In 1990, she visited in Israel. Since the 1990s, Rita has lived in Germany.

Tamara Buchman, who was a counselor with me in the HaShomer HaTzair clubhouse in Wałbrzych, uprooted herself with her husband, my friend Meitek Weinreich, from Israel to Toronto, Canada. Our friendship has continued to this day.[3]

Mr. Stulgiński crossed my path on a Tel Aviv street about five years after I arrived in Israel. Just as in Poland, he invited me for dinner and a game of chess. As before, I inquired about a job, this time for me, and once again, he knew of one. Thanks to him, I got a good job, which was my start in accounting. A coincidental meeting in Poland and a continuation of such in Israel: two chance meetings engraved in my memory.

—∿∿—

Peretz Kaganovsky and I met in Łódź in 1947. A chance meeting was the beginning of a strong friendship. Our paths to Israel were interconnected. Our beds were together in the army barracks. Our rooms were adjacent in the kibbutz shacks, we worked in the same building in Tel Aviv, we lived in the same city, Holon, within walking distance of each other, and we enjoyed many happy moments together with our families.

As I recall my memories of those days, the memories of my hardships in Poland give way to the memory of my friendship with Peretz. His influence on me was great and blessed, and I cannot help but remember him with longing. Our friendship was interrupted with his untimely death in 1987 at the age of fifty-nine.

—∿∿—

Matityahu Mintz has been a Jewish History professor at Tel Aviv University, Professor Emeritus since 1990. My meeting with him in Poland in 1948 was the beginning of a wonderful friendship, which delights me to this day. Matityahu has been my teacher and my friend.[4]

—∿∿—

My family.

As you have already read:

My father, Menachem Fein, died in Dachau close to the end of the war. He was sixty-four years old when he died.

My brother Zvi (Hirsch'keh) Fein was murdered in the Fourth Fort, apparently on July 20, 1941, at the age of nineteen.

My mother, Ronia Fein née Braude, my oldest sister, Vera (Devorah), her husband, Fima (Ephraim) Chagall, and their daughter, Lia, returned from their Siberian exile to Kaunas in 1955.

—∿∿—

My mother immigrated to Israel in 1964. At that time, the Soviet border was locked tight, and her exit was made possible by the intervention of high-ranking officials: a senior Yugoslav Army officer, General Colonel Vojo Kovacevic, my cousin Mina's (née Braude) husband, asked his friend, the Yugoslavian ambassador in Moscow, to take action. The ambassador informally contacted Anastas Mikuyan, a senior official in the Kremlin, and my mother's departure for Yugoslavia was arranged and approved within a few weeks. After a month-long stay in Yugoslavia, she immigrated to Israel. My mother passed away in 1972 at the age of eighty-two.

Vera and Fima immigrated to Israel in 1971. Fima passed away in 1986 at the age of sixty-nine. Vera has three grandchildren from her daughter, Lia. Vera lives in Bnei Brak.[5]

Yehudit, Yeshayahu, and their baby son, Reuven, immigrated to Israel from Norway in 1949. Their daughter, Nava, was born in Israel. Yeshayahu passed away in 1997 at the age of seventy-four. Yehudit has four grandchildren from her daughter, Nava, and four grandchildren from her son, Reuven. Yehudit lives in Petach Tikvah.[6]

February 2004[7]

NOTES

Chapter 1. Who Was This Man?

1. The Molotov–Ribbentrop Pact was a nonaggression agreement made between Nazi Germany and the Soviet Union that included a covert division of various territories: the Baltic States were to be part of the Soviet Union, and Poland was to be divided between the two countries. The Soviets annexed the Baltic States (including Lithuania) in 1940. The pact was broken by the Germans when they invaded the Soviet Union on June 22, 1941.

Chapter 6. The Great Action and the Looting of Those Who Remained

1. In the nineteenth century, the Russians built nine fortresses around the city of Kaunas. During German occupation, some of them were used as execution sites.

Chapter 7. The Separation from My Parents

1. *Judenrat* (meaning the "Jewish council") was imposed by the Germans in all the ghettos. A few of them may have collaborated with the Nazis under threat of death or punishment. This was not the case in the Kaunas Ghetto. In any case, the author has chosen to use the Yiddish term to avoid this association.

Chapter 19. About Anna, Oscar, and Otto

1. See a photocopy of the certification on page 88.
2. By summer 1942, Lithuania had already been under German occupation for a year.
3. See a photocopy of the letter on page 102.
4. My family made contact with the decedents of the Müllerschkowski family in 2020. They graciously provided some details and photos of Anna, Anka, and Otto. Omama, Anna Seitz, passed away in 1950, not in 1964 as

Freida, Oscar's daughter, thought. Otto passed away in 1985; Anka passed away in 2008.

Chapter 20. The Sixteen Survivors

1. "The Internationale" is the international anthem of left-wing movements. It was also the anthem of the Soviet Union until 1944.

Chapter 21. About Hideouts and People

1. Righteous Among the Nations is an honorary award given by the Israel's Holocaust memorial (Yad Vashem) to non-Jewish individuals for risking their lives to aid Jews during the Holocaust.

Chapter 22. The Paulavičiuses

1. A Yiddish word meaning someone who does shady business.
2. Kęstutis passed away on July 21, 2019, at the age of 92.

Chapter 24. Gražina

1. In many languages, a gymnasium means a school.
2. Vilnius was a part of Poland until World War II. So Vilnius residents from that time could claim to be Polish.

Chapter 29. Goodbye, Lithuania

1. During Stalin's rule, approximately 5–10 percent of the population in the Baltic states were sent to Siberia for a variety of reasons—or at times, for no reason at all.

Chapter 30. Strangers in Poland

1. HaShomer HaTzair (the Young Guard) is a socialist-Zionist, secular, Jewish-youth movement.
2. A minimum number of ten worshipers required for traditional Jewish public prayer.

Chapter 31. At the Children's Home

1. The Bund ("General Jewish Workers' Union in Lithuania, Poland, and Russia") was a Jewish socialist, secular party. Bund opposed Zionism and Zionist movements like HaShomer HaTzair.
2. Haganah ("Defense") was the main semimilitarized Jewish organization in Mandatory Palestine and became the core of the IDF (Israel Defense Force) after the establishment of the state of Israel in 1948. Palmach was the elite fighting force of the Haganah.
3. *Yiddishkeit* means "Jewishness." Typically, it refers to the traditional Jewish way of life. In this case, the author refers to secular Jewish culture.

Chapter 35. Goodbye, Poland

1. Bronisław Huberman (1882–1947) was a Jewish, Polish-born violinist. He is considered to be one of the great violinists of the first half of the twentieth century. He is also known for founding the Israel Philharmonic Orchestra.

2. A *meshuggeneh*—a crazy person in Yiddish.

3. DDT (Dichlorodiphenyltrichloroethane) was a white powder that was used during and after World War II to control malaria and typhus.

Chapter 36. Me and My Past

1. The English edition of the book was completed in October 2020.

Epilogue

1. Tanya Ipp died in 2005 at the age of ninety-five.
2. Miriam Krakinowski died in 2010 at the age of eighty-six.
3. Tamara Buchman died on January 20, 2017, at the age of eighty-six.
4. Matityahu Mintz died on February 16, 2017, at the age of ninety-three.
5. Vera passed away on April 12, 2011, at the age of ninety-one.
6. Yehudit passed away on January 31, 2017, at the age of ninety-three.
7. The comments were added to the English edition in October 2020.

Born in 1929 in Lithuania, YOCHANAN FEIN was just a boy when he was forced into the ghetto and his parents were taken from him. After surviving three years of peril at the hands of the Nazis, Yochanan was approached by a stranger with a miraculous claim: that as a prodigal violinist, he was chosen to be saved.

Following liberation, Yochanan fled Soviet Lithuania in secrecy. He immigrated to Israel in 1950, where he joined the kibbutz movement and married his late wife, Nurit. Yochanan lives in Holon, Israel, and has two children and six grandchildren.